THE
SHAPESHIFTER

the Shapeshifter

A Tale from Glitter to Light

CLAUDIA NAVONE

Waterside Productions

Printed in Canada

First Printing, 2019

ISBN-13: 978-1-939116-37-6 print edition
ISBN-13: 978-1-939116-38-3 ebook edition

Waterside Productions
2055 Oxford Ave
Cardiff, CA 92007
www.waterside.com

CONTENTS

THANK YOU NOTES

I wish to express my gratitude to these beautiful people who supported me during the creation of this book:

To Peter Adler, my rock in every given moment.

To Charlotte Gordon Cumming for being my first editor, encouraging me on a daily basis and opening the first of many doors into the publishing world.

To Gillian Mosely for being my second editor and believing that my story could touch the hearts of many.

To Jan Olesen for his super special and inspiring friendship and constant support in many practical and spiritual matters.

To Amaya Ma for offering her incredible Spiritual Knowledge and her home in the Pyramid Portal so that I could complete this book.

To Charlotte Tilbury for being such a bright light embracing me with her generosity of spirit and great humor.

To Roseline De Thelin for channelling the subtitle with such Divine Inspiration.

To my sister Francesca Navone for being my mirror and for forgiving me so easily and gracefully.

To Monique Arcand and Laura Micozzi for patiently listening to me while reading for hours the first few chapters when the book was still in its infancy stage.

To Marianna Tufarelli, Donatella Piccinetti, Fiammetta Parri, Alice Alexander, and Alethea Gold for being the pillars of my life.

To Bill Gladstone, agent extraordinaire, for his guidance, clarity, and honesty.

To Ken Fraser for having effortlessly created a cover that I love so much!!!

To everyone at Waterside Publishing for their kindness and superb work. Especially to Kenneth Kales for his brilliant editing skills and infinite patience in dealing with me!!!

And finally to my beloved family, my fellow mentors and all my precious friends—Angels and Fairies spread around the world ... you know who you are.

PREFACE

A message from Spirit:

> *Are you ready to sing my name*
> *From the depths of your soul to the tip of your lips?*
>
> *Are you ready to sing my name*
> *To join your body, soul, and spirit with mine in a wild dance with*
> *sacred fire that shall burn what is no more?*
>
> *Are you ready to sing my name*
> *To let yourself go to a passionate embrace, to the eternal kiss*
> *of Light?*
>
> *Are you ready to sing my name*
> *To surrender your internal fight and just feel Oneness?*
>
> *Are you ready to sing my name*
> *To listen to the endless words of an ancient wisdom, to ride upon*
> *the wave of change?*
>
> *Are you ready to sing my name*
> *To face your shadow without tears, no more illusions and no more*
> *fears?*
>
> *Are you ready to sing my name?*
> *I am ready for you.*

Beloved Reader,

Please try to imagine this rather unusual scenario. A spoiled and successful *fashionista* receives a radical Spiritual Awakening, calling her to trade her glamorous lifestyle for a very deep Spiritual Path that will eventually require her to give away all of her prized possessions and to abandon a world of luxury forever, in exchange for an uncertain future simply guided by faith and her direct contact with the *Enlightened Masters* and the *Family of Light*. Yes, I agree this sounds rather unconvincing. And yet I promise you it is the absolute truth, as I am that being and this is my story.

History is filled with the names of those who walked upon the earth in a similar manner, and this is the reason why I never thought of myself as either brave or original. But a couple of years ago, a group of *Enlightened Masters* from the *Brotherhood of Light* visited and asked me, to my greatest surprise, to write this book with their full support through channeling.

They explained that it was important to share my truth with others as so many were suffering deeply from the same symptoms and conditions that had also affected me greatly before my Awakening.

They told me that in this moment in time, humanity greatly needs to know that nobody has to be a prisoner of internal mechanisms and unresolved karma and that it is very possible to co-create one's own reality with the help of Spirit. A *New Education* is in place and anyone can benefit from it, not just a few souls but all souls, as we are all equal. I knew in my heart how much I had personally received from this *New Education* and how grateful I was for the immense freedom and lightness of my being.

So even if I dreaded the idea of exposing myself so deeply, at least at first, I also understood that the *Enlightened Masters* had Higher Reasons and my only choice was to yield to their wish, starting with the laborious process of channeling this book through them. While the story unfolded, the thought that some of my experiences would be hard to believe constantly crossed my mind.

Since I was a child I have had the ability to see the unseen. My seership has also gifted me direct contact with Spirit. My visions, dreams, and mystical encounters belonged more to a fairy tale world than to a story set upon this earth where everyone is brought up only knowing life in a three-dimensional reality. But strangely enough, it is this exact exploration of the concept of realities that has become one of the prime subjects of this first book in *The Realities Trilogy*.

Ultimately we all are multidimensional beings and Planet Earth is only one of many other dimensions, a world inside many other worlds, and a reality inside multiple realities. It is the raising and expansion of our consciousness that takes us beyond the façade of this reality, opening doors to the otherwise hidden Dimensions of Light for us so that we may obtain the endless gifts of love and wisdom. The more our consciousness is expanded, the more we can travel in these different dimensions and receive the sacred teachings that, after a very long time, are finally coming back to us all.

Once upon a time I was hiding behind a mask, a false identity that kept me captive to a way of being that looked superficially perfect, but inside so much was deeply unresolved. My wounded soul carried the signs of an invisible illness that was gradually eroding my being. I was unable to show my true self, unable to give or receive love in a profound way, and unable to see or speak my own truth for fear of being either judged or ultimately rejected.

Restricted by all of these fears, illusions, and desires, I was ruled and controlled by them from childhood and into adult life. Losing the pure essence of my being and ultimately closing my heart because of the illusion of self- protection were the two most severe side effects caused by the sickness in my soul and the karma associated with it.

Ultimately Divine Intervention broke this stagnant circle, lifting me up into the world of love and Light that first challenged all of my previous beliefs, and later systematically liberated me from each of my heavy burdens.

The construction and deconstruction of both my being and my reality, and the powerful Spiritual Awakening that shifted me beyond any possible mental comprehension, are the humble offerings that I wish to share with you.

To realize that the trigger of our internal revolution is the alchemizing of the heart and mind, to learn to create in a new way without any limitation, and to see beyond the boundary of our mind, are indeed great blessings that I have been fortunate enough to experience; and with all of my heart I would now like to present you with these same possibilities for yourself.

Beloved reader, it is time to wake up and feel the immense power that already resides in each one of us. The golden key to our happiness, fulfillment, and freedom is to simply reconnect to what is already within us. Going through this process will support the dissolution of your ego and all of your original patterns, blockages, and fears in order to uncover your true self.

It is purely the song of your heart and soul that will lead you towards change—if I did it so can you, as we are all equally divine. Please open your eyes, delve into your heart, and start to perceive all there is.

To be awake and aware is of the now. You are so precious and only you have the power to rediscover the pure unmasked beauty of your true self and to manifest the reality that you wish for with all the magic and grace that goes with it.

In Truth, Light, and Service,
Ishkah and the *Enlightened Masters*

DEDICATION

To my mother Giovanna, who taught me freedom, giving me the courage to follow my own destiny.

To my Spiritual Mother Qala, who taught me the strength of an open heart and the Infinite Power of the Light.

And to my seven Knights—each one of them a wonderful teacher of the many lessons in love.

I am forever grateful....

PROLOGUE—
THE
INVITATION

Beloved Reader,

Life can be easily compared to a geographical map. We are walking on our paths through the mountains, rivers, and oceans of our existence while constantly searching for the right way forward. Every decision we make can lead us on a different trajectory, and consequently towards different realities either filled with ease and grace, or filled with hardship and struggle.

Believe it or not, in both the positive and negative, we are always truly responsible for our choices and outcomes as ultimately we are the creators of our own realities.

Journeying like pilgrims on our chosen road map, many of us are determined to reach the Holy Land of our dreams. But blinded by our desires we are often prone to miss or ignore signs that could be of great importance.

Spirituality is simply the unified map of Heaven and earth, the torch of Love and Light that eternally illuminates everyone's path through the earthly and cosmic universal highways, gently revealing the way forward towards a fulfillment that goes far beyond the mirage of all of our wants and desires.

May this scroll be your inspiration to travel within the unexplored landscape of your own heart, helping you to recognize and embrace your own authentic self. Word by word, chapter after chapter, I am sharing with you the story of how I embarked on my own life journey.

From Darkness to Light, this is a tale of Awakening and remembering that the power of love resides equally within each one of us without exclusion, even when we may have forgotten what love means and how it truly feels to love and be loved in deep acceptance of ourselves and all beings.

So let us begin, let us unfold the events that brought the winds of change to my life. The whispers from another world that grew so loud and clear, that in time each one of the chains that kept me captive to countless fears and illusions dissolved into the Light.

I am not the chosen one, we are all the chosen ones and my Higher Purpose is to simply pass on this message.

My tale begins in the magical land of Australia on a clear winter's morning, a morning like many others in the Southern Hemisphere. And yet it was a symbolic point in time when unbeknownst to me, the fortress of my beliefs was destined to crumble and be taken apart via the most unexpected twist of fate.

I remember the sun shining brightly in the vast turquoise sky, coloring Sydney with a multitude of golden hues. Light and shadow were running after each other in a playful game of dramatic contrasts, adorned with mirrors of infinite reflections on all the shiny surfaces along the tall glass buildings.

Like most mornings during the working week, I was sitting quietly at my usual table outside my favorite café. Enjoying the tepid warmth of the winter sun, I often gazed across the busy road where a luscious tropical park was home to many venerable trees. Those trees possessed the most intricate roots and they were as imposing in their regal beauty as the surrounding skyscrapers, the proud guardians of one of the few patches of land still left in the city centre by now transformed into a conglomeration of glass and steel.

I love Australia, this ancient land where the power of nature is in stark contrast to the power of men in an eternal struggle for survival. And so there I was sitting at the edge of two opposite worlds eating my breakfast and reflecting on my state of being while so many around me were coming and going, chatting, laughing, filling the air with a multitude of sounds; a symphony of human voices, car engines, and the sweet songs of birds. The city was vibrant, but I was not.

At that moment in time I ached deeply. My heart was broken and I did not know how to mend it. Considered successful in my chosen career, I secretly viewed myself as an absolute failure because the man I loved had rejected me, preferring to marry someone else.

And yet on that particular morning somehow I was feeling a bit more cheerful as an unexpected proposal had brought me a new wave of excitement, instantly lifting some of the sadness that was burdening my heart. Suddenly, invigorated by a sense of renewed optimism, I took off my jacket and rearranged my body in a more comfortable position. With half a smile painted on my mouth, cappuccino in one hand and cigarette in the other, all my thoughts started to drift into a daydream about the impending weekend.

A few months before I had befriended a charismatic man named Giovanni.

An intriguing character, he had just invited me to Coorabella, his magnificent property in the tropical hills of Byron Bay, the Ibiza of Australia. As I was imagining all the possible scenarios of my imminent visit, a virtual fashion show was simultaneously playing over and over in my head with me serving in double roles as model and stylist. *What could I wear to impress Giovanni* I was wondering while mentally scanning my vast wardrobe.

In those days I used to express myself through the language of fashion. Like an actress with her roles, I acted out my own life according to my very precise sartorial choices. Clothes were my body armor, used as a tool to put distance between myself and others. In order to conceal my own fragility and insecurities, I only felt safe when hiding behind a fabulous outfit, deceiving people by superficially presenting myself.

In fact, I was extremely adept at projecting a powerful and manipulated image of myself that had nothing to do with my inner reality. The most intimate part of my being was indeed my secret domain, never to be exposed, shared, or discussed with others, even those closest to me.

A complex character is how I would describe myself, somebody who lingered on the surface; too fearful to confront what was hiding beneath my shiny upper layer of illusions carefully constructed to disguise the truth of my real identity. Pretending to have a perfect life, I was mainly fooling myself. In truth, I was lost and deeply dissatisfied.

I had the tendency to focus only on what I couldn't have instead of being grateful for what I already possessed. Trapped inside my own ego, my mind and heart were severely disconnected; I inhabited a golden tower of my own fabrication, where simultaneously I was the master and the prisoner. I say the master as without a doubt I was the creator of my own reality and therefore responsible for it. And I say the prisoner as I was living within endless self-imposed limitations that severely restricted the freedom of my heart and soul, creating high walls of separation between myself and others.

But I was too scared to leave, too scared to unlock the Pandora's box of my emotions. In fact, I would go to great lengths to control every aspect of my life as the illusion of being in control made me feel safe; even though at times it produced massive internal clashes. As a result, I was feeling unhappy and unfulfilled yet incapable of doing anything about it.

Because I remained hidden behind the veils of this fear, others could not see me or receive me. Inside my soul I longed to meet somebody special who could pierce through the veils and witness my vulnerability. But I was so skillful at revealing only what I wanted to show to others that almost no one was capable of reading what was behind my mask. And let's face it, there are not many individuals who are inclined to be the detective of their own soul, let alone the souls of others.

This particular condition, the inability to express myself in alignment with my deepest truth, the truth of my heart, had especially manifested through the unfolding of each of my intimate relationships. I wanted so much to love and be loved back but I could not let go of either my pretenses or controlling patterns, often causing a lot of grief for everyone involved. These intimate relationships repeatedly ended in tears, each time leaving me feeling more lonely and misunderstood than before.

Fashion was simply my refuge, both a world of creation and a temporary Band-Aid helping me to distract myself from the real issues and uncomfortable state of being that I was unable to shift. Therefore, that morning I was once again playing one of my favorite fake identity games, the one in which I carefully edited aspects of my persona: *Which one should I present to Giovanni this weekend? Which mask should I put on next?*

But while I was lost in an ocean of thoughts about fashion and the opportunity of birthing a new romance, the world of the unseen made its Presence very clear to me when all of a sudden fantasy collided with reality and I shifted dimensions....

Since I was a child this mysterious world had been open to me, inviting me to explore beyond the veils of our present reality. Blessed by many supernatural encounters that helped me to navigate the map of my existence, I was about to receive the most extraordinary of all visitations, the one that would trigger the greatest change in me.

It all started with the sensation of being literally invaded by something made of the coldest energy. This something was rapidly filling me—I felt impaled and could not move. Silence enveloped me and the outside world went strangely quiet until the present reality just faded away in slow motion to be replaced by an unseen realm of Light.

My body was frozen, my cappuccino and cigarette left in mid-air. I was no longer in control. All the fashionable and romantic ideas that had dominated my mind till a second ago, vanished with everything else I had sensed as I went blankly into a trance. I could not see or hear anymore. I could not feel my body and my mind was so still, so silent, as if all thoughts had been surgically removed.

After a few moments that seemed to have lasted forever, I perceived the sound of a voice emerging from this void of nothingness, while a winged being was the only shape that I could now distinguish amidst a sea of fog. Next, I found myself face-to-face with this unusual visitor. He was standing tall and regal in front of me in his robe of white and blue light. His wings were large and made of the purest white crystalline texture. His eyes, luminous and kind, were gazing upon me with celestial beatitude. Then I heard his angelic, yet authoritative voice clearly address me:

"I am one of your Guardian Angels," were his first words to my complete surprise! "I have come in order to deliver a very special message to you, so dearest one please listen carefully. The moment has arrived and your life is about to move in an unexpected new direction. In Divine Time and in Divine Order you will undergo a process of great transformation where you shall evolve and shift in ways you cannot possibly imagine at present."

The Angel continued, "Very soon you shall meet a great teacher. She will show you a new way of being, as you are meant to walk a deep Spiritual Path in order to accomplish your mission here on earth. This teacher will be guiding you step-by-step. She too came to earth with an important mission, the *New Education*, to educate many to be *New Humans*, to teach them to live through the way of the heart.

"Don't be afraid, your time has simply arrived for you to fulfill your destiny and honor your sacred contract. You shall remember the truth of your being and you will learn to live, to act, and to speak in full open heart, as now your heart is very closed, dearest one."

In case this was not enough news, the Angel explained to me how Mother Earth was also shifting, and how a new era of great Awakening for humanity—an era described by the Angel as the *Golden Age*—was fated to take place at some stage in the future. And his last words to me were that my help was needed towards this great Awakening.

I was completely and utterly astounded by all of these revelations. But as fast as I had been taken over by this invisible Presence, I was suddenly dropped back into earthly reality, and slowly recovered my sight and hearing. After regaining full command of my body and senses, I immediately asked myself *did anybody else witness this strange event? Did anybody see me with the Angel?*

The café was full of people by then, but once I checked my surroundings with a quick and furtive look, it became obvious that nobody had paid any attention to my supernatural adventure. Then I looked at my watch and discovered that I must have been in a trance for at least half an hour, if not longer. Myriads of questions surged through my mind: *was I just subjected to a state of temporary insanity or did something of huge importance just happen to me?*

It was certainly not the first time that I had experienced this kind of phenomenon. And yet this day felt completely different perhaps in part because according to my Guardian Angel, my whole life was about to change.

What was this contract and this mission? Who was the mysterious teacher that could transform me into a *New Human*? And what was the meaning of being a *New Human*? Quite frankly I could not handle the Angel's message, as fear and distrust started to overwhelm me.

I became enraged with the Angel. How dare he interfere with my life, that, by the way, was already complicated enough and didn't need any extra aggravation! How dare he say that my heart was closed when I was the one suffering! Looking down helplessly to what was by then a cold cappuccino and a cigarette butt, I took some deep breaths and decided to go back to my office at *Harper's Bazaar*, hoping that my Fashion Director's duties might push me in to my normal state of being. But I was wrong. There was no escaping from the Angel's message.

The rest of the day went so slowly that I could not concentrate at all. The meetings I had to attend were never-ending, and even the gorgeous Chanel dress that had just arrived from Paris failed to excite me. Luckily, no one noticed my lack of enthusiasm and my total lack of Presence.

At last the end of the day came marked as usual by a flock of fruit bats starting their nightly shift across the dark blue sky ... it was time to return to my beautiful apartment perched above the rocks of Tamarama overlooking the Pacific Ocean. There, on my own with just the sound of the crashing waves as company, exhausted by hundreds of unanswered questions, I went to bed and fell into a dreamless sleep.

I woke up the next morning promising myself to keep the Angel's monologue a secret. Nobody would have believed me anyway, and at that stage I was not too sure of what had actually happened either. Maybe it was just a lucid dream?

The day went smoothly, no Angel in sight, no cryptic messages to decipher. I felt relieved and started to prepare myself for my trip as careful planning was needed in the clothes department. The next day, Friday, I was to fly to Byron, and was not due back in Sydney till the following Tuesday. I felt a small rush of excitement going through my spine. Coorabella seemed full of promises.

It was dusk when Giovanni called. To my utter disbelief, he asked if I was interested in going to a spiritual workshop with him. My friend often mentioned this woman named Qala, apparently gifted with mystical powers. Now Giovanni was trying to convince me to accompany him to a program that Qala was teaching in Byron on Saturday and Sunday. His weak selling point was that I was presented with the perfect opportunity to meet her. As if I cared!!!

But Giovanni was not giving up. "If you don't like it, we can easily leave the workshop any time you want," he added almost apologetically, a trace of guilt in his voice knowing very well that half of my holiday would be gone, swallowed up by the very inconvenient spiritual retreat. Not being interested in the slightest, and practically on the verge of being rude, I was just about to tell him "no, sorry, not for me but maybe another time," when instead I heard myself say, "Yes! I would love to join you. Thank you, it sounds really different I mean … I would love to try."

Giovanni was relieved by my positive answer and our telephone conversation ended soon after with his promise to collect me from the airport the following day. Staring in dismay at all my hippy chic clothes in lovely outfits so neatly packed, I began to wonder *what do people wear to a spiritual workshop? And why did I say yes? What came over me? Was the Angel responsible for my answer?*

Being a control freak, I detested any kind of surprises. What I originally had in mind was in fact a very different kind of weekend, but yet again I had been taken over by something else, something that I could not see or manage in any way; but this intangible

Presence was real and worst of all, somehow capable of influencing me.

While all these questions were resurfacing, I started to pack for a second time, coming to the conclusion that undeniably, spirituality and fashion did not go well together. Therefore, I removed nearly all of my glamorous garments from my suitcase and replaced them with a few tracksuit bottoms and oversized t-shirts. *This is not a good look* I thought, my mood gloomy, my fashion vision in shreds.

Later on I went outside onto my apartment's terrace. I needed some fresh air while I frantically tried to work out if this unforeseen invitation to the spiritual workshop was somehow related to the Angel's prophecy. The view from the terrace was spectacular and took my breath away. In the darkness of the night, the ocean roared beneath me. The waves were enormous, pure white foam erupted from each one of them, in stark contrast to the pitch-black seawater.

I looked up in wonder at the stars cast across the firmament in a geometric pattern of shimmering webs of light. The almost full moon was suspended above me, like a precious luminous jewel set against the black velvet mantle of the southern sky. Surrounded by such intense beauty and the sheer raw force of nature, I felt emotionally charged.

Then, just as swiftly, loneliness enveloped me and I became sad. Both loneliness and sadness, my best-kept secrets, had been deeply rooted in my being for as long as I could remember and often haunted me. I felt utterly alone. The pain of rejection, still fresh in my heart, had created an open wound that was not healing. I longed for something, but this inexplicable something had thus far eluded me.

Slowly, I lit up a cigarette, my constant companion in those days—this act of self-abuse somehow helped me focus. Then suddenly an insight flashed in my mind and I began to see more clearly. I realized that the Angel was the last link in a chain of paranormal events that had occurred since my arrival in Australia. In the past three years I had witnessed a crescendo of Spiritual Manifestations culminating with the Angel's visit.

Have I been truly prepared to receive a new life? I asked myself with some trepidation. *This cannot be a coincidence. I don't believe in coincidences* I repeated silently over and over again, in the manner of reciting a sacred mantra.

My heart skipped a beat and a profound sense of mystery bound me. In that fated moment under the shadow of a silver moon and the brilliant light of so many stars, I became certain that my encounter with the Angel was indeed a heavenly sign of great significance.

The next day I boarded the plane to Byron Bay feeling rather apprehensive. Changes were ahead but I could never have predicted what was about to unfold. My life as I knew it would be no more, as something so powerfully divine was about to rise from the ashes of my shattered illusions and rip open my heart. Veils would be lifted, truths would be revealed, and my mask would fall off to at last liberate the real essence of my being from the darkest depths of my soul memories. The Angel's words had marked the beginning of a new journey....

My Journey back home....

IN THE
WAITING ROOM—
FLORENCE

Beloved Reader,

This tale is told in chronological order from the very start, from my first breath. Like so many of us, I was born bound by countless veils concealing the Divine Nature of my being. Consequently, this lack of awareness produced a series of internal struggles augmented with false beliefs about my own identity. I was fighting against the essence of my true self, often lost in a labyrinth of endless fears and illusions.

Constrained by society's rules and codes of behavior, I walked my path with a closed heart, often fearful of being judged. Yet, I judged others in the blink of an eye. Seeing my reality through the distorted reflection of my ego's mirror also became a way of life in which lessons were rarely understood or learned because of my pride and the shadow of my own ego.

Those were the years spent in the *Waiting Room*, not living in my full potential, not knowing about the power of Love and Light,

the power of the heart's dreams. To exist, to be, is not an easy task as each one of us is affected by something that is intangible but intrinsically there.

Through my unfolding personal story, the purpose of this book is simple but profound. We must learn that we are truly powerful beings, the creators of our own reality and fear does not have to limit us in any way. All we need, we already possess. The switch is inside our own hearts, ready to be turned on.

And now, I invite you to live beyond your own preconceptions and travel with me through the pages of this book. To honor yourself and your own truth is the most unique of gifts. We are all equally divine.

This story began with my appearance on Planet Earth on the 6th of May 1964—I landed on Gaia under the identity of "Claudia Navone."

My point of arrival was the ancient city of Florence, the cradle of the Italian Renaissance. Through the pages of history, men and nature harmoniously co-created a town of great beauty set amongst an exquisite landscape of undulating emerald hills. A small gem, it still stands today in its full splendor despite the ravages of time. Florence was to be the very first dot on the map of my earthly adventures.

Several years later, during my twenties, I experienced my own birth all over again but this time in full consciousness. I was shown the exact moment of the fusion between my soul and my tiny new human form, as I traveled at great speed inside a bright and luminous corridor. This galactic highway was the link between the earthly dimension and all other dimensions. At first I was just a Body of Pure Light, as I only merged with the physical part of myself when bursting out into this reality. Then, surrounded by a very different kind of light, the artificial light of a hospital room, I saw myself safely held by human hands beginning my new incarnation.

At the time, I remember being rather besotted by this unexpected insight that somehow made perfect sense to me. I had been given a tiny piece of the puzzle of this fascinating mystery called life.

What was shown to me was in fact one of the fundamental Spiritual Truths: we are all beings of light visiting this planet under a temporary human identity.

Yes, dearest reader, your own temporary identity, your own family and path here on earth are no coincidence. All is predetermined by our soul prior to our arrival back here, in accordance to the contracts we need to fulfill, the lessons we need to learn, and therefore the karma we need to dissolve. As with most of us, I started this earthly journey unconsciously, with no memory of my true origins or the real reasons for my visit.

My chosen family for this particular lifetime was a melting pot of interesting individuals. Not the easiest of families, I must say, but indeed the perfect one for the purpose of my learning. This cast of characters, who from the very start shaped my life in a multitude of ways, helped me carve the raw diamond of my being into both luminous and darker facets—*human nature is a nature of duality where the Shadow and the Light are equally represented within us.*

My mother is named Giovanna. Beautiful, elegant, spiritually-gifted and free-spirited, she is quite an exceptional being with a very unique outlook on life. Also gifted with seership, her behavior can at times be rather unusual, as she is often guided by powerful insight.

From a very young age, my mother has experienced much upheaval in her life journey. Born just before the explosion of the Second World War, she suffered illness and deprivation in wartime. Later on she lived through the loss of a stillborn child and the fear of being unable to conceive.

She was born rich, and yet when much was lost, she didn't show any attachment to material things. My mother is a master of positive thinking and possesses both an indomitable spirit and a selfless heart which allowed me to explore different realities and gave me the freedom to follow my own destiny.

Paolo, my father, was the offspring of a wealthy Italian-American father and a Russian aristocratic mother. Sent to a severe boarding school at the tender age of six, the trauma of the forced separation from his parents closed his heart very early on. The feeling of abandonment, and later on a brutal encounter with war, scarred him deeply. As a result, my father created a world of his own that he left only very occasionally, choosing very carefully to whom he gave the entry key.

My mother was eventually the one who received this key. She was truly adored by him and his love was so exclusive that somehow he forgot that he also had two daughters. But unlike my mother, he has been unable to see life through positive eyes. Like my mother, he had Spiritual Gifts of his own.

Rita, my maternal grandmother, was a refined woman possessing both an intellectual mind and an artistic temperament. A muse and great beauty, many of the painters, writers, and composers of her generation regularly convened at her elegant home.

But underneath all the glitter, Rita suffered great loss. Both her parents and one of her siblings died when she was just a child. Heiress to a great fortune, she experienced financial adversity as her wealth slowly vanished amidst two world wars, as well as poor fiscal administration. Her nervous system was fragile and she frequently suffered from acute depression and anxiety.

To me she was like the sun, so warm and loving, a source of endless inspiration. Her husband, my grandfather Piero, was a believer in justice and freedom. Born into an ancient aristocratic family from Tuscany, he was involved in politics before Mussolini created the fascist state. Eventually Mussolini came to power but Piero refused, point-blank, to be part of the new regime.

A man of great principle and integrity, he lost his position and became an outcast. Hunted by both Nazis and fascists, he lived through the wartime in hiding while the new government confiscated a large part of his family's assets. He worked tirelessly behind the scenes saving many from certain death and helped to organize the local resistance that eventually contributed to the overthrow of Mussolini.

After the war, he worked with great enthusiasm as a lawyer helping many people for no compensation. But suddenly, one day my grandfather died in a fatal car accident—I was two years old.

An aura of mystery surrounded my paternal grandmother Maroussia, a Slavic aristocratic beauty with striking violet eyes. Hiding behind the superficiality of appearances, Maroussia was in truth numbed by grief, and abused herself throughout her life with a toxic combination of alcohol, pills, and cigarettes.

She was just a child when forced to flee from Russia, her beloved country ravaged by the Red Revolution. My grandmother lost everything she knew and loved. The only member of her family to survive the carnage, she reached France, where with the help of a family friend, found safety in a boarding school on the Riviera.

An orphan, with no country and no fortune, in due course Maroussia was taken under the wing of the kind school owner who became a second mother to her. The lady's plan was to eventually marry her off to a rich man who could offer Maroussia a new life. That man appeared when she was barely eighteen years old in the elegant shape of my grandfather Stefano. He fell in love with her at first sight and instantly offered Maroussia a glamorous new world.

However, theirs was not a fairy tale because nothing could cure the addictions that had sprung from her feelings of loss and abandonment and that subsequently produced perpetual self-abuse.

Stefano, a gentleman from a bygone era, never worked a day in his life. The son of an Italian father and an American heiress, my grandfather spoke five languages fluently and cut a dashing figure amongst the fashionable set that gravitated along the French Riviera during the twenties and thirties.

It was in Nice where he met and wedded Maroussia in a whirlwind romance. Interestingly enough, both my father and grandfather were instantly besotted with their future wives, and consequently their all-consuming love excluded their respective children.

In 1929, with the crash of Wall Street, Stefano lost much money but his wealth remained large enough to allow my grandparents to carry on with their extravagant lifestyle, although it slowly depleted their fortune. This merry-go-round hid a darker reality, as his beloved wife was unable to stay sober, and unable to stop anesthetizing her pain with her other many addictions.

During the Second World War, they settled in an ancient villa amidst the Tuscan Hills, close to Pisa. My father, who was born in France just before the family moved to Italy, was eventually sent to boarding school in Florence where he was destined in Divine Time to meet my mother.

Francesca, my only living sibling, wasn't born yet. A very sensitive and highly complex soul, she also felt the pungent sting of loneliness, abandonment, and rejection from an early age. I did not accept her. To me, she was the usurper of my righteous place in the family, as I was the eldest child and in my mind should have been the only daughter. My lack of love and consideration hurt her deeply.

When Francesca was ten years old, I left home in pursuit of my own destiny. From then on our difficult relationship became even worse, creating a deep fracture between us, filled up only with

endless fights, jealousies, and misunderstandings. It was only after my Spiritual Awakening that my heart finally opened to her and I made amends.

Francesca taught me to apply the *Universal Laws of Love and Forgiveness* to my daily life and to be much more aware of the undeniable truth that we are all just a reflection of each other. My sister was my first mirror, the first of many with whom I would reflect all of my own unresolved issues, judging her and others without compassion.

There was also an outsider who became part of our family long before I was born. Tata Anna, a saintly figure that knew only love, kindness, humility, and patience. She deeply influenced me. One of my first Spiritual Educators, she taught me to have faith and imparted some of my earliest lessons on Love and Light. A mystical being devoted to Saint Francis of Assisi, she embodied these virtues daily, with a serene smile on her face. Tata Anna was originally employed as a cook for my maternal grandparents. She came from a simple background, but her knowledge of the heart was far deeper than any of ours. The keeper of all the family's secrets, she was truly our Earthly Angel.

This colorful cast of characters, each could have easily belonged to a film or a work of fiction, was indeed my beloved chosen family—each one of us linked and intertwined through the spider's web of karma. Dearest reader, there is a precise reason for describing my family members to you as I would like to share some essential information that will support your better understanding of the many parts of our own nature:

At birth, we automatically inherit the genetic patterns of seven previous generations from both our mother and father's lines. We are therefore the recipients of many of the gifts, and many of the unresolved issues or energies of our parents, grandparents, and ancestors. These patterns are multilayered, reaching a greater depth than just the physical and personality traits that we share with our bloodlines. The genetic patterns I am talking about lie hidden in the depth of our soul, DNA, and cells.

You will soon see how the energies of loss, abandonment, rejection, addiction, loneliness, and much more played a fundamental role, not just with my parents and grandparents, but also throughout my own life and my sister's life. The strong undercurrent of unresolved energy from both my genetic heritage and my soul's karma affected me deeply, at times dragging me down into a vortex of self-abuse.

We don't need to be full-fledged drug addicts or alcoholics to abuse or sabotage ourselves. These energies can be very subtle, but equally toxic in the way they interact with our beings, often putting a negative and heavy spin upon our thoughts, feelings, and views of both others and ourselves. Although it is truly possible to heal our internal mechanisms by raising our consciousness.

As you journey deeper into this tale, you shall find out how we can each free ourselves from these layers of old stuff, cellular memories, patterns, blockages, fears, and anxieties that no longer serve us. Yes, you will indeed discover that a happy heart, a peaceful mind, a loving soul, and a joyous spirit can become your daily reality.

But ultimately, what really supported me through those thorny years in the *Waiting Room*, was a mysterious inner guidance that came from somewhere else, sometimes through dreams and unusual encounters, and at other times simply through knowing; a strong knowing that I could neither explain nor silence and that would eventually always steer me in the right direction.

This inner guidance was to be my saving grace, illuminating my path even in the darkest night of my existence. It doesn't matter if your heart is only partially open, if you learn to listen to it, you may find the answer that you are struggling to receive—your mind is young and has limitations but your heart is ancient and wise.

Staying with matters of the heart, I shall now describe to you some key moments during my childhood when my persona began to experience karma and therefore the rise of multiple internal

mechanisms and challenging situations. At the same time, the first signs of magical celestial guidance were manifesting to support me on my life journey.

I was born with a silver spoon in my mouth. Those early years evoked in me the sense of being completely loved, cocooned, and protected by my family. But this idyllic life came to a halt when my younger sister was born.

I was three and half years old and felt betrayed like the Trojans when the Greeks invaded their citadel, tricking them with their infamous wooden horse. Like the Trojans, I stared for days at my mother's tummy without realizing that the enemy—my innocent sister—would come out of it, changing drastically the dynamics of my family's life, and my way of being.

Of course my parents prepared me for my sister's imminent arrival. And yet, somehow the theory, the idea that was formed inside my head regarding the meaning of this event was totally different from the reality that suddenly hit me with full force when the mother I loved and adored disappeared in order to give birth, and I lost access to her for what seemed like an eternity.

This forced separation was what prompted the first closure of my heart as my reaction was violent and resentful, my hypersensitivity deeply exposed. I went into a rage and mistreated whoever was trying to calm me down, trying to assure me that I would see my mother soon enough. I believed my mother was my own property and I was not at all ready to share her with a newly born intruder.

For the very first time, I felt an array of emotions previously unknown to me. The flames of anger, jealousy, rejection, betrayal, and abandonment rose up fast and furious through my infantile ego, and burned me deeply. The birth of my sister triggered something inside of my being that was wild and incongruent with the sweet child I was. With this episode, a part of my innocence was lost and immediately replaced with a certain lack of compassion.

This event activated the initial seeding of my unforgiving nature and marked the time when the first layers of protection were originally woven around my heart.

But why did I react in such a way? Where did it come from? I was just a small child when, beyond my understanding, an ancient aspect of my being already looming within me was swiftly reactivated by particular soul memories. This aspect fed my ego in a negative way, giving me the illusion that I had the right to possess somebody else. Consequently, this aspect dominated my personality for many years, causing me much heartache.

An aspect is a part of our soul's consciousness from a previous lifetime that has lived through certain internal or external experiences which were never resolved. Therefore, this unresolved energy has been traveling with us from lifetime to lifetime activating negative mechanisms and behavioral patterns within our being. These parts of our soul influence us to the best of their ability, trying to protect us from that which hurt them so long ago, when they were unable to deal with their own internal issues or external actions.

In doing so, an aspect may create all sorts of blockages and limitations within us. This part of our consciousness needs to heal so we may also heal our fears, insecurities, and unconstructive states of being which can deeply affect us, sometimes on a daily basis. It is often these intangible shady feelings that are contaminating us, making us feel small, unwanted, unworthy, abandoned, lonely, jealous, and envious of others, filled with anxieties that we are not enough, and ... the list is endless.

Dearest reader, after just a few pages, you may start to understand the truth of how complex and multilayered we really are, and how, even as children, we could already easily be under the influence of our aspects, karma, and genetic patterns.

We are indeed the product of so much more than just the present physical form which holds our temporary incarnation. As

my story unfolds, this will become more apparent and hopefully you will receive a better understanding, supporting you to comprehend at a deeper level your own state of being and your own aspects.

So from that moment on, my own large aspect took control, viewing my sister as a rival for my mother's love and attention and instigating within me a devouring uncompassionate nature—this illusion of owning another, the energy of being possessive with the people I loved, would ultimately create a strong controlling pattern that would very much constrict my happiness, especially in intimate relationships where I frequently reflected my deeply rooted fears of loss and abandonment upon many of my lovers.

Then, a time of prophetic dreaming entered my young life….

Going to bed became the equivalent of playing Russian roulette, as I could never guess who was waiting for me in the darkness. Angels or demons?

The dreams started when I was about four years old. They came to me in the most peculiar way, which can only be described as watching my own TV series. Every night, upon falling asleep, a new episode would unravel, either to my delight or horror. The sensations were incredibly real. I was consciously living every moment. I was soul traveling.

At times, simply by closing my eyes I was immediately transported into an unknown reality where I saw myself as a winged child flying around the most phantasmagoric worlds. I was not traveling alone. My trusted friend, a golden lion also winged, faithfully followed me around in each one of these delightful journeys.

Every dream took us to a different realm and to such breathtaking scenery painted with endless strokes of the most luminous and vibrant colors. The deep green of enchanted forests, the aquamarine of pristine waterfalls, the indigo of lakes, the crystalline beauty of tall ice-capped mountains. Each one of these landscapes created the enchantment of faraway wonderlands.

And a great number of fantastical creatures dwelled amongst these magical places. Fairies, elves, giants, unicorns, dragons, all became the companions of my nocturnal adventures and the guides to these wonderful realms where flowers and trees were often made of precious stones and the waterways were the playground of golden baby dolphins and iridescent mermaids.

To fall into this dream, to experience the freedom of flying, of not being bound by the physical body, awakened inside of me a feeling of remembrance.

And yet I didn't realize at the time that I was exploring different realities, Dimensions of Consciousness that coexist within our Earthly Reality. I did not know that we are multidimensional beings in a tri-dimensional world, that we are so much larger than what our physical body may contain. Nobody teaches us at school that with the physical body we are also equipped with a Light Body, which represents the entry key to our multi-dimensionality.

So dearest reader, if you have children with an overactive imagination, maybe it is time to be aware that what they see sometimes it is not just pure fantasy. Certain visions may simply be fed to them from somewhere else, a different Plane of Consciousness that is as real as the Earthly Dimension we live in.

The other fascinating detail about my early soul traveling was the golden winged lion, my mysterious friend who in Divine Time would return to show me at last the truth of his identity.

A different sequence of dreams also revealed itself to be prophetic and started the process of bringing inside my consciousness the holy Presence of my future teachers. Dressed in long white robes with a small floral tiara adorning my head, I often wandered inside vast marble and crystalline temples; supported by giant pillars and crowned by large domes of all sorts of colors and shapes. Sometimes, I took part in ancient rituals amid those temples and streets of the cities of lost civilizations in the company of many other children.

I shared this dream with a very different set of beings. They were both male and female of exceptionally tall stature, wearing long tunics so shiny that the garments appeared as if made of light. Some of these magnificent beings wore metallic pendants around their necks in the form of solid gold or silver disks. They were so kind to me, either guiding me through the temples or allowing me to touch their jewelry. Often they also gifted me with the most beautiful flowers to toss during sacred ceremonies.

It was during these dreams that the *Enlightened Masters* first revealed themselves within my consciousness, switching on the connection with the child I was, gently preparing me for things to come.

And there was also something else in these dreams, something that manifested itself in my early life here on earth. Frequently, from beginning to end during rituals, I danced wildly and freely, spinning around the pillars of the temple, my long Titian hair flying in all directions. I was floating, moving my body with such precision and lightness that my soft white robe gracefully molded to the shapes I created with these different movements.

Profoundly imprinted upon my soul, this part of the dream was indeed so compelling that I started to dance incessantly around my family home. Till one day my mother asked me if I would be interested in properly learning how to dance. I immediately agreed and my first great passion in life was born.

Another recurrent dream was dramatically different from all the others and filled me with fear. This dream haunted me for very long periods of time in which I would dread going to sleep, as I would consequently plunge into a rabbit hole of strange and scary nightmares.

I adventured by myself in the darkest woods where monstrous creatures were hiding behind trees. These evil beings were out to get me and at times seemingly came close to accomplishing their deed, though somehow never could. In the dream, I was not aware of the danger and kept walking deeper and deeper into the mysterious forest.. But the other side of myself consciously witnessed the horror of my circumstances and the perils I was about to encounter, yet was unable to communicate this.

This situation put me in such a state of sheer terror that I could hardly breath, in fear of being caught by wicked creatures. Pure agony enveloped me for hours, till I fell into oblivion. This nightmare was to be as equally prophetic as the other dreams, because it is our Shadow that prevents us from seeing our own Light—where there is Light, Darkness also exists.

After a few months of such horrible dreams, I was exhausted and distressed. Desperate to confide my troubles in someone, I turned to Tata Anna. I felt she could understand how disturbed I truly was while the rest of my family would have likely dismissed the situation as childish nonsense.

It was in that moment in time when Tata Anna taught me how to pray, telling me with confidence that the power of prayer would dispel the Darkness with Light. Despite not yet having a clear understanding of Dark and Light, I felt a deep resonance with these teachings and intuitively understood that to pray was indeed a potent form of communication with the Beings of Light in the Heavens. And so I prayed, I prayed with all of my heart to God, Jesus, Mary, the Angels, and all the Saints I knew.

By some kind of miracle, the nightmares soon vanished, and from that moment on I always prayed before falling asleep, asking for the Light of God to protect me from the Darkness. This episode marked the beginning of my official relationship with God.

This sacred relationship was to become a tormented one, moving through so many ups and downs, so many twists and turns, as I saw myself separated from God. I believed that God inhabited the realm of Heaven and from there he looked down on me with a benevolent smile when I was good, or he shook his head in disapproval if I was naughty. Sometimes he could be a clement God and other times I felt utterly let down and abandoned by him.

Eventually, this credo would shift beyond everything I originally per-
ceived as truth, to ultimately fully embrace the fact that God is inside us
and in all there is. It is simply this Oneness, this union with all parts of
ourselves and with the Universe, that allows us to touch the divine with-
in. This extraordinary expansion of our consciousness then reveals that
the truth of the Love, Light and Power of Creation of our own Source, is
all we really need and already within us.

With the nightmares now gone, I was free to resume my life
concentrating on all the new exciting things I was so keen to learn.
Unlike other children my age, I had no concern for toys. What interested me were the magical stories told by books recounting the
legends, myths, and fairy tales of a mysterious world that was long
gone and yet very alive in my heart. The dreaming heavily influenced my choice of books and I became so drawn to those publi-
cations that I soon expressed to my grandmother Rita my burning
desire to learn how to read and write, hoping that she could teach
me well before I was supposed to start my official schooling.

She was immediately responsive. What I received was a great
deal more than what I had originally asked for. In fact, Rita also
introduced me to art, music, history, and encouraged me to dance,
escorting me regularly to ballet classes and to the theatre where I
could witness dancers in action. The theatre held a particular kind
of fascination over my child-self.

I was spellbound by the magical atmosphere and the delicious
surprises that unfolded in front of my eyes. Once the red and gold
velvet curtains were lifted, a doorway was revealed leading me
into an enchanted world of endless possibilities.

Filled with anticipation, I would gaze upon the stage, repeatedly smitten by the fusion between the music and the dancers'
bodies; each of their steps executed in such perfect harmony and
synchronicity. I was not yet conscious of the existence of the alchemical process between music and creation, yet the power of
sound already influenced me, its vibrations raising mine, opening

my vision, inviting me to glimpse future possibilities. It would evoke all sorts of feelings within me pervading my being with a profound sense of longing for something that I did not have any explanation for or understanding of—something mysterious was a trigger for the romantic nature of my soul, intensifying my emotions with every note, every sweet new melody.

Music also often brought tears to my eyes, as a sense of remembrance took a stranglehold over my being. This was rather bizarre. I was so young, what was there to remember? But soul memories were unfolding and sometimes faces and places that I did not know appeared in front of my eyes in a fast sequence of images resembling faded pictures. Time after time, I travelled within my imagination inventing new circumstances for myself in the shape of daydreams.

I loved to dream accompanied by a piece of music or a song, as this was in fact stimulating my Power of Creation. Because when we dream we create with the Light. And when Sound and Light work together, powerful frequencies are produced to support more possible manifestations.

So, both music and dance became my first true reason to exist. My heartfelt wish was to become a ballerina, unifying the movements of my body with the sound of music.

To have received such purpose so very young was a precious gift that would eventually teach me how to direct my energy powerfully in order to accomplish what was needed. Besides, I was infinitely blessed to have my grandmother sharing with me both her artistic sensibility and her love of beauty. Together, we frequently visited museums, palaces, and churches appreciating some of the most extraordinary architecture, paintings, and sculptures ever made by man.

Growing up in Florence enriched me with a strong sense of aesthetics that later on would shape-shift into a sort of obsession, where beauty and superficiality of appearance became far more important then the beauty of my internal state of being. But those were years of great discoveries, and my grandmother's teachings inspired me to recognize that knowledge was power. She was the one who instilled within me the seeds of the intellectual mind and through this process she became my first mentor. A very strong bond forged between us, and as a result I became extremely attached to her.

If my grandmother had at heart the mentoring of my intellect, my mother was indeed a teacher of the soul. Life with her was never dull, always reflecting the various facets of her sparkling personality and eclectic nature. Her point of view on many things was different and more daring than others. The range of her individuality spread from the way she dressed to the way she taught my sister and I. Her methods of education were far more modern than what was considered to be correct at the time. There were so many rules regarding how to mentor children and Giovanna liked to break most of them. My mother was an original thinker and this originality also extended to her spiritual beliefs such that she had nothing to do with the Catholic Church's dogma.

So while Tata Anna taught me how to pray and indoctrinated me with religion in her own individual way, my beautiful mother instead presented me with the concept of a most unusual Spiritual World, certainly not the one I would eventually learn from catechism. She believes that souls return to earth time after time through reincarnation, and that in the course of our lifetime we would again meet the souls of those we had previously encountered.

According to Giovanna, many unseen Spiritual Presences were guiding and protecting us on our paths and it was very possible to communicate with Spirit if one possessed particular gifts. But ultimately, my mother truly inspired me to dream of my own destiny, teaching me that we do have a predetermined destiny. And that to find the faith, courage, and freedom inside of myself, to follow my destiny, was of vital importance in order to live a fulfilled life.

Utterly mesmerized by all of these revelations, I absorbed the essence of each of her words like a sponge, feeling resonance with them at the core of my being. Soon enough, I started to ponder my own destiny daily, feeling that dancing was somehow part of it.

My mother's knowledge came from her teacher, a powerful medium named Vincenzo. In his youth, Vincenzo became a disciple of the Italian Saint Padre Pio who trained him in mediumship. When Vincenzo met my mother, he was quick to detect her strong spiritual predisposition, passing on to her some profound teachings that awoke in her a higher level of awareness.

Despite being totally disinterested in the Catholic way, this very unique woman that I called mother recognized the teachings of the Christ, calling him the first revolutionary, the one who came to earth in order to bring us the revolution of the heart. My mother carries deep inside of her the seeds of Christ Consciousness, a special Light that holds the qualities of the Spiritual Education of love that Christ brought to earth to support us in opening our hearts.

Also, one of my mother's greatest understandings is about equality, shared as well by Tata Anna. These two women, so opposite in everything, from social status to interests, perceived and treated all others as equal in identical measure, possessing the gift of compassion for both humans and animals.

Unfortunately, these wonderful qualities were lacking in many other members of my family, who instead were only interested in others according to their social status and wealth. Especially my paternal grandparents who firmly believed that if you were born aristocratic or rich, somehow, you were automatically better than those of more modest birth or means. As my paternal grandparents did, nowadays many people still hold this idea of *birthright* that gives them a sense of fake superiority—it is one of the many illusions that humanity still holds in the banks of our collective memories, this perpetual judgment measuring others according to their social status or bank accounts.

I have a confession to make though. While I was still in my sleeping state, I too used *birthright* as a shield to hide my low self-esteem in order to look more interesting, more special in the eyes of others, as I did not feel I was enough. And when you don't feel enough, it is also difficult to be able to give enough of yourself to others.

Both conditions would personally affect me in a deep way, creating a system of false beliefs within me that I would abide by for many years to come. This false belief system led me to put others in so-called categories. There were some individuals I considered inferior, some I considered equal, and some I saw as better then me. I would feel very intimidated and threatened by those who could trigger all my mechanisms, causing me to go into a negative and depressed state. And dearest reader, this is the truth of exactly what happens when the measurement cup is out and we insist on comparing ourselves to others, refusing to see our own Light.

There is also another side of the coin for my mother, a more abstract side to her: physically she was aloof. Touching, hugging, kissing, or any kind of physical affection was not part of her vocabulary and as strange at it may seem, both my sister and I were hardly ever touched by her.

So, Francesca and I both grew up with much to stimulate our brains and inspire our souls but the affection on offer was almost nonexistent, too indefinable and far too conceptual for two young kids who also wished to be held by their parents, to feel the warmth of an embrace, the softness of a kiss. My father was largely absent of affection too, often locked inside his own world and only devoted to our mother. This meant it was up to Rita, our beloved grandmother, to come to the rescue by saturating us with physical expressions of love and gifting us with the reassurances that we were both cared for on all levels.

A year or so passed. By then I was going to school and attending ballet studies with constant dedication, when out of the blue I began to suffer excruciating pain inside both my legs. This pain would come and go in waves, exactly like the nightmares had previously. The family doctor visited me several times but could not diagnose the cause of my illness.

After awhile I started to deteriorate. My body weakened as the pain spread all over my body. High fevers were constant, devouring all of my life force and restricting me to my bed most of the time. Descending from the picture of health, I became a sickly child unable to dance or to attend school for long periods.

Confined to my bed all day long with not much company, I experienced more loneliness and a sense of separation from others. Feeling punished by God, I could not understand what I had done wrong. *What had I done to deserve being pushed away from everything I loved and cherished?* In my own mind I was convinced that nobody would truly be able to assist me because no one could possibly feel my pain, anxiety, and hopelessness. I was also fearful that my illness could be grave, and that my parents did not want to tell me the truth. *Maybe I didn't have much time to live or much to live for.*

The reality was that my family looked after me as best as they could but all their kindness did not make me feel any better as loneliness and separation cut deep wounds inside my heart, along with the illusion that nobody could possibly understand me. The disease acted as a cellular memory trigger that reactivated old memories within me, causing all the beliefs that I was feeling at the time.

You must understand, dearest reader, that sometimes what we may feel or think is not necessarily the truth but just an illusion created by an old program in our being

While I was left in this limbo, I became angry with God as I felt totally abandoned and started to wonder what his purpose was—when I needed him the most, he was not there for me. Tata Anna sensed that I was in trouble and once again took me under her wing, elucidating the meaning of being tested in life, and how it was of utmost importance to have faith and trust in God so I could be supported to receive the best possible outcome. "Even Jesus had been tested" she used to say to me matter of fact. Her simple words somehow impressed me enough to give me courage and hope.

So I prayed with renewed fervor—it took a little while but I was finally heard. At last, after almost two years of misery, the doctor discovered that my tonsils were rotten and had infected my blood causing rheumatic fever. I was immediately operated and soon after started to rapidly recover my health . In no time, I was back inside my ballet shoes pirouetting my way into the future, my spirits uplifted in a state of pure joy, and my faith in God temporarily restored.

I say temporarily because the wounds of loneliness and separation, so deeply entrenched in my soul, were not at all mended as this was part of my karma and many lessons would be required to finally liberate my being from the grip of those ancient memories.

Now, for the next few pages, we are going to travel outside of Florence, across the freeway of our imaginations to a small country place that had great relevance in my younger years.

There is a tiny village set in a most picturesque valley guarded by the Apennine Mountains, between the cities of Florence and Bologna. It is called Covigliaio. From the 1800s, Covigliaio became a rather fashionable holiday destination and every year my maternal family would leave the torrid Florentine summer for the scenic beauty and fresh air of this enchanted village. It was there where I developed my passion for walking and discovered that nature was powerful, and held many secrets. And it was there where I also encountered and embraced a few fundamental realizations that had deep impacts on my future life. Furthermore, Covigliaio offered the first clear picture of my paternal grandparents.

Stefano and Maroussia didn't spend much of their time in Florence.

As I mentioned before, their main residence was the ancient Badia, a stunning villa, once a monastery, perched on top of a hill close to Pisa. My grandparents were not greatly interested in children, including their own, my father.

But for some odd reason they became very fond of me. So, every summer in June, Stefano and Maroussia travelled to Covigliaio especially to visit their granddaughter.

Both deeply intrigued me, especially Maroussia with her fascinating stories, violet eyes, and impenetrable sphinx-like personality. Constantly holding a cigarette in one of her well-manicured hands and some sort of drink in the other, my Russian grandmother represented to me an ideal of utter sophistication; her foreign accent was music to my ears. When my grandparents were conversing between themselves in either French or English, a strong conviction rose inside of my being: *One day I will be able to speak those foreign languages. I will travel all over the world as they have, and enjoy an international and glamorous lifestyle.* I was indeed a dreamer, a daydreamer as much as night dreamer, spending large amounts of time lost in a fantasy world, my imagination running wild with the visions of how I sensed or wanted my future reality to be.

What I didn't know then was that hidden somewhere inside of me lay the power of manifestation, the ability to create my dreams, to shape-shift the present reality into a different reality that suited me better. This awareness would arise with time, but for a long while I would still be unconscious of the most important thing: the knowledge of the difference between the dream of the mind versus the dream of the heart. This would only be discovered in Divine Time.

In those slow and lazy summer days, I amused my grandmother greatly, and in exchange she could be rather indulgent, often letting me play with her real and rather extravagant jewelry. Maroussia would tell me stories of how some of those precious objects had saved her life in the distant past when she had fled from Russia dressed as a peasant girl in the company of only one trusted servant. The revolution was about to start and her parents had sent her away to safety making sure that she had several diamonds sewn in the hem of her simple dress to provide her with something of substance, as nobody knew what the future might hold in those unstable times.

My grandmother narrated this tragic real-life event as if it was almost a fairy tale. Occasionally I could sense her sadness, but I would instantly brush it aside. Through my childish eyes, her stories were adventurous and incredibly romantic. Afterwards, I would play for hours pretending to be a runaway princess with all of my grandmother's jewels hidden inside the pockets of my jeans.

Remember, I loved the theatre; I had a sense of drama and a fertile imagination. And most importantly, what I wanted to see was only the aura of glamour that surrounded Maroussia, and not the uncomfortable truth that would have shown me a very different and disturbing reality.

Though I was just a little girl, to see only what I wanted to see, the partial truth, was also to become a deep pattern in my adult life and accordingly one of my biggest lessons. To see the truth from every angle and not just from our own narrow corner can open our views to a much brighter Light shining on the truth about ourselves and others, supporting us to interact with more awareness, more acceptance, and more understanding of what is needed in order to create more harmony.

Every morning I impatiently waited for my grandfather to pick me up and take me for a long walk. He always appeared at the gate at the same time impeccably dressed in a light-colored cotton suit.

A panama hat sat elegantly on top of his head, revealing a flash of rebellious white thick hair from underneath the straw. I would immediately run towards him with all of my youthful enthusiasm and then we would always walk hand in hand for a short while on the main road under a clear cerulean sky.

After awhile, we would enter a country lane framed on both sides by endless golden wheat fields. This idyllic scenario became the unusual setting of the seeding of many of my new dreams. Because my grandfather was not particularly adept at handling children, he would address me as an adult, and in a strange way I benefited from this situation. I was allowed to ask him all sorts of questions, and being very inquisitive I would comply with his requests with great eagerness.

Above all, I was especially fascinated by the stories of his many excursions around the globe and his childhood tales of growing up in Australia and California. Stefano's father, my great-grandfather, owned a large business trading in exotic fruits between Australia and America. Stefano's mother, Catherine, the American heiress, was bequeathed an estate in Santa Barbara on the northern coast of California, and his father spent his youth travelling between these two continents.

Imagining with open eyes these mysterious and faraway lands, I was completely absorbed listening to every detail, every single word of these family stories. My grandfather gifted me with a larger vision of life. During our walks, we mentally journeyed together all over the earth, helping me to expand my horizons across a world that was still mysterious to me in its vastness.

Genetically, I felt a strong resonance with my grandfather's lineage filled with adventurous characters that stopped at nothing to manifest their ideas. And eventually I would fully inherit my ancestors' strong spirit of adventure, the courage to leave everything I knew and loved behind in search of my own destiny.

Sadly, those summers with Maroussia and Stefano were short-lived. Cancer devoured my grandmother and soon after my grandfather committed suicide. He could not conceive of his life without her. My family was both devastated and horrified by his act. Personally, I thought it was the most romantic of actions and also wished one day I would have such passion for someone. Though in time the chimera of romanticism revealed to me a darker side through a series of illusions about the nature of love that would profoundly affect my behavior in several of my future intimate relationships.

With Stefano gone, I lost the support of the most active male figure in my life. My other grandfather Piero, who had perished in a fatal car accident when I was just two years old, had become only a vague memory. My beloved father was of course there, but he very much blended into the background, too busy, and too absorbed in showering his love exclusively onto my mother.

I was eight and my sister was five when our lives started to unfold within a matriarchal society where the Presence and influence of men was rare. And with time, the nature of men became more and more of a mystery to me while the many examples of strong women taught me how to be independent. This period also marked the beginning of a great imbalance between the masculine and feminine energies within me. This imbalance eventually produced the struggles I was to encounter in expressing myself emotionally, as my masculine side would often crush the needs of my feminine side, and vice versa.

What I later grew to learn is that independent of which sex we are, each of us carries within us both the masculine and feminine. Therefore, all unresolved issues between these energies are fundamentally key players in some of the negative dynamics that may affect our being.

In my case, to brutally hide my vulnerability and loving ways from the eyes of others and instead show a fake version of myself only helped to increase my loneliness and cause misunderstandings with the ones I loved. The Shadow of my ego and pride often rejected my female energy, forcing my masculine energy to bear the heaviness of responsibilities alone; the weight of duty and all the anxieties that go with it. Thus, I became resentful of always needing to show my strength and providing for myself, but simultaneously I was incapable of showing others my deepest wish to be held and taken care of as I was terrified of losing my independence and ultimately giving my power away to a man.

With the death of both of my paternal grandparents, the first losses were received while my personality was slowly forming, and my heart closed down a little bit more. Season after season, the months disappeared at such a fast pace till another year went by and a very special day was about to arrive. But stormy weather was quickly approaching the serene sky of my childhood.

September at Covigliaio was stunning. This was the time when Mother Nature morphed the colors of her dress from summer to autumn, spraying endless rainbows of yellow, red, and orange across the land. A tinge of coolness was in the air mixed with the strong musky aroma of the woods, while the earth was gifting us with the most delicious mushrooms, sweet berries, and figs. While Gaia was crowned by such beauty and abundance, I was to celebrate my First Communion. After an intense training in religious studies, I was soon to receive the body of Christ according to the rituals of the Catholic Church.

My mother dressed me as she had envisioned: white embroidery angles in the lace of the dress, with a matching bonnet and white leather boots peeking through.

Giovanna loved clothes, and her daughters at times were her fashion dolls fitted by a seamstress for every important occasion. My First Communion gave my mother the perfect opportunity to exercise her fashion skills. On the other hand, I sulked as her choice of my Communion dress was the cause of much discontent for me.

I have to admit that my own fashion ideas were still in an embryonic state. I had only recently started to experiment on my new imaginary friend Barbie. The doll was given to me as a Christmas present and in spite of my general dislike of toys, Barbie with long blonde hair caressing her tiny waist, endless legs, and fabulous outfits, somehow stimulated my sense of aesthetics and love of glamour. In fact, she appealed to me to the point that I started to spend hours putting her looks together, becoming quite obsessed with my newfound passion for styling clothes.

Because my mother imposed her sartorial choices on me most of the time, Barbie came to represent my first attempt to master the fashion language and supported the development of a precise thought process that would later become a very important form of my self-expression. But my ideas and my mother's ideas on fashion matters clashed and so a battle of wills began.

Why could Giovanna not understand that this was my big day? I wanted tulle, not embroidery angles. I wanted pretty silk slippers, not white lace-up boots. But most of all I wanted a veil and not that ghastly bonnet. *Would Barbie wear a bonnet? Not even in her worst nightmare* I thought cringing with embarrassment and anger. In desperation, I ran to Tata Anna begging her to explain to my mother that as a new bride of Christ I was meant to wear a veil. But all was in vain and Giovanna was unmoved.

Finally, the fashion battle was lost and I was gutted, yet to receive the final blow. The fateful day arrived at last and I walked slowly towards the simple country church, facing the rest of the children in my silly bonnet and white boots. All the other girls were adorned with gorgeous fine veils and delicate silk slippers. I felt so inadequate and was grateful and relieved when nobody actually ridiculed me—after all, it was a special day and all the children were on their best behavior.

I sighed and finally decided to enjoy the moment, after reproaching myself for being concerned with superficial details when I was about to experience the Holy Sacrament for the very first time. *What would I feel?* I spent so many days and nights dreaming of that moment and imagining all kinds of different scenarios where I would fall into ecstasy like Saint Bernadette of Lourdes did in the film that I recently saw on TV with Tata Anna. My excitement became uncontainable and I couldn't wait any longer to be fed by the body of Christ.

After a never-ending mass, the priest finally arrived in front of me and with great anticipation I ate the white paper-thin bread. I swallowed it, my eyes still closed, savoring the sacredness of that moment and waited to receive a Divine Sign. But nothing of what I was promised during the endless hours of catechism arrived. *Where was the feeling of ecstasy, the vision of Jesus, the immense happiness in my heart?* Quietly I went back to my seat and kneeled down in prayer. Still nothing. *How could that be possible?* The only thing I truly felt was massive disappointment and aching knees.

With each minute ticking away, a sense of emptiness instead of joy grew inside me. I suddenly stood up and looked around at the other children. They were all radiant with satisfied looks painted upon their faces. *Did God forget me?* The shadow of doubt descended upon my soul, obscuring my mind and heart and crumbling one by one each of my religious beliefs in a domino effect of absolute destruction:

How many times had I heard my father's negative opinion about religion—his distrust of priests? I never saw him attend mass once. My mother hardly ever went to Church either, and certainly her credo was very different. Am I being cheated by God or by men? Is it all a lie? But no! It could not be!! Tata Anna and my beloved grandmother Rita loved going to church and found comfort in it.

All these different thoughts were pulling me apart. Feeling utterly lost, I needed answers fast. But what was I to do in the meantime? The service was about to end and everyone was brimming with happiness, apart from me. *Why am I so different, so complicated?* That was a question I kept asking myself. In truth, I often sensed separation from others and felt alone, disengaged at times even from those closest to me.

I was not a loner. A loving family surrounded me—I was a popular student, bright academically, and a gifted dancer. People, in fact, gravitated towards me, and yet loneliness inhabited my being. I had received the first symptoms of the solitude of my soul when I fell gravely ill with rheumatic fever and that disturbing feeling had never left.

My Communion was to be the day I expected the Light of the Christ to fill the hole in my heart, but instead I felt abandoned, unworthy of God's love and once again on my own. *Was I going to admit defeat and tell my peers and family that nothing had happened? That I felt no different?* Can you imagine their faces if I implied that the sacrament of Holy Communion could be a masquerade? I thought, *so why not just pretend? Pretend to be as ecstatic as the other kids. That will make it so much easier and, most importantly, nothing needs to be disclosed or explained.*

So I did. I pretended and realized I was excellent at it, a born actress. That day one of my primary patterns, pretense, hiding behind a mask, resurfaced in the stream of my consciousness, and the first of my many performances worthy of an Oscar was offered to a willing public. As a result, I also suffered a further closure of my heart.

In retrospect I wish I could have hugged the child I was when I felt alone and not worthy of God's love, of any love. How was I to know that God was already within me? That we already own our divinity and that none of this was an exterior act that can be received from others outside of ourselves? I believe my soul carried that knowledge but my young mind got in the way of the truth, frantically searching for a logical explanation that I could not find then because that explanation lay hidden in the Akashic Records of my soul.

It was, in fact, the process of my mind versus my heart that in time caused me so much grief and confusion. It was my strong mind that led me further from the path of the heart. In a few words, what I thought with my mind and what I felt with my heart were to be two disjointed factors in my daily existence and bound to remain separate for a long while

That day I felt disenchanted and betrayed, losing another piece of my pure child innocence. Furthermore, I promised myself from that moment on I would never set foot in a church ever again, and so it was. That I was reliving something that had happened to me exactly three lives earlier was a truth I would discover about myself in the future.

In the meantime, something else fierce and hard-edged began to take shape inside the traits of my character, slowly molding the sweet dreamy child into the warrior woman that I would become shortly thereafter.

It was around my tenth birthday when the uneasy feeling of separation pushed me to build an even more impenetrable, invisible barrier to protect myself from others. Ultimately it was constructed as a defense against the energy of judgment, especially the one coming from the environment of my new ballet school.

I had recently started to study with a well-known English teacher. The school was located inside a grand old Florentine palace and the ballet classes were held in a stunning space beneath a high ceiling decorated with original frescoes. There was a large mirror covering the entire width of one of the walls and wood barres were all around the perimeter of the room.

This place was to become a temple where I forged myself in more ways than one. The physicality of dancing would give me a lean and strong figure and gift me with command and awareness over my body and mind, teaching me to control them simultaneously and to stay focused. But above all I would be taught discipline. In this temple of dance, I developed an iron will and powerful determination. I learned not to give up but instead to be strong and to endure.

With time, strength became one of my most evident trademarks, sometimes to the point of hurting both others and myself deeply just for the sake of keeping up the appearance; to show weakness was to be almost shameful. I learned from a young age never to give away my inner thoughts, the inner truth of my being, so that others could not take advantage of my vulnerability. Consequently, this was another vital reason that pretense became a way of life to the extent that masking and hiding my real self became one of my biggest skills.

In the beginning of this transformation I was only trying to protect my hypersensitivity from all the judgment and jealousy that I was exposed to in a very competitive microcosm. The ballet world was extremely tough and I was not spared any of the harsh realities that came with it.

To help me rise above the pain, I soon developed another weapon of self-defense. Aloofness together with an attitude of superiority became my bow and arrow constantly directed towards anybody who threatened the fortress fully constructed around my heart. The young warrior woman was secretly training. She might have worn a tutu and ballet shoes but underneath the froth, she was getting ready to conquer whatever awaited her on the battlefield of life.

Despite all these hardships, to dance was also a source of immense joy for my being. It was again, as fate had decided, lighting up the sacred fire of Terpsichore in my heart. To design with my own body the most harmonious of shapes, to fly across the air and land on the ground as light as a feather, to pirouette at great speed with such precision, and to master it all to the sound of wonderful music utterly inspired me—it made me feel alive.

Dancing represented the freedom to express myself but strangely enough it was also about to bring me some unexpected surprises tainted by the invisible veils of unresolved karma.

A few more years passed without much disruption till the moment when an unwanted guest came knocking at the door of my family home. It was death. And as only death can manifest, it brought an ending and a new beginning.

A new phase, a new initiation of my young life was about to commence.

The transition from child to teenager was the beginning of a profound personal metamorphosis. I went through an existential crisis and rebelled against the norms and any predesigned road map that was not the one my soul had truly chosen.

A fresh idea had gradually taking possession of my mind: My future did not lie in Florence. Instead, I was destined to live abroad, maybe in one of those faraway lands described by my grandfather. To dance was to be the key to my freedom and my inner desire was to study full time at a prestigious international ballet academy.

Of course I had no idea how this was going to unfold. But what I knew for sure was that I felt constricted by the thought of living in Florence and that my wish was to walk my own path. The concept of finishing school, university, possible marriage, children, and so on, was alien to my being. I became totally disinterested in the approved way of living and instinctively recognized that my mother would be the one to help me fulfill my new vision.

Giovanna was also different. I understood that if my mother could have had a chance earlier on in her life to break free from all the rules and regulations she would have done so gladly. Often she talked about freedom, explaining to me that to be free at all levels was the most important of all achievements. She also pointed out that with freedom came great responsibility and that it was critical to make wise choices. I truly wanted this freedom, the freedom to walk upon my chosen path, not the pre-established route fundamentally accepted by most individuals.

Those were the times, especially in Italy, when parents mapped out the futures of their children, disregarding what their sons or daughters truly wished for—the thinking then was that children could be dismissed exactly because they were children and could not possibly know any better. Many young people were utterly crushed by the hopes of their parents.

So I say, dearest reader, if you are indeed a parent, don't ever forget to be a loving and compassionate guide so that your children can achieve their Highest Potential. The young ones may already know in their hearts their own truth and a good parent needs to individuate this truth, nourish it, and not repress it or replace it with what they think could be best.

The day soon arrived when I fully opened up to my mother, telling her what was weighing on my heart. Luckily I found in Giovanna a very receptive listener. She understood that I was different and therefore needed an alternative educational system that would help me truly express my heart's dreams. She understood my artistic nature and my Spiritual Turmoil, and never forced me to go back to church. I will be forever grateful to my mother as she made it all possible for me. Certainly we had plenty of disagreements and arguments, but still I felt so profoundly supported by her—she is indeed a great blessing I was graced with from the very beginning of my reincarnation.

While Giovanna started to investigate various potential foreign ballet schools to further my education, my grandmother took ill. It all began rather casually with a simple visit to the family doctor. Rita was gradually losing her energy and appetite and the cause of this was yet to be detected. The doctor sent her to a specialist followed by another specialist but no one could establish what was wrong.

In the meantime, my beloved grandmother, like a wilted flower in the heat of summer, was slowly drying up. It was heartbreaking to witness her deterioration, to see the life sucked out of a woman I loved so very much; a second mother to me. My grandmother was not only my mentor but also the only source for my physical affection that was otherwise nonexistent. It was her touch, her kisses, and her hugs that my sister and I would impatiently wait for every day, especially before bedtime where a ritual of love, a great display of affection, was always exchanged between the three of us.

Then one doomed morning the news that nobody wanted to hear arrived and crushed us all. My grandmother had cancer and it was incurable. Soon after, I found my mother alone crying and realized that death was on its way. I pleaded with God to not take my grandmother. Despite being angry with the Church, I still believed in the Almighty. I told God that this was his chance to show his mercy and if he truly loved me he would leave her alone. *What was the point of such an early departure? It would not make any difference if Rita were to join you much later! You must already have plenty of company up in the Heavens!* Night after night, alone in bed, I would make all sorts of deals with God in order to keep my grandmother alive and it seemed to work for awhile.

Till one day I came home from a ballet class and saw my mother standing at the top of the staircase leading to our apartment. She was silent, staring at me with glassy eyes and tears streaming down her beautiful face. I ran past her and into Rita's bedroom, almost believing that I could stop death from taking my grandmother. There she was lying on her bed, as if she was asleep. I stood motionless looking at her peaceful face, trying to take in every single detail of her features because I never wanted to forget her. Memories of all the wonderful moments spent together were rapidly passing in front of my eyes. And though I felt such pain piercing my soul, I could not cry.

The day of the funeral I was numb to the point of no return and felt utterly abandoned by God. I did not go to church. Only afterwards I joined the rest of my family for the burial. My grandmother chose to rest eternally in the small country cemetery at Covigliaio, a peaceful place surrounded by cypress trees and fields. While I observed the coffin disappear into the earth, I felt a distinct mechanism of closure inside of me; that was the final turn of the key that sealed the vault of my heart.

The impact of my grandmother's death would violently reverberate through my soul with increased strength through the years and bring me to a new and deeper level of loneliness, as well as to a new false credo: I came to the conclusion that I would never give my heart fully to anyone else, as my fear of losing them became insurmountable. "I shall not feel therefore I shall not suffer" became my shield as hard as a thousand diamonds around my heart to seal an invisible fortress.

The days and months that followed were the saddest I can ever remember. I felt defeated, angry with God, and in a state of denial. My grandmother left a big empty space inside our family's heart and consequently I was even more compelled to leave home and follow my own path.

Death imparted in me a deep realization—time was truly precious and given to us only in limited amounts. Therefore, I was never going to allow myself to waste anymore time in doing things that were meaningless to me. This insight, on one hand made me very focused and determined to achieve my goals, but on the other hand transformed me into a selfish person. Giving to others or compromising for the sake of others became increasingly difficult because I was so driven by my own wants and desires, and by the credo I lived by—please myself first since life is so brief.

The energy of loss rampant in the genetics of my family tree had scarred me badly. But for all the protection I had raised around my heart, I still had to discover that suffering is unavoidable when you are a human being, and my fear of not wanting to recognize this truth, would not serve me at all well.

A few weeks later I had another revelation. I had fallen into a deep sleep and dreamed I arrived in a magical garden in the company of one of my school friends. We were walking around exploring the beauty and lusciousness of the surroundings. There was a towering wall at the back of the garden covered by a multitude of rambling roses embellishing its ancient stones with their ephemeral beauty. I looked up and noticed the wall was so high that the top was hidden amidst the clouds. I asked my friend if she wanted to accompany me, as I was curious to discover what I might find all the way up there. She declined so I decided to go on my own.

It was not easy to climb such a steep wall, but gradually, step-by-step I advanced while underneath me the garden slowly disappeared, fading away in the distance. Those roses had plenty of thorns which cut through the fine skin of my hands and caused them to bleed. But strangely enough I felt no pain. At last I reached the clouds wondering how much further I still needed to climb, and then finally came to a golden door carved in the stone. I opened it with a mixture of fear and excitement. I entered the unknown, and my hands, as if by magic, immediately stopped bleeding.

To my great surprise I also found myself in the most exquisite palace where gallery after gallery contained many important works of art hanging from the walls. Many other individuals were there too, walking through the large corridors admiring the paintings. I tried approaching some of the other visitors to ask them where I was, but it was in vain as I was invisible to them. An abundance of light poured from a large window so I went in that direction to investigate, trying to find out a little bit more about this mysterious location. Sprawled in front of my eyes was the breathtaking sight of a city of great beauty. Built on the bluest of water, temples, palaces, and bridges stood in all their magnificence.

I opened the window to admire this spectacle with more ease. Then all of a sudden I felt somebody's strong Presence. I looked around but the palace was empty. All the visitors had vanished. What a strange place indeed.

I looked up at the sky and there he was, this giant Being of Light dressed in a regal way, suspended amidst the clouds. He was young and very handsome. His eyes were like sapphires, his hair

golden, and his smile gentle. I was fascinated by the vision and wanted to reach out to him. *Who was he? Where was I?* Then, it all started to fade away and I was back in my bedroom wide-awake, safely tucked inside my bed .

Instantly it all became clear. I would leave home soon and climb high upon my path. I felt blessed and protected by the mysterious being. *Was he an Angel? Perhaps not, as he possessed no wings. One day I will find out* I promised myself.

But for the time being I was getting ready to move forward and stride across the uncharted territory of the map of my existence. I knew my journey was about to start....

IN THE
WAITING ROOM–
MONTE CARLO

$\mathcal{S}$oon after the passing of my beloved grandmother, my parents announced their imminent departure to an unknown destination. When I questioned them on their whereabouts, they only gave a vague reply. *What was the reason for such secrecy?* I kept asking myself while wandering in the limbo of my curiosity. But just a few days later upon their return from the mysterious journey, I was rewarded with a piece of the puzzle of my future existence. The magic wand of fate touched me, and in a split-second fantasy was alchemized into reality as I became the bearer of a special gift.

The Accademie de Dance Princess Grace, one of the most prominent ballet schools in Europe, was to be my summer destination. I would spend the school holidays in Monte Carlo training with Marika Besobrasova, the formidable director and world-renowned teacher.

Since the death of my grandmother I had descended into a spiral of desolation, a stark landscape of the soul where the spring of

faith had dried up and all hope seemed lost. In those bleak hours, I first turned against God, as I judged him responsible for my suffering. But later on I had a change of heart influenced once more by Tata Anna. I renewed my faith in him and prayed incessantly to receive Divine Help. And yet again I was heard: The answer swiftly delivered, wrapped in the translucent frequencies of grace. A small miracle finally lifted me out of the black hole of my sorrow, once more gifting me with a sense of purpose and a clear direction.

I was convinced that this unexpected surprise was most definitely orchestrated from the Heavens. What intrigued me the most were all the strange coincidences that played a part in this fateful chain of events. Firstly, my future teacher shared a very similar background and history with Marussia, my Russian grandmother. Because of this, Marika had expressed to my parents immediate interest in meeting me. And secondly, I would soon travel to a place deeply aligned with my paternal genetic lineage— the French Riviera, a coastal land of legendary beauty set between high mountains and cobalt blue sea.

Dreaming with open eyes, I often imagined my grandparents plotting away from the Spirit World. I also suspected that the mysterious luminous figure from my latest soul journey was somehow involved in this celestial conspiracy. Certainly, not long after his visitation, my wishes had materialized out of thin air; it was hard to believe that after being crushed by such sadness and hopelessness that my dream of studying abroad was becoming my new reality.

Mysterious forces were at work. I was sure of that.

Summer came, announced by the sweet fragrance of nature in full bloom.

I arrived at *Casa Mia* on a fine day at the end of June and entered the threshold of a new chapter of my young life with confidence. I had no fear, only eagerness to launch myself into an exciting new adventure, guided by a strong conviction that I was exactly where I was meant to be.

Casa Mia was perched above a promontory at the edge of a curve, elegantly standing where the road gently rolled down to meet the sea. A pink Belle Époque-style villa, once home to the famous dancer Isadora Duncan and her wealthy lover, the school had commanding, sweeping views of the Mediterranean. The imposing building with its harmonious proportion and gothic arched windows, emanated a certain air of mystery that immediately captured my imagination. I felt strangely at home in that foreign place and could not wait to be on my own and out of parental sight—my independent spirit already smelling the exotic scent of freedom and all those infinite possibilities that could blossom upon my path.

Soon after our arrival Marika made a grand entrance into the hall of the school to greet my parents and I. Oozing abundant charisma, her distinguished features gave her an air of great authority. Without missing a beat, she scanned me with her intense gaze and in that very instant when our eyes met for the very first time I felt electrified with a new sensation that was hard to define except to say our souls recognized one another, and for a moment time stood still.

Dearest reader, you too may have found that some individuals touch us only superficially and others immediately strike a deep chord within our beings. The reason must reveal itself in Divine Time but be assured that there is always a motive for our reaction, as nothing is without purpose on this earth. There is a meaning for every word, every action, every thought and feeling, and of course every encounter. Both individuals and circumstances are brought to us so we may learn continuously and grow on our paths of evolution, because when these lessons are understood, this process will support the dissolution of the karma we have previously created.

Consequently, almost at first sight, I was about to be served with exactly one of these karmic lessons as I experienced with Marika an acute sense of remembrance, one I had never sensed before with a total stranger. I felt I knew her, clearly perceiving that Marika was the mentor I was searching for, somebody who could take me by the hand and guide me to the next level of knowledge that I was striving to reach. Though intuitively recognizing the powerful soul connection between us, I was still unaware of the many dynamics that would convey with time the far more complex nature of our encounter in which more karma would ultimately reveal itself in a rather abrupt way.

Marika immediately began to show me what was required to move forward in life, and that life itself was neither straightforward nor fair. She was skilled at empowering those already showing signs of strength. Equally, she possessed no patience for anybody with a weak predisposition, dismissing whoever did not pass her tests. The warrior woman was growing steadily inside of me, fed by Marika's teachings and uncompassionate philosophy. I wanted to be just like her, strong and powerful. And when the moment came to go home, I knew I would return to my chosen teacher—that time it would be for good, or let's say for as long as it was needed.

After my dazzling summer in Monte Carlo, going back to Florence felt like stepping backwards. School was uninspiring, the other teachers a pale imitation of Marika. All I wanted was to dance, pushing myself harder than ever, as I was determined to go back and study ballet full-time. But at home the situation was degenerating into a reality with which I could no longer identify. With all my grandparents gone to a different dimension, my mother and father were harshly introduced to serious financial problems. Both their inheritances had resulted in more debts than cash and much had to be sold off.

On top of this, grave internal family issues between my mother and uncle had created an uneasy situation that potentially jeopardized the ownership of our only remaining property.

My mother, who until then had a leisurely lifestyle, was forced to work as extra income was urgently needed to pay additional expenses to allow us to keep our family home. Giovanna had a resourceful character and without hesitation fought against this adversity with creativity, transforming her passion for fashion into her new profession. Her business was designing and making clothes for all of those society women who always admired and envied her style. However, her new role was demanding, leaving my mother less available to both my sister and I.

This radical shift in our family dynamics destabilized Francesca's fragile internal mechanisms. My sister, also deeply wounded by the loss of our grandmother, felt abandoned, and in time developed the burden of not being heard and a certain form of victimization. The changes touched me as well but in a very different way. I simply closed my self off in my own world. Driven by the burning desire to go back to Marika, I focused all of my energy on manifesting my intention. Unfortunately, ignoring my younger sister was a normal state of affairs, making me utterly blind to her sufferings and sense of loss. In order to compensate for the imbalance of Francesca's frail personality, Tata Anna began to spoil my sister rotten, trying to accommodate all of her whims and her ever-growing cries for attention. In the years to come, Francesca would hold huge resentment towards all of us, at times causing terrible rifts and harsh exchanges filled with regrettable words.

And on top of everything else, as a result of the precarious financial situation, our parents started to fight, sometimes violently, leaving me rather disturbed and incapable of coping with my new reality. The stress on them must have been enormous but instead of feeling compassionate towards my mother, father, and sister, I decided that nothing resonated with me anymore. It was simply time to quit and go back to Monte Carlo as soon as I possibly could. I was desperately seeking some form of order in rejecting my disgruntled family. The peace and harmony that had once existed among us had disintegrated rapidly, torn apart by a tsunami of unresolved negative energy that was reclaiming everyone's loving heart.

It was harrowing to witness this reversal of fortune, as underneath it all I was hypersensitive and both my reaction and my wish to leave were partly dictated by a self-defense mechanism. Furthermore, because of my own selfishness, I failed to see that I was not the only one suffering and feeling displaced, as each member of my family was hit as hard as I, if not harder. Still, my mind was made up. I was unhappy and unable to handle this new situation, therefore I was determined to shift my reality. Finally I struck a deal with Giovanna. I was going to complete one more year of academic studies in Florence and after that I would be free to move to Monte Carlo where Marika had already accepted me as a full-time student.

The ability to radically change what did not suit me anymore became in time my gift and my curse. These manifestations were mainly dictated by my mind and not my heart, therefore they could never be fully successful as I was lacking the immense grace that one can only experience when co-creating with Spirit. What I mean is that when we create on our own, something will always be missing from our lives. This sense of incompletion occurs because the unresolved nature of our karma brings us continuing internal struggles that affect our reality in that particular area of our lives.

The real changes only arrived when I finally realized that my shape-shifting needed to come from within. It was the liberation from these internal mechanisms, karma, and core wounds that would actually affect my external reality in a positive way across all areas. This truth was to be found only in my very distant future—this new way of creating that would dismantle the old paradigms, freeing me from the limitations created by the mind.

It must have been tough for my mother to let go of me especially during such challenging times, though she never showed me her pain of separation. She had lost one after another, her own father and mother, her first son, financial stability, and now, one of her daughters was also about to go. Although there was an invisible cord of Light between us, threaded like a bridge that connected our souls deeply, the love we had for each other was universal, reaching a far greater depth of mutual understanding at all levels. I knew that Giovanna, despite her physical detachment, was the person I felt the closest and most similar to. She was the one I trusted implicitly. My mother's most special quality was that she practiced what she preached. She was a giver, gifting me with the promised freedom even if it came at a high cost to herself.

She always encouraged me to explore life and to go on my own journey without any fears or regrets. Occasionally I might have seen glimpses of her very well-contained sadness, but don't forget dearest reader, I saw only what I wanted to see. In fact I had convinced myself of quite the opposite—that she would not miss me at all as she was far too busy with her new business and the social life that supported her flow of clients.

My own personal version of the truth was not the truth at all, but simply what matched the creation of my illusions in that precise moment in time; and this mismanagement of the truth eventually brought me several painful lessons—the truth cannot be manipulated for our own personal benefit or to make us feel better. To seek truth outside of our being is simply another illusion because the ultimate search for such truth should always begin from within the depths of our own heart where each one of us possesses the key to ancient wisdom.

While all hell was breaking loose on the home front, an interesting scenario presented itself at school. My class was divided between friends that supported my decision to leave Florence and others who believed I was insane to leave my academic studies for such an uncertain future. There was a boy who tried to put me down at any given opportunity until one day I had had enough. I should have let go and just told him to mind his own business—after all, everyone is entitled to their own opinion. Instead,

I decided to punish him because my ego was not going to be undermined by any kind of criticism from him or anyone else. I was not just going to punish him, but I was going to do it in front of the entire class.

I waited for the right opportunity and when it presented itself I was ready to strike. My cold icy voice, almost metallic in sound, rolled out in a sequence of words that were like well-aimed bullets firing upon the chosen target, repeatedly perforating and trashing his confidence and his ego. There was no need for such cruelty, but in that moment something else had taken over and blinded me. This aspect of my consciousness was determined to have the last word in unleashing its full power in the most damaging of ways. I will never forget the face of that poor boy, so humiliated by the sheer fury and cruelty of what came out of my mouth!

Dearest reader, I was not yet aware that sound is a potent tool and needs to be used wisely. Words carry frequencies and if we speak to another in unconstructive terms using cruelty, anger, jealousy, manipulation, and lies to name but a few, we activate a powerful transmission of negative energy that will consequently sit deeply inside the consciousness of everyone involved. If you give negativity you will only receive negativity.

What I also received that day was the bitter aftertaste of revenge—it gave me no joy. Afterwards a little voice inside suggested I apologize to this boy, but the voice was a whisper compared to a louder one that insisted instead that he fully deserved to be treated in such a manner and not to waste anymore time with such a loser.

Another one of my patterns was clearly rising to the surface. This particular one was extremely ingrained in my being. It was about power, or shall I say the misuse of power. At the dawn of a new chapter of my

young life, the shadow of forgotten memories from the past were coming back to haunt me.

In my case, I brutally imposed my opinions, disregarding the views of others as a defense because I did not like being judged. Most probably, I was unfairly judged in past lives. Regrettably though, I was quick to condemn whoever acted in the same manner towards my persona, becoming in return, a very harsh judge myself.

The cause and effect of the Law of Karma were clearly at work as many unresolved energies were subtly controlling my behavior, influencing me to be uncompassionate and unkind each time I felt threatened or judged by others.

After this unpleasant episode, doubts started to creep into my mind. *Could the boy be right? What if I failed?* I had never thought about failure before, but through my wrong action I had brought upon myself the energy of failure. Acting badly towards others is the perfect way to bring negativity directly back on ourselves. It is the Law of Reflection and it acts like a boomerang.

So now I was stuck with this uncomfortable thought that would plague me constantly, drilling the seeds of doubt deeper and deeper into my consciousness.

The power of negative thoughts, words, and actions is such that these can instantly manifest substantial blockages and obstacles.

This state of being lasted awhile till one day I realized that if I carried on following these trails of unconstructive thought, I eventually would really fail. Fortunately, I was guided to quickly redirect myself to my usual positive mode. Unfortunately, I never apologized to that boy, holding on to the illusion that I was right and consequently created a pattern regarding always being right, even when of course I was not. Once this specific process was integrated, something else presented itself to my consciousness; a

decision that in due course would bring deep turmoil to my future actions.

With my relationship with God, by then, on shaky ground, what happened in my life gave me the false belief that I needed to have much more faith in myself than in God, as I thought God was mostly unreliable. *What was he doing while my family was collapsing in every possible way? What was he thinking when he let my grandmother pass away?*

Haunted by these questions at a very young age, I rejected my own divinity because I saw myself as separate from God and chose to walk my path alone, scattering into the wind the sacred gift that is given to each one of us; the possibility to always co-create with God/Spirit. To forget our own Divinity or the Divinity within others is the cause of most of our problems here on earth. When we live in separation from God it is so much more difficult to access the flow of Grace and Synchronicity offered by the Universe. Each time we refuse our own Divinity we take a much longer and difficult route along our life's map.

Since I did not know this yet, I felt God had let me down too many times and had no trust in him and no trust in the Universal Support—so I made the decision to only trust and have faith in myself. Eventually I found out what it all meant because in reality my choice to only rely on myself led me on a steeper path filled with misconceptions ruled by many illusions, anxieties, and fears. And still unknown to my mind, my own disconnection from God—from all there is, letting me experience separation instead of Oneness, leaving me scarred inside my soul and hiding behind a mask—was exactly what I had come to mend.

The rest of the year went by in a flash. It was time to say goodbye to my family and fly the nest. An uncomfortable nest it was but still the only one I truly knew and called home. I suddenly felt heavyhearted, almost as if the gravity of my decision had just sunk in, hitting me with the full realization that a new period of my life was about to start in which I was to trade everything I knew and loved for the unknown. This produced in me a sense of anxiety that I could not share with anyone, as it contradicted everything I had just manifested. In the end there was no alternative but to simply plunge into what I had created, hoping for the parachute of grace to open up and help me land on the soft grass of my new life.

This was my first victorious attempt to tap into the *Universal Law of Manifestation*. I had succeeded in shifting my present into a new reality, the one I had wished for, even if I felt fearful and insecure about it.

The Law of Manifestation states that ultimately we are only able to fully manifest what is in alignment with our life's destiny or Divine Plan—otherwise it will only be partial manifestation, or none at all.

Monte Carlo represented the next dot on the map of my destiny—a time and a place for me to learn. So it was simply meant to be. At last I left the city of my birth migrating to my next destination. What I treasured the most about the past, my grandmother and a serene family life, had been taken away from me. I had no choice but to move forward and face the future alone. The school of life was opening its doors to me, and entering meant never looking back.

Life at *Casa Mia* started well. I was undeniably looked after by the Heavens because as soon as I left my family I was blessed enough to encounter someone very special, my first best friend and confidant Alejandra. Although we could not have been more dissimilar, she and I truly found each other.

She was a dark Mediterranean beauty while I was pixie-like with the fairest of skin and Titian hair. Her family had plenty of money and mine had lost it all. My new friend had a sweet disposition and open smile while my own attitude was reserved and distant. But most strangely, Alejandra was a churchgoer and devoted

Catholic and I certainly was not. And yet despite all of these differences our connection was strong. At first, when I had just arrived at *Casa Mia* feeling a bit low and insecure, I carried myself around defensively and with my usual air of superiority, but Alejandra was not fooled one bit. Instead, she saw straight through my veils of protection, offering me her sincere friendship and generosity of spirit.

The sweet memories of those times will forever remain impressed on my heart, as the joy and pain of our daily discoveries filled us to the brim and made us grow fast. We never had a dull moment, constantly sharing our thoughts, hopes, dreams, and of course teenage angst, relentlessly questioning each other on what the future might bring. With Alejandra I discovered the meaning and value of having a real friend and the importance of all the codes of friendship like loyalty, trust, acceptance, honesty, and discretion.

With time all of my friends would come to represent my family, my support system, my home away from home, my exodus just unfolding. Some individuals grew up in the hearts of their families, firmly rooted under the shadow of their family tree, but I had chosen to walk alone from a young age. Along the way I have met so many precious friends to whom I am deeply grateful for helping me to evolve and for easing my lonely path. All of them have enriched me in the most wonderful ways with their love, patience, and compassion. So Alejandra and I became each other's Guardian Angels, stepping together, hand in hand into the treacherous waters of our chosen profession.

At *Casa Mia* the days began early with the first ballet class starting promptly at 8 a.m. After getting up at dawn, I would usually climb the elegant staircase spiraling all the way to the top floor of the villa where an enormous room filled with light had become my new sanctuary. On my own, my being still drifting on the edge of the dream world, I was rarely fully conscious of this reality. Resting upon the stillness of daybreak I glanced through the arched window, as the rising sun cast its soft golden light over the sea. Underneath, the shimmering water reflected at times a glowing soothing light on my soul, inducing me to peacefully reflect on the stream of thoughts that flowed freely upon the wings of my imagination.

In those early morning hours with just the sound of silence as my friend, strong yearnings arose from the core of my younger self. Wondering about the future was my favorite pastime, often to the point of preventing me from being fully present. In those quiet moments, so many scenarios were presented in front of my eyes. One in particular deeply excited me. I was just a child when an unexpected thought had suddenly appeared in my head and never left me. The notion that somebody special destined for me existed and when the time was ripe we would meet.

Romantic love was on my mind. Over and over again I was consumed with the idea of this mysterious soul mate and the parallel lives that we were simultaneously living. *Where is he now? What does he look like? What's his name?* I was in love with the idea of being in love and this simple thought excited me into a state of great expectation.

Romantic love was to become one of my greatest obsessions, a magnet for all my wants and desires, a mirror to reflect endless internal mechanisms and dynamics, and a battlefield where I would fight many lost wars against my own unresolved karma with men.

In those peaceful mornings in Monte Carlo, once the sun was higher in the sky I gradually left the world of my imagination for my preparatory routine. Starting with a series of stretching exercises, I would slowly get my body ready for class and in doing so helped myself fully return and ground into the present moment. Then one by one the other pupils would enter the room, breaking

the silence and dissolving the enchantment of those magical moments that came to mark my daily meditation.

A kaleidoscope of many races was the tribe that inhabited *Casa Mia.* In our microcosm each one of us was a little piece of the jigsaw puzzle of humanity, with so many different languages, cultures, and traditions all fused together into a giant melting pot of young people united by the wish to dance.

It was priceless to be exposed to this international cornucopia, learning and absorbing many valuable new things. French and English were slowly integrated into my daily dialogue, giving me the opportunity to connect with a larger number of students. My mind expanded and my curiosity more fulfilled as endless talks with my foreign companions revealed much to me. Throughout those conversations I slowly realized that staying abroad would offer me so many more possibilities for an interesting life and career. Italy felt rather stale and old-fashioned in comparison to the rest of the world.

At that point in time, technology was a remote concept. There weren't computers and easy access to all sorts of information like nowdays. But to have the opportunity to be under the same roof with like-minded young people from all over the globe truly changed my perception of life. Many fresh thoughts fermented inside my mind and eventually morphed into ideas that would ultimately shape my future. As a matter of fact, I had already mentally projected myself onto my next unknown destination, knowing perfectly well that Monte Carlo was only the first step on the ladder of my ambition; merely the beginning of a long and mysterious journey.

This constant projecting myself into the future was another one of the patterns that I developed early on. So often in the course of my existence I missed out on some precious points in time, simply because a part of me was just not there. This created a true lack of Presence. To experience the current moment is important, as everything only happens

in the now; and to trust this truth is an essential key to our own peace, supporting us to overcome the anxiety that the future may bring, or regrets about the past as what is done is done. To be too engrossed in the future or past only creates obstruction to the beauty and magic of the present moment, and the many surprising gifts that life itself brings us in each one of these unique moments.

The ballet classes were highly energetic, and Marika would lead us in the manner of an orchestra director, each of us her precious instruments. Every single day I couldn't wait to be such an instrument, to be fine-tuned by her, able to create perfect shapes and movements with my body, and to understand new and exciting concepts. Always thirsty for her knowledge, I loved learning all that was truly inspiring and interesting to me. This was the engine that pushed me forward, the intellectual food that nourished me. By then, Marika had also largely replaced my grandmother in fulfilling the role of mentor.

Although when I was alone I could be a rather melancholic young girl, suffering deeply from numerous anxieties and insecurities, I longed to receive a warm embrace, a tender kiss—now only distant memories from that period in time when my grandmother was still alive. This lack of love in its physical expression weighed heavily upon my heart, enhancing the energy of loss and loneliness that was claiming an even larger space within my soul. I relentlessly pushed these thoughts away but they always sprang back, especially triggered when I listened to certain pieces of music as melancholic as my own soul. These melodies never failed to reach the core of my being, unleashing the sorrow that would abruptly embody me like a dark veil, quickly obscuring my Light.

Marika, an original cross between despot and mystical being, was certainly nourishing my intellect, but unlike my grandmother Rita, she was unable to feed my desperate need for affection. Consequently, I was always extremely careful to disguise any kind of behavior that could show the truth of how I was really feeling. I knew well that Marika would judge this condition as weakness, and that to appear strong was crucial in order to survive in the school's tough environment.

Despite these complexities, I was indeed one of my teacher's favorites, not just because of my talent but more because of our soul connection—the mysterious bond that could not be controlled or explained and yet was strongly felt by us both. However, this privileged position did not do me any favors with my classmates. Instead it made me into a target of jealousy and envy as an energetic imbalance was manifested. Apart from my faithful Alejandra, I soon discovered that the friendships I felt with some of the other students were not reciprocated, and I often felt betrayed. This caused my heart to close down even further.

Dearest reader, not until later did I come to better understand that favoritism can negatively affect the dynamics of any group, where lack of fairness does indeed produce an energetic imbalance for every member of the group. To be aware of treating everybody equally and without preference is a vital Universal Truth that should be applied every day of our lives if we wish to create a loving and harmonious environment both at home and at work.

Since a tender age, I had spent endless hours looking at my reflection in the mirror, scrutinizing every inch of my body while trying to achieve perfection in my dance poses. With time, this narcissistic relationship with my own body image magnified the negative traits within my personality. Sitting at opposite ends of the spectrum of my character, self-criticism and self-obsession started to feed each other in a very unhealthy way, simultaneously conveying to my persona a sense of great insecurity because I was never happy with who I was or what I possessed as I felt I was not enough or did not have enough, versus absolute self-assurance bordering on arrogance.

Comparing myself with others was a potent way of sabotaging my own being. This particular deception of the mind was firmly established in the fabric of my consciousness where everything was put on a scale to be measured and judged against others. My arrogance stemmed from this deep state of insecurity that needed to hide and compensate for my uncomfortable feelings of being less or having less.

Of course all of these illusions seemed very real to me at the time as I was not aware that in our equality, each one of us carries a unique Light and unique gifts that makes each of us special. So to compare ourselves to other beings is indeed an illusion created by the mind, as there is nothing to compare when everyone is irreplaceable in their own distinct Light.

I was rapidly growing up to be a rather complex young person, extremely skilled in concealing my true self, the deeper nature of my soul, with layer upon layer of thick protection. But this was only the beginning of my troubles.

As a child I used to be slim with long legs and a swan-like neck. I had a perfectly proportioned dancer's body. Soon after my arrival in Monte Carlo, I began to experience a great physical change as my body shifted from child form into a more feminine shape. To my horror a fuller breast was pushing its way up, making me feel rather strange. I detested having my monthly bleeds and blamed my body continuously for making me feel so unsettled. Plainly I was not in acceptance, rejecting womanhood and contracting and repressing my feminine energies even if this was in direct contradiction with all of my romantic dreams about my future companion. My wish was to remain androgynous in form, but my hormonal system in full swing was not listening to my wants and instead kept creating havoc. Worst of all, I started to put on weight.

If we don't love our body, our body may have a strong reaction to our refusal, as all is energy. To live in full respect of our being, meaning body, mind, and spirit, is indeed one of our deepest lessons. I personally had to walk a long way before even catching a glimpse of this truth, and eventually fully understand its profound meaning.

Marika, also alerted by my suddenly plumper shape, promptly imposed a strict diet. I became even angrier towards my body because I wasn't able to control it anymore. Besides, I could not stop myself from wanting food, especially the forbidden kind. The diet had the opposite result for me, simply because I could not resist the impulse to do just the opposite of what I was asked to do. Feeling frustrated and resentful, I started to sabotage myself even further. Banned on Marika's orders from all the tearooms in Monte Carlo, I sent Alejandra on secret missions to my favorite patisserie, and then gorged on mountains of sweet delights, purging myself afterwards.

Soon, a very important dance exam was approaching as fast as my waist was expanding. In truth I was battling a serious eating disorder, reflecting my own emotional disorder and the lack of physical love that had left a deep void within me. But at the time this subject was still taboo and consequently was not handled very well. No support system was in place to help me come to terms with my bulimia. Interestingly, while I was getting bigger some other students were shrinking because of anorexia. The school was fertile ground for the growth of such illnesses that came directly from the unhealed wounds of the soul, as so much was triggered daily in this challenging profession. But nothing was implemented to resolve this dire situation, not even in basic terms. What happened during that period would deeply harm my personal relationship with food for years to come—I would live in terror of gaining weight, triggered first by being a ballerina and later on by being part of the fashion business.

In the meantime, Marika couldn't understand why I was not losing weight, no matter how severe my diet. Instead of looking like a swan, every day her beloved pupil resembled more and more like a force-fed goose ready to become *foie gras*. For the first time in my life I felt totally at a loss in a very confrontational situation, battling with failure and guilt because above all I felt I had failed myself, let alone my teacher and mother who had always trusted me implicitly. On top of everything else, I felt ugly and disgusted with my heavy figure, choosing to be as far away as possible from my beloved mirror, no longer able to recognize my own reflection, by then a distorted version of myself bordering on the grotesque.

Then the day of the exam arrived. This was publicly held in a theatre. While I was making my way from the changing room to the stage, I felt like Marie Antoinette advancing towards the guillotine. I knew that I had to face my family, and a severe panel of examiners who would pronounce me guilty of being too fat to dance. Because I had nothing to lose, in spite of all my extra kilos, I performed brilliantly and consequently, by some kind of miracle, passed the exam. Marika was relieved. But Giovanna, who hadn't visited me in awhile, was furious and traumatized by the sight of her bloated daughter. My darling mother asked me how I could have done this to my own body in such a short amount of time. Frankly, I could not explain myself, as to fully admit my self-loathing would have been far too shocking for her. So I just stood in front of her in silence, pushing the tears back and silently praying to God to help me as I could not help myself.

Every time I felt defeated I always called for celestial support despite my wobbly relationship with the Almighty, and every time I was truly blessed to be heard once more. But God was really only in my mind if needed. After all, I was angry with him, holding him responsible for much of my suffering. Feeling greatly disconnected from God, I convinced myself that it was his duty to always get me out of trouble whether he liked it or not. In those years the word "gratitude" was not a part of my vocabulary. I firmly believed that everything was owed to me, both by God and by man.

We all have some strange illusions, and this was definitely one of mine, sprung from the separation from my own Source and this inexplicable sense of rejection that many of us might feel when we distance ourselves from the acknowledgement of our own divinity.

That summer, under the strict guidance of Giovanna, I finally succeeded in shedding the extra weight, and regained both my svelte figure and my self-confidence. However, that was only a small victory in a long war. My body's struggles had just begun.

Battling with weight was not my only body issue. The entire classical ballet repertoire required female dancers perform *en pointe*. Unfortunately, my delicate feet had developed a very unpleasant relationship with pointe shoes. At the end of each class I would be in agony, my toes raw with open wounds that would not heal fast enough. But this kind of torture didn't stop at my feet. There were also injuries, and plenty of them, regularly afflicting different parts of my body because so many of the poses I needed to achieve were extreme and unnatural. Constantly aching, I had no alternative but to endure the pain, and bypassing my mind became a daily exercise.

To be a dancer was not an easy choice. And to have the soul of an artist was both a blessing and an agony, as suffering is intrinsically part of the artist's nature. Though the seeds of understanding this, were just planted in Monte Carlo, soon I began harvesting their deeper insights that would continue to apply throughout my life:

When art is your mistress, you learn fast how to please her as she wants everything from you, giving very little in return. The few times that she does allow you to receive fully flowing preciousness, such magic

is created! Such a high is reached! Then, like an addict, you only live for your next fix, for that elusive moment when once again you feel touched by her Divine Perfection. My soul wanted to dance and my body had to obey no matter what the price.

To achieve artistic perfection became one of the many obsessions that in time controlled me in a subtle but hard-core way. My disturbed relationship with food opened the door to my numerous addictions, as the energy of addiction was already part of the genetic structure of my being through the female line of my family. The chains of obsession and addiction would both play important roles in my future, building around me an invisible prison that I could neither avoid nor escape, because after all this was to be a crucial part of my journey, and later on, one of my most significant liberations.

So taken with the training, for awhile I forgot about the Spirit World. Till one day I suddenly realized that *Casa Mia* was a place of hidden secrets and unexposed supernatural mysteries.

Since my arrival I had often felt observed by invisible eyes and sensed the tangible Presence of something that was concealed but undeniably there. I was not alone while wandering the long corridors at twilight. I was not alone in the big room upstairs in the early hours of the morning when silence still ruled supreme. Just before falling asleep, I could hear whispering voices so soft that it was hard to know with certainty if they were real or just pure deception. Other times, in the middle of the night, I used to catch glimpses of bright white lights dancing in the dark and then vanishing as quickly as they appeared. Our personal items were also mysteriously disappearing, only to be found a few hours later in the most unusual places. There were even reports that a few students felt touched and pushed while walking up and down the stairs. There was some kind of mysterious phenomenon at *Casa Mia* and I was determined to find out more.

Around that period I became an avid reader of gothic literature. Edgar Allan Poe, H.P. Lovecraft, and Bram Stoker were the writers who most inspired me with their dark fantasies of surreal worlds where sinister Spiritual Manifestations made my heart skip a beat. Ghosts and vampires fascinated me. Gone were the memories of my childhood nightmares as a new wave of strange creatures of the night lit up the flames of my imagination. The bloodstained romanticism of those tales enthralled me to the point of obsession and a more obscure, more hidden side to my nature slowly resurfaced. With the passing days I became more and more certain that I was experiencing in my daily life comparable situations to those described in the books I felt so absorbed by.

At *Casa Mia* an eccentric woman called Dora looked after us, making sure that all the school's rules and regulations were respected at all times. Many strange stories were circulating about Dora and truly there was something rather peculiar about her. I was firmly convinced that she was also the keeper of some of the secrets I was trying to uncover. Occasionally she would disclose to those of us who would listen, some puzzling pieces of information, but never gave too much away. Alejandra thought her mad and warned me that I should not believe any of her silly tales. I disagreed and instead suspected that Dora could shed some light on this unusual situation. I started to question her at any given opportunity, making sure she knew that I was well aware that something of a paranormal nature was going on.

At first she was reluctant and feared that I would repeat well-kept secrets to everybody else. So, I was right—there were secrets! For days I begged and begged her, and finally so exhausted by my persistence, she gave in and confirmed that what I felt, heard, and saw were not just illusions, as the school was indeed haunted.

A terrible event had taken place during the Second World War when Nazi soldiers had brutally killed an innocent group of Jewish children temporarily hiding inside the villa, en route to safety in Switzerland. According to Dora, the bodies could still be buried somewhere underneath the school. I was deeply saddened by the story, but equally, in a state of great surrealism. This made perfect sense to me. The children wanted to interact and most probably this was the simple explanation of why things kept appearing and disappearing. It was their way of communicating their Presence to us, trying to secure our attention. And so, for me being able to communicate with them, became my wholehearted wish.

When alone, I would softly call upon the children. After a few trials where nothing much happened, finally one day I could sense them gathering around me and all of a sudden I glimpsed their faces. They were playing with me, caressing my face and gently pulling my long red hair. It was like being touched by the impalpable lightness of a butterfly's wings, and brought tears to my eyes and deep emotions to my heart. In the depth of the night I kept hearing their murmurs, but never clearly.

Till one early morning, for a fleeting moment I saw them running in front of me all the way up the staircase. Once they reached the top they chanted my name several times before disappearing from sight. The vision was brief but crystal clear. The children were all different sizes and between the ages of maybe nine to fourteen. They were boys wearing clothes that resembled a school uniform and each one of them was smiling at me with an open expression in their faces of Light.

I was astonished, marveling at what was being offered to me— the spirits had just demonstrated that their existence was as real as ours, and communication between us was undoubtedly possible. I kept my promise to Dora and never breathed a word to anyone else. And yet, all the other pupils commented on the fact that suddenly the only belongings that remained untouched by some strange phenomenon were mine.

I couldn't stop smiling, thinking of my invisible new friends and feeling that somehow I had been invited to be a part of the mysterious world of the unseen, because this world was familiar to my soul and slowly it revealed itself to me.

With my head filled up with dark romance, I often floated in and out of different Planes of Consciousness, slowly opening my mind to the possibility that alternative realities could truly exist. Every day through dancing I was learning to transcend my own body and mind, to transcend the physical pain. And while a part of me was propelled upwards towards the unexplored planes of the unseen, another part of my being was pulled down by the heavy roots of loneliness and melancholy that were constant weights upon my heart.

Visions of the dead children, dreams of blood on the whitest snow, the inexorable decay of the most ravishing of roses, the sorrowful melody of an exquisite piece of music; there was such fatal beauty, such depth in loss, in the idea that all on earth will meet their end—that human life is transient. Since the passing of my grandmother I had become acutely aware of death, of human fragility, of those fugitive moments that could never be recaptured but sometimes replayed in our minds over and over again like an old faded movie. One day when I encountered a very unique being, I was reminded even more of the melancholy of loss, of the solitude of the soul.

One of Marika's most treasured friends was Rudolf Nureyev, one of the world's greatest dancers, and in that moment in time, my absolute idol. To me Rudi represented the essence of *The Spirit of the Rose*, the immortal symbol of Terpsichore reborn. I had worshiped Rudi since I was a six-year-old baby ballerina, learning the first simple steps at the barre. Around that time my grandmother escorted me to the theatre to watch him perform *Swan Lake*. In the exact moment I cast my eyes on Rudi, I fell in love with him. What he filled me with was something that is indescribable, something that only a great artist is able to transmit to his adoring audience. A gift of Presence, a special Light that reaches the souls of others.

So you can imagine my utter wonder when suddenly one day Marika invited both my mother and I to meet him. Barely in my teens, I could hardly believe that my dream was about to come true and only a few hours were separating me from being face to face with him. In spite of the excitement that vibrated in every cell of my being, I also felt fearful of disappointing him, such were my insecurities. He was my idol after all and how can someone measure up against a demi-god? But unbeknownst to me I was about to receive a deep lesson in human nature.

We traveled in Marika's car all the way from Monte Carlo to San Remo where Rudi was giving a rare performance of mixed dance at the local theatre. During the journey I experienced a state of anxiety like never before, trying to imagine how the encounter was going to unfold. Finally the fateful moment arrived during the interval between the first and second acts, when without warning, Marika grabbed my mother and I and dragged us backstage.

We were standing in semi-obscurity at the edge of the stage, when from the shadow into the light Nureyev emerged like a Divine Apparition, gracing our group of mere mortals with his Presence. Still wearing his corsair costume, with an exposed gleaming torso contoured by perfectly shaped muscles, he slowly moved towards us in the manner of a feline. Rudi's charisma was palpable and immediately I felt his full energetic blast affecting me to my core. I was magnetized by his strong sensual features, and perceived in him a raw kind of beauty; a primordial force of nature amalgamated within the most sensitive of souls.

Apart from his dancing that was almost faultless, there was nothing else that was polished about him as you could almost smell the latent wildness inside his being, the intensity of his soul, the unpredictability of his character. He possessed an unruly spirit that gave him an edge, making him a cross between an exotic bird of paradise that could not be caught and a dangerous panther that could not be tamed. Through my young eyes this is how I saw him: wild, elusive, enigmatic. So lost was I in these personal observations, that I became totally unaware of the fact that Marika was about to introduce me to him when unexpectedly I felt his strong arms hugging me, his embrace taking me back to the present moment. When I looked up I was gifted with the most radiant smile and a few words in Russian spoken to me in a warm tone. Then he was gone.

In a catatonic state, I followed both Marika and my mother back to our seats and only then heard that he had invited us to join him for dinner afterwards. Still recovering from the apparition, and in shock at the idea of dining with Nureyev, I was relieved when the curtains slowly rose, unveiling a scene from *La Sylphide* that marked the beginning of the second act.

While a sweet melody lingered in the air, Marika's whispering voice reached my ears with a powerful message: "Feel your *dusha*. The Russian soul is also inside of you and it will help you to understand yourself." My teacher knew me better than I thought. The *dusha* might have given me my melancholic nature and might have been what bonded Marika and I so deeply, but it was surely the only true reason why my mother and I received this precious invitation.

Later on, I was sitting at a corner table of a small restaurant with Rudi opposite me conversing in a mixture of English, French, and Italian while eating a plate of food with much gusto. He looked tired and this made him more vulnerable, less god-like. To realize that he was, after all, of this earth, helped me feel much more relaxed in his Presence. Marika then described the story of Maroussia, my Russian grandmother, in dramatic tones. It was evident that Rudi enjoyed hearing anything about Russia's past or present. Constantly engaging in the conversation, he kept asking us questions. I could feel his emotions rising, his passion unfolding. My family tale provoked his strong reaction, acting as a magic key that unlocked floods of memories from his past, his triumphs, and his regrets.

He had paid a high price for his choices, ones that bound him to a similar fate as those of both Maroussia and Marika. I was flabbergasted, witnessing my idol holding on to so much anguish and sorrow for all that he had sacrificed in order to gain his artistic freedom. To be unable to see or talk to his mother was one of his deepest regrets, and this touched me profoundly because of the closeness I shared with my own mother sitting just beside me.

I guessed the combination of him being so fond of Marika and the knowledge that we were all united by loss, made him feel more comfortable to freely express his melancholy and pain, knowing that he would be fully understood and accepted.

That special evening I discovered that no matter how famous or successful an individual may be, no matter how many adoring fans a person may have, if their soul is deeply wounded, all else is utterly insignificant, just a temporary bandage, an illusion to help forget and soothe the daily grief.

Rudi's saving grace was dancing. To dance was his cure against the torments of his inner being and what kept him sane through the darker shadows of his past. To dance was all that he truly possessed, even if he owned so much materially.

There was also a powerful mystical side to Rudi that somehow helped him accept everything he needed to accept. He too believed in destiny and in the irreversibility of it. During our profound exchange, I started to understand a little bit more about the source of my own sense of loss and solitude. The Russian soul was in part influencing me, but there was so much more hidden in the multiple layers of my consciousness that were still inconceivable for my mind to comprehend

In the next few years I saw Rudi occasionally, spending some brief moments with him, here and there. Often a veil of sadness would cloud his eyes, so imperceptible at times and yet always there. It is not easy to hide the reflection of one's soul in one's eyes.

He was to be my first and last idol as he showed me an important truth. There are no idols upon this earth, only gifted human beings searching upon their path for that which eludes them the most, as each

one of us, no matter who we are carries both the burdens of karma and equally the keys of transformation and rebirth.

My time on the Riviera was flying by in a whirlwind of classes and bountiful moments of laughter and tears. Almost three years passed till one day the shadow of death spread her black wings across Monte Carlo: Grace Kelly died in a car crash. Monaco lost its beloved princess, and I lost my generous benefactor. Yes, dearest reader, the princess had been gifting me with a scholarship since my arrival at the school. The ex-Hollywood star was truly like a fairy-tale princess, fair and kind, coming to visit us regularly and always encouraging us with plenty of advice from her generous heart. I fondly remember her sitting patiently for hours watching us dance. It was very upsetting to know that she was no more.

Death reminded me, yet again, that our time on earth is limited, and that from princesses to paupers we are all equally bound by mortality and by the mystery of when the end will come for each one of us. So once more the bell of my own destiny rang loud and clear, awakening me to the full realization that a new period of my life was soon approaching.

For awhile, even before the tragic passing of Princess Grace, I had started to feel restless, engrossed in a growing state of dissatisfaction. A few months before I had been deeply fulfilled, learning a little bit more every day. But lately, I became afflicted with an inexplicable feeling of stagnation and a sense of boredom that made me resent the routine of my everyday life.

Superficially, nothing had changed in my relationship with Marika. I say superficially because in reality several undercurrents were already boiling up to the surface in my mind. Without a doubt my teacher adored me, but concealed inside the fabric of her love lay some subtle control mechanisms that could be suffocating at times. She liked to be in charge of all parts of my upbringing, but some of her views outside of dance were often rigid, verging on being seriously old-fashioned.

This feeling of being restricted by too many rules had provoked in me the wish to be utterly liberated from the heaviness of her strict disciplinary methods. A cry for freedom was rising from the core of my soul and getting so loud that it was almost impossible to ignore. I started to feel more and more conflicted by the way she wanted me to be, and my frustrations were growing stronger as my own dreams became less and less compatible with hers.

In the beginning I would listen to her philosophy as if it was gospel but now new ideas, independent ideas, were seeding their rebellious germs of freethinking inside my mind, rejecting her attempts to mold me in her own way. I was rapidly becoming my own person and sensed that I was trapped in a golden cage, my aspirations had rapidly outgrown my situation. Even Monte Carlo itself had lost its glamorous sugarcoated *patina* and all that I could see was a small place that restricted me, a ghetto for rich people that lacked soul. I needed to expand, and a fated encounter had propelled me even more towards a new vision for my future.

The previous summer during a school break in Florence, I met Tina, the sister of my mother's American best friend Joan. Tina was a well-known soloist with the New York City Ballet and her way of dancing made a great impression on me, her technique being so different from what I was studying with Marika. There was something so light and free about Tina that I wanted to emulate. I would question her endlessly about her life in New York, and felt an instant attraction to this city that was influencing the rest of the world on so many levels. According to Tina, the best ballet schools were all there and she implied that if I was interested in moving to NY, she could easily help me secure a place in one of the top schools. Since receiving this offer I couldn't stop thinking about the possibility of having an exciting new experience, and when Princess Grace died I interpreted it as a sign of change that inspired me to put my ideas into action.

But a few major obstacles were standing in the way of this appealing future. There was my mother who thought I was still too young to go so far and that I should remain in Marika's safe hands for at least another couple of years. And of course there was Marika. In spite of my desire to alter my present reality, I loved my mentor deeply and nervously wondered if she could possibly understand her rebel daughter's wishes to explore a different direction. Time ticked away and a deep sense of guilt engulfed me to the point that to look straight in my teacher's eyes became challenging, as deep inside I felt disloyal towards her.

From a young age I had been single-minded and adept at getting my own way. But there was also a certain degree of fairness and justice in my character that made me respect those who had helped me along the way. In this case, I felt a burden of betrayal as if I was a wife or a husband who wanted out of a relationship because of a new lover.

After all, my mentor had cared so much for me in spite of her controlling manner. I needed to come clean with her as soon as possible in order to release these heavy feelings of cloudiness and guilt. Against my mother's advice, a few weeks after the princess's funeral, I asked Marika if I could have a private conversation with her. What I couldn't foresee was that I had greatly miscalculated my teacher's personality, and there was to be a high cost for my juvenile oversight. In fact, I was about to discover how ego, selfishness, and lack of compassion, often some of our primary flaws, blur the truth and in doing so create the nonacceptance of truth.

The fateful meeting took place in Marika's elegant white and gold office on a sunny autumn morning. From the very start my mentor looked slightly uncomfortable, staring down at me with a puzzled expression on her aristocratic face, a faint smile on her thin pale lips. She sensed trouble but I don't think she was quite prepared for what I had to say. I began the difficult conversation by thanking her for everything she had done for me. But unfortunately I did not know how to speak from my heart, and had no understanding of being grateful, truly grateful, to somebody who had done so much for me. The words that came out of my mouth didn't carry any vibrations of love, instead they were flat, stale, and formal.

"To say thank you without love is to not say thank you at all."

It was not how I felt inside, but it was more about my inability to express myself in the true Light of my heart. I was also defending my point of view, which caused me to be controlling over the way I delivered my words. In the meantime, not one sound came out of my teacher, so I carried on, launching myself into a full description of my next opportunity and how I couldn't possibly miss out on experiencing life in NY.

By that point, I had become so fired up talking about my future without her that for awhile I failed to notice the cold and distant expression on her face, and above all her absolute silence. My selfishness prevented me from reflecting on the fact that Marika might feel hurt by my desire to leave her for some unknown teacher. But being too deeply concerned about others' feelings was not my *forte*, as I was only thinking about what I required.

Wanting to leave people or a situation that did not match my expectations would become another of my future repetitive patterns. To escape what did not suit me anymore would be modeled in years to come in my early life behavior of trading realities, always in search of the next best thing. I traded my life in Florence for my life in Monte Carlo and now I traded Monte Carlo for New York. Whomever or whatever disappointed me had to be replaced by somebody else, somewhere else, or something else.

It does not matter how young we are, as so much is seeded inside us from the very beginning. Karma, aspects, personality traits, soul wounds, genetic inheritances, all are already there formed inside of our beings; all these parts of us already created from many existences prior to this one.

Yes, my destiny was calling me. But the way I was dealing with Marika definitely lacked love and wisdom. In youth arrogance sometimes exists in plenty. On the other hand her reaction was equally wrong, as she should have understood that I was young and therefore prone to act unwisely.

An ice curtain descended between us—an ice curtain that belonged to the lands of perennial snow where nothing could ever melt. In the moment that Marika felt I was slipping away from her tight grasp, she also rejected me. If she was to lose me, then I would also lose her so that the burden of loss would not just be hers. My teacher's uncompassionate nature matched the selfishness of my own nature and so we produced an irreparable break. In my blindness, I just wanted to have my own way with everything, meaning to both receive her blessing and my freedom. But Marika felt betrayed as she had given me so much and almost saw me as the daughter she never had. She was not aware that love cannot be measured and that it needs to be given freely without conditions or expectations. And I was not aware of how much I had hurt her.

My careless words reactivated her own cellular memory around her wounds of loss that were already deeply seated in her consciousness from childhood—because of the Russian Revolution she had experienced much loss. Marika patiently waited for me to finish my long monologue, then she whispered in a dead calm voice that I was dismissed and to let her secretary know which date I would be departing from the school. And that was it. No more words were said, however her coldness and indifference hit back at me hard. I left the white and gold office in a state of shock feeling the brutal emotional blow, but still hoping that somehow she would calm down, forgive me, and love me again. Though it was not to be.

That same Monday afternoon I went to class as usual, only to find what it meant to be on the receiving end of Marika's cruel behavior. It was painful to witness the chilling detachment of somebody I had adored and felt so close to until a few hours before. The loving teacher that I once knew was no more, now replaced by a very different uncompassionate being who mocked and ridiculed me in front of everybody. The rest of the week went from bad to worse as she decided to make an example of me, reminding everyone else what to expect if they displeased her. I endured the psychological torment in silence—after all, I was the creator of this situation. By Friday I had had enough of trying to handle her rejection and decided to put an end to the agony by jumping on the first available train the next day to Italy.

On my last night at *Casa Mia* I could not sleep. Floods of tears ran down my face. While sobbing away and feeling dead inside, I suddenly received a surprise visit from my special friends, the ghosts. To my complete astonishment, they surrounded my bed, each of them holding a flower made of Light. The children had come to say goodbye. When I woke up in the morning I discovered a pink rose placed at the end of my bed. I immediately asked the other girls, but they all denied having placed the rose there, looking at me as if I was insane. I went back to my room and cried softly.

It was time to go. The pain I felt was acute but my mind was made up. I asked my beloved Alejandra to keep my departure a secret from everybody else at school. Then I took just a few of my personal belongings including the pink rose and left without giving a second glance to the villa that I had called home for the past few years. I was hurting terribly and couldn't stop feeling that the way Marika had treated me was utterly unjust.

She had warned me all those years ago that life was neither straightforward nor fair. It was a bitter pill to swallow and in retrospect an important rite of passage from the golden world of my childhood to the real world where happy endings are not always dispensed, especially if certain lessons need to be deeply understood through the Law of Karma. Sometimes we have to make difficult choices that may hurt others. And yes, it is important to always speak our own truth, but at the time I did not know the Spiritual Golden Rule that says we speak our own truth with love and only love.

I was growing up fast, learning the hard way how to be my own person, standing by my own vision and not by anyone else's.

The disappointment I felt in that instant was deeply entrenched, with the negative energies of anger and frustration defining the state of my bruised ego. Nevertheless, I had to take responsibility for what I had created even if accepting the truth was hard.

The easy option is to constantly blame others without taking responsibility for our own actions. But in doing this, we remain stuck in a place of deep unawareness, relegated under the shadow of an ego that stops us from truly evolving in alignment with our own Light, our own Higher Consciousness, and our own great potential to love with an open heart.

We are The Creators of our own Reality in every given moment.

And so I returned home to face my parents who had no idea of my escape from *Casa Mia*.

IN THE
WAITING ROOM–
NEW YORK

At first, my parents were surprised to receive my unexpected visit, welcoming me back with great delight. But as soon as they found out that I was a runaway, a tidal wave of serious concerns regarding my future education instantly swept away the brief joy of our reunion. Apart from reaffirming my desire to change schools, I was unable to explain myself properly. I was in limbo, in a state of deep turmoil, which created pressure in my heart and even greater confusion in my mind. A few days later, Marika telephoned my mother asking her to escort me back to Monte Carlo as soon as possible. She was convinced that I must have suffered some kind of temporary crisis, and would eventually realize that I had made a terrible mistake. But I was no prodigal daughter. I simply told my mother that if she forced me to go back, I would run away again.

Yet, I felt utterly miserable every evening when I was alone in bed, missing terribly my mentor and old life at *Casa Mia*. Doubts crept into my mind regarding my next step. *Do I to go back or move forward?* I was so afraid of making the wrong decision, the wrong turn on my path, that I was torn apart by these opposite choices. Then one day for some strange reason I placed the special rose given to me by the ghost children under my pillow. I had preserved it like a mystical object of great power and perhaps this was the time to witness its real purpose. Waiting for a Divine Sign, I had a premonition that the young ghosts could well be the messengers of the next phase of my life. And so it was, because approximately a month later a special dream did materialize.

I was transported to a small tree that was standing alone in the middle of a bucolic landscape surrounded by endless fields of wild flowers. The children were waiting for me in this mysterious place and for the very first time they addressed me with great affection—they all chanted together in their sweet voices: "Small trees do grow and you shall grow tall and strong." As if by magic I saw the small tree shape-shifting in front of my eyes into a much bigger tree with very deep roots and many branches covered in emerald leaves. The children's chanting continued: "Don't be afraid to follow your destiny and don't look back. We will always protect you." Then, one by one, they kissed me goodbye and vanished.

My strong intuition was guiding me to recognize that dreams were the chosen form of communication between the Spirit World and my being, therefore it was of great importance to pay full attention to their meaning.

So in the darkness of the night I saw Light—wide awake, an insight flashed in my mind: It was growth that held me back from returning to Marika, or rather the knowledge that in order to grow like the magical tree, I needed to move forward on my life's path without being limited by my teacher's domineering manners. This clear new vision powerfully integrated in my mind and my newfound awareness showed me that if I returned to Monte Carlo I would delay this vital process of personal development. The signs had been sent, giving me the faith that I would soon be able to move out of this dead-end situation and onto the pathway of the next part of my journey. Somehow NY had to happen, and once again I knew that my mother was the key to manifesting this new reality.

Giovanna, after digesting this latest turn of events, also concluded that sending me to America would, after all, be a positive experience, one supporting my budding dance career. The financial situation at home had improved a little and my parents were now prepared to cover my expenses, hoping that at some stage I could win another scholarship. In order to organize the trip to NY, the following months revolved around a beehive of activities and by springtime all of the practical requirements were sorted out.. I had a student visa, a place to stay in the Upper West Side, and an excellent ballet school arranged by my mother's friend Tina.

The Spirit World had sprinkled its magic once again, removing all potential obstacles from my path. A new reality was about to unfold and NY was to be the place on the map holding the key to the next stage of my evolution. I often thought of my grandfather Stefano and his American heritage, of how I had been dreaming since childhood of this faraway land, sowing the seeds for future manifestations.

I was simply learning to read the secret language from another world, despite my fears, illusions, and plenty of internal dynamics still governing my being. Dearest reader, coincidences do not exist! Everything in life is preparing us, step-by-step, for the next installment of events.

Before leaving for NY that upcoming September, I was to spend the month of July in Genoa, attending a ballet workshop with an impressive list of international guest teachers. It was essential to arrive in NY in top physical shape, and the opportunity to study with such illustrious names seemed to be an obvious reason to participate. Or so I thought.

One day I noticed a tall blonde boy who was training at the opposite side of the room. A sense of recognition invaded all of my senses and as soon as the class was over I felt moved by some invisible force to cross the room and make contact with him. In truth, I was very reserved and felt almost embarrassed to approach a stranger with such directness. But I need not have worried as the striking young man received me with an open smile and soon the conversation was flowing. His name was Lorenzo, and he was equipped with both charm and physical beauty. But the best was yet to come. Towards the end of our talk, to my greatest surprise, he told me that he actually lived in NY. My heart jolted, but with extreme self-control I veiled my excitement pretending to be cool, when in fact I was over the moon and could not believe this extraordinary twist of fate. After accepting with great anticipation the piece of paper with his phone number, I promised Lorenzo that I would call him as soon as I arrived in NY.

Remarkably, after Marika, this was the second being that my soul recognized straightaway. I did not know Lorenzo and yet there was something intangible about my new friend that once again was so familiar to me.

Soon after, I left Genoa and spent the little time I had left before my departure reminiscing about Lorenzo's mischievous green-blue eyes framed by long dark eyelashes. I felt euphoric and sensed that I had a lot more to look forward to in NY than just dancing. Around me Angels were flapping their wings and a few feathers landed inside my well-guarded heart causing an unusual tremor that gifted me with a resplendent lightness of being. My romantic nature was blossoming and I could not wait to begin to explore it.

I was seventeen year old when I landed in New York City on September 1st, 1981. At the very beginning, an amalgamation of fear, excitement, and loneliness were my daily companions in equal measure. The city was bursting with such high energy that this overwhelmed me at times. I had never experienced so much chaos, and such an abundance of everything—people, cars, shops, lights. I found my new environment harsh yet irresistible and when I had settled in a bit more, my sense of being lost was swiftly replaced with the discovery of a newfound freedom embodying every atom.

Being completely on my own became the most liberating and exhilarating of all my previous experiences. In NY it was fine to experiment, fine to be different, fine to express yourself in the most extravagant style. Individuality, inquisitiveness, and open-mindedness were celebrated and not judged, and I absorbed this new reality deeply as it allowed me to flourish in many new and unexpected ways. Feeling light-headed, I realize that to be a ballerina was just one path amidst multiple choices and endless possibilities. In fact, studying classical ballet seemed to be the least interesting thing I could do in this extraordinary place that had shaken me to my core.

I experienced an internal revolution. Day after day, my eyes were wide open collecting information of all sorts and slowly transforming my personality and aesthetic into something more daring than just the diligent young dancer I used to be. As I was birthing new parts of myself, still unknown to me, fate was already grooming me for things to come.

My new residence, a posh boarding house for young women with artistic dispositions, was conveniently located between Central Park West and the Lincoln Center. In the very beginning I was shy and riddled with insecurities, choosing to isolate myself from others. But soon after my arrival, a couple of lively girls from California who occupied the bedrooms closest to mine warmly introduced themselves to me, and new friendships were soon forged. One of them was studying fashion, the other acting, and we were soon like The Three Musketeers, fencing our way through the concrete jungle. I was truly living the life of one of the characters of those American TV series so popular in Europe, where youth was celebrated.

Although I had one big worry. The school that Tina had chosen had failed to inspire me. I felt so guilty as my main reason to be in NY was to further my dancing career. Because of the discipline I had formerly acquired, I was forcing myself to attend the ballet classes daily, hoping that I might change my opinion and like my new teachers a bit more. Usually I trained in the morning so I could have the rest of the afternoon free to wander around, absorbing the electrifying atmosphere of my new surroundings.

It was in NY where I initially became fascinated with fashion, where some of my favorite destinations had names like Bergdorf Goodman and Bloomingdale's. At first I was rather intimidated by these megastores. In the past I had visited plenty of elegant shops in both Florence and Monte Carlo with my mother, but nothing had prepared me for the magnitude of these American temples of style, small citadels of luxury goods.

To be exposed to such an endless choice of products had an intoxicating effect on me, as I was suddenly infected with the desire for material things.

This ultimately created within my being a craving for possessing everything I liked such that spending hours browsing inside the crowded stores trying on clothes, makeup, and perfumes became a compulsory daily ritual.

On the wave of an economic boom, the beginning of the eighties brought an exaggerated form of fashion and makeup that was supposed to empower women. There was nothing subtle about the so-called trendy look of that era.

Very pail geisha skin, multi-colored eye shadow, and a dash of bright pink or red lipstick were *de rigeur*, matched by impossibly large shoulder-padded jackets and very short tight clothing. This was the mood of the time where every female on the planet dreamed of being a "Glamazon."

Personally, I had known how to apply makeup from a young age because it was necessary for stage performances. Intuitively, I understood that it was possible to virtually create a new identity with an appropriate outfit and made-up face. After all, when I was on stage I was not presenting myself, but the character I was impersonating. And now I was on the verge of discovering that acting a part could also be extended to real life. Though I had become quite skilled in the art of not revealing my real self to others, and at this point in time, I was about to learn how to go a step further, reinforcing the mask that was already on with a stylishly appropriate extra layer of artifice.

This narcissistic aspect of my being, that till then had been relegated to my ballerina self, started to spread to the rest of my persona as I became obsessed with the way I superficially looked. Clothes were also wonderfully inspiring but I had very little money so could only lust after them, touching the soft fabrics and imagining how they would look draped on my body, especially the gorgeous long gowns so beautifully displayed in the windows of the most elegant and expensive shops.

My new life was opening me up in many new ways, but not always positive ones because there and then the illusion of possessing things in order to be happy crept into my consciousness, together with the desire for all that I didn't have, leaving me feeling stranded and with a strong sense of frustration that would last for a long while until I gained an understanding that it is indeed all of our wants and desires that create our various unhealthy attachments; and therefore the many conditions that subtly control us on a daily basis, restricting the freedom of our being with invisible heavy chains.

Since my arrival in NY, I had toyed with the idea of calling Lorenzo but was battling with another one of my many illusions, the illusion of being unwanted. This deep-seated fear of mine constantly sabotaged my wish to dial his number. Finally, one day an American girlfriend of mine who was very matter-of-fact and bored with my indecision, took the number from my hands and dialed it for me. As if by magic Lorenzo's voice appeared at the other end of the line inviting me to his house the following Saturday. I was ecstatic, wondering why I did not have the courage to do it sooner.

Immediately I wished I could go shopping and buy something special for the occasion, but financially it was not an option. After debating with my girlfriends on what to choose from my own small rail of clothes, a simple chic dress of my mother's design eventually made the final cut. Saturday came and my friends helped me with my long unruly hair, braiding it to perfection. Then, my baby features got an overall transformation as I morphed into a replica of a silent movie temptress with big golden eyes rimmed in jet-black kohl, and a heart-shaped scarlet mouth. Several sprays of Chanel No. 5 later, I was ready, done-up to my satisfaction. After much thanking and kissing the girls goodbye, I decided to not take a taxi but instead to stroll across Central Park to Lorenzo's house as I badly needed fresh air to calm my nerves.

It was a stunning day. The entire park was washed in a cloud of golden sunlight—a place of ethereal beauty, a magical landscape straight out of a fairy tale where, of course, I was the princess about to meet her prince. To walk amongst nature in all of her autumn glory had a soothing effect on my soul. On the ground a carpet of dead multicolored leaves reminded me of how life and death were inextricably bound together in an eternal circle of creation, destruction, and rebirth. *Life and death, new beginnings and new endings, this is what life is made of* I thought while secretly hoping that my meeting with Lorenzo would bring me a romantic blossoming of some sort.

When I finally arrived at his house, I pressed the doorbell with anticipation and waited, my heart pounding inside my chest. After a few moments he opened the door and looked stunned, hardly recognizing me at first. A very different girl from the sweaty young dancer that he had briefly encountered back in Genoa was now standing in front of him. Oozing confidence from every pore of my made-up skin, this image of sophistication I projected truly worked on him, perfectly covering the truth of how I was really feeling inside. All my insecurities and nervousness had been camouflaged by this pretend version of myself. I felt victorious, as I knew that the message I wanted to give him had been delivered. When Lorenzo finally recovered from the shock of meeting my new persona, he kissed me lightly on my cheek and kindly invited me inside his home.

Knowing very little about his background, as soon as I entered I was utterly taken aback by the elegance and opulence of the interior. Lorenzo's family held an old aristocratic Italian name and riches acquired over generations. They had purchased the townhouse in the Upper East Side a few years before, transforming it into a small palace. The house had several floors, and below was the most enormous reception room and a den of preciousness where many valuable works of art and beautiful objects had been gathered together with exquisite taste. Large portraits of family ancestors dominated the room keeping the past alive, their imperious personalities so well captured by painters with names even more illustrious than their subjects.

The impact of such grandness took me by surprise and immediately set in motion a range of mechanisms rooted in the deepest recesses of my consciousness. Part of me felt immediately at home. Because of my own background I was familiar with wealth and titles. But another aspect of my being was cruelly reminded that my family had lost almost everything we once possessed—this produced within me a sense of tremendous loss, and dare I say, a sense of inferiority as often I felt I was not enough compared to others.

This Cinderella complex had been instilled inside my being since I was at boarding school in Monte Carlo, where many of the other students had come from very wealthy families. Now this illusion of mine was about to expand to the next stage. In fact, my friendship with Lorenzo was to be my personal introduction to a glamorous and rarefied international society that often made me feel out of place, constantly comparing myself to others.

The energy of separation had cut a profound division within me, and consequently I unconsciously reflected this personal condition upon everyone; some of whom would trigger the internal dynamics of my hidden insecurities. As soon as this occurred, in return, I was quick to judge the culprits, as judging others was my personal defense whenever I felt threatened in any way.

To feel separate made me feel lonely and misunderstood, giving me the impression, at times, of being a solitary soul wandering the earth in search of something that was yet unknown to me. I was not aware that my quest needed to be internal, and not an external search, and that what I was so hoping to find was simply the rich treasure of my own open heart.

Despite these struggles, almost immediately Lorenzo and other members of his family fully accepted me, and became a sort of second family to me. I was therefore blessed with a new earthly Guardian Angel and a very inspiring companion.

I had come to NY with great hopes of furthering my ballet career but instead received a different gift in the form of a wonderful romantic friendship stemming out of a fated encounter.

Lorenzo and I became inseparable, and although we were the same age, curiously enough, he started to fulfill the role of my next mentor with NY as the perfect backdrop for all of our exciting new lessons. My friend loved art and beauty in every form and shape, and for somebody so young, he had vast knowledge and very sophisticated taste. We also shared much more in common because of our similar approaches to life.

Lorenzo and I had both chosen to be our own person and not to follow the accepted rules and roles of many other individuals in our age group. We became life explorers, tourists of human creativity. Visiting museums and art galleries, going to movies, concerts, and plays, became our daily reality; but we lacked the dedication required for our dance studies—though he did introduce me to some excellent teachers and my ballet training somehow continued. But it wasn't my primary focus anymore, surpassed by my newfound passion for living. NY had a lot to offer and while I uncovered many interesting new facets to life, simultaneously I also journeyed deeper within the mysterious landscape of my own persona. I was feeding my being with a much broader education that alerted all of my senses to a wider horizon of choices and interests.

Nightlife was another welcome novelty on the spectrum of my experiences. Those were the last years of disco and Studio 54. Lorenzo and I often danced the night away in all the hip clubs. There was something so liberating about moving my body freely to the rhythm of the music. The songs pulsated through my being, sending me into an almost hypnotic trance where I was improvising all kinds of movements without the restrictions of ballet's severe rules.

The scene was hedonistic and pretty wild but by some kind of miraculous intervention neither Lorenzo nor I wanted to try drugs or alcohol. Even smoking cigarettes didn't interest us. But we both had voyeuristic streaks, which when combined with old-fashioned educations made up of solid principles, drew us together pretending to be sophisticated grown-ups. In reality we were still children, and this was also reflected in our relationship; loving but purely platonic. Yet, both of us were highly intrigued by sex—we would talk about it a lot, however we were far too shy to even consider kissing each other. On one occasion we found ourselves in the red-light district on Broadway, watching some soft porn show, thinking that we were quite daring to be doing such a thing.

To explore the forbidden gave me a real adrenalin rush, and part of me was quite shocked at the realization that my nature had a possible decadent side to it. Obviously, there was much more to myself than met the eye, as multiple hidden layers of my personality were slowly resurfacing creating an internal shift that was not all of the Light. In truth, I didn't know myself or what I could be capable of. Both my mind and soul appeared as mysterious to me as the future, secretly holding my destiny like a white sheath of paper with the ink of life just starting to write my story.

Lorenzo's father had a vast collection of precious antique books about the Old World history and myths. I had never forgotten my own passion for ancient civilizations, and often used to converse with him about the many theories encircling some of these mysteries. One day he showed me one of his most priceless manuscripts. I was immediately intrigued by the title, carved in golden bold letters: *Atlantis*.

I listened rapturously to every detail of the story of this kingdom inhabited by a very advanced society around 10,000 BC. This land had suddenly sunk beneath the ocean, taking with it all of its inhabitants and their powerful secrets. The Greek philosopher Plato was the one who first narrated this tale and since then the world has been divided between those who believed in the existence of Atlantis and many others who thought it was simply a legend. I was mesmerized by the idea that this lost empire had completely disappeared without leaving a trace. *How was that possible? What could have caused such an immense catastrophe?* In my heart I sensed that the story could be true but maybe it was just wishful thinking. And yet this mythical tale deeply resonated with me.

That same evening Lorenzo and I were walking towards my boarding house and ended up sitting on the ledge of one of the Lincoln Center's fountains. It was a balmy night, unusual for that time of year. In the darkness, the purple, white, and blue artificial lights added a surreal touch to all of the fountains' aquatic displays. It was as if amethysts, diamonds, and sapphires were dropping down like falling stars from the sky creating a waterfall of magical blessings from the Heavens. And it was indeed the Heaven, the esoteric, that was very much on my mind while sitting underneath that dazzling shower of light.

I opened up to Lorenzo, telling him for the very first time about my unreligious beliefs, my encounters with ghosts, my strange dreams, and my impulse to always follow my destiny without hesitation.

"Was I mad to believe in such things? To sense that there was so much more beyond what we could see or perceive?" I asked.

He listened carefully, agreeing that "it would be quite impossible to explain everything in a logical way."

Encouraged by his positive reaction we spoke more about Atlantis, trying to comprehend why this legend had made such an impression on me. Did I have a past life in that ancient land?

In truth, for a while I had also experienced recurrent dreams of giant waves coming towards the shore, and of course there were the vivid dreams of my childhood that I never forgot. *Could this be my link to Atlantis or simply the fantasies of an adolescent girl with a fervid imagination?* For the time being my life was an ocean of unanswered questions. But I was increasingly thirsty for this kind of alternative knowledge—knowledge of the unknown and unseen; the most secretive and hidden truths only revealed to the *High Initiates of the Mysteries.*

Through another of his father's books, I learned that in ancient times the spiritually-gifted young were sent to study in temples. These were called *Mystery Schools*, where the unknown and unseen was taught as a normal subject like history or math. *Where are these schools now?* I wondered with a hint of sadness and frustration. I was a modern girl living in a modern world where the other side was often considered pure invention. And yet I felt such a strong attraction to everything that was not of this earth, experiencing at times the magic hidden in those alternative dimensions through my dreams and ghostly encounters.

That night I couldn't fall asleep, and while tossing from side to side I made a promise to myself. I would never follow religious beliefs again, because this was not my credo. What I believed was the extraordinary world of alternative realities that might seem like a strange choice to others, but one which I knew in my heart was not only real but had the power to support and guide us.

Winter came bringing snowfalls and icy winds. A soft white blanket regularly covered Central Park. Snowflakes laced the bare tree branches with crystalline decoration of such delicate beauty, works of art that only nature could have conceived. It was then that I left the boarding house and moved to Lorenzo's home. I took up residence in the luxurious attic, feeling like a princess in an ivory tower and distancing myself from my present reality. I was slipping away into a dream world as soft and silent as the land covered by snow. I was dreaming of strangely futuristic-looking cities suspended across the Universe. I was dreaming of tall Beings of Light, exactly the same as the ones I had encountered earlier in my childhood visions. And I was dreaming of being surrounded by Books of Light upon which I could place my hands and receive strange symbols that filled me up, gifting me each time with a knowledge that changes were ahead and that this particular phase of my life was about to end.

I became much more introspective and could no longer deny that despite having a wonderful time, I was not progressing in my efforts to become a professional dancer. The fear of failure once again made its Presence strongly felt in my consciousness. Something had to be done—I needed to acknowledge the signs.

Lorenzo was also well aware of how NY had been terribly distracting to his own goals. Suddenly we both felt we had lost our way. Funnily enough, my tales of Marika always intrigued him and he was seriously considering going back to Europe and enrolling in her school in Monte Carlo. But I could not conceive of NY without Lorenzo, so if he was really thinking of returning to the

Old Continent, I would follow him. I thought to myself *maybe this is the push I need to shift my own stagnant situation.*

A few more months went by peppered with an infinite number of discussions about our future. In the end it was decided that going back to Europe would be best for both of us. Our amazing holiday was officially over. My American adventure had been brief but deeply impactful. The girl that arrived in the USA six months previously had shed her old skin and was now reborn—I'd experienced a slow loss of innocence but also a new way of being.

I did not understand at that time the normalcy of positives and negatives. Dearest reader, earth is simply the planet of duality upon which we all carry the Shadow as much as the Light as both sides need to be embraced if we wish to find Oneness within.

Alone on the plane back to Florence, I felt such sorrow staring at the NY skyline swiftly disappearing from my sight and vanishing from my reality. But the change in me had become deeply instilled in my being: I had an insatiable hunger for individuality and freedom together with the notion that I could be who I wanted to be.

IN THE
WAITING ROOM–
LONDON

My homecoming was not a glorious one. My parents were not impressed and according to my mother I'd infringed upon their trust. It was obvious to her that in NY I had a ball without my ballet shoes. I could not deny that there was truth in what she was saying, but at the same time I could not explain to her that my lessons were of a different kind, yet equally valid. There was no point in arguing so I put my head down, knowing that I was simply buying time till the next move. Reintegrating with my family proved to be a challenging affair, especially after having sipped the intoxicating elixir of absolute freedom. I had no choice but to regain my mother's confidence by going back to the discipline of dancing.

There was an excellent ballet academy in Florence belonging to an eccentric Florentine countess. The academy, built inside the ancient walls of her palazzo, attracted a very professional crowd of dancers; and through starting a brand new chapter in my young life I felt more aligned to her teachings than those of my original British teacher. The countess and I understood each other well. She encouraged me to recognize and embrace the talent I had relegated to the bottom drawer of my priorities during my NY adventures.

Gradually I rediscovered the joy of dancing and soon felt the urge to be on stage, the only place where I could truly fulfill the expression of my chosen art. I had heard from my new companions that during the summer season there were always abundant ballet festivals requiring a large number of dancers to perform at various theaters and amphitheaters all over Italy. Shortly, plenty of auditions would be held, and with everybody's encouragement I was now ready to secure a role for myself in one of those productions.

My mother was relieved by my renewed enthusiasm and grown-up aspirations and so when I asked her if I could go to Monte Carlo to visit Lorenzo for a few days, she immediately gave me permission. By now he was enrolled at my old school. Feeling the burden of separation, Lorenzo and I had constantly exchanged passionate letters that fueled our tentative romance, still alive in spite of the distance. So off I went to Monte Carlo where an unforeseen message awaited me.

The start of my Monaco interlude was marked by a rather dramatic event. As soon as I arrived Lorenzo broke the news that Marika had banished me from both her Presence and *Casa Mia*. Feeling despondent, I could hardly believe that my beloved teacher still had no intention of forgiving me. In truth, the other motive behind my visit had been to reconcile with her. But my wish was not to be granted.

At the time, I lacked any real understanding of cause and effect. I thought of karma as a simple word, failing to realize the deep impact that such a word can have on our lives and that I clearly held an ancient

Karmic Debt with Marika. Of course karma can be balanced but then I had no awareness regarding any of this.

Feeling like a general who had lost the war, this was the final blow and I cried my eyes out. I knew there and then that she was lost to me forever. Her rejection of my persona was absolute.

In that moment I learned that there are many different kinds of death. The one I experienced with my former mentor was strange in its finality. I lost somebody who was alive and available to everybody else and yet denied to me as if I didn't exist. And dearest reader, to be cast away by a person we love is the harshest of punishments.

The pain of being rejected and humiliated a second time around was acute, an invisible thorn in my heart that led to an even bigger closure. In this state of pure misery, I took up residence in Lorenzo's small apartment in the center of Monte Carlo. As a male, he was not allowed to board at *Casa Mia*. Even so, the time we could spend together was limited since he was training daily at the school. Also, Alejandra had gone back to Barcelona and the others were too frightened to see me in case they were caught and might suffer a similar fate to mine.

Thus, my visit turned out to be a rather solitary affair where I mainly wandered the streets of Monte Carlo, lost in the memories of happier times. I was drifting away—a twig in water transported by strong currents with no particular direction, and no alternative but to be swept up in the crushing realization of defeat.

One day my aimless walk took me past the casino and onto the promenade by the sea. It was a stunning morning, but under the flawless blue sky I was wrapped in gloom, only aware of my own grief and confusion. Loneliness and the uncertainty of the future weighed on my shoulders like a ton of bricks.

Did I make a huge mistake leaving Marika? My head, filled with this question and so many other unresolved issues, was throbbing. I sat down on one of the many benches along the promenade, staring at the brilliant indigo sea sprawled in front of me like a giant pool of liquid light. *Why can't I have the knowledge of what is hiding behind the horizon of my own fate?* I asked myself, gazing upon the bluish silvery infinite line that divided the sea from the sky.

Deeply immersed in my thoughts, I failed to notice that an older lady elegantly dressed in black had sat beside me on the bench. She was smiling with great kindness in my direction, and in spite of my sadness and bad headache, I responded to her with a timid smile and a *"Bonjour Madame"*—hoping to be left alone after the quick exchange of courtesies. The woman looked rather fragile although her luminous eyes observed me intensely, lighting up her pale wrinkled face. I'd never seen so much sparkle in a person's eyes before and for a moment I was certain that the sun was playing tricks on my sight. Feeling rather embarrassed, I was unsure of what to say or do as she kept looking at me perhaps thinking that staring upon strangers was the most normal or polite thing to do.

Finally she broke the silence and addressed me in Italian. "Why are you so sad? You are young, your whole life is in front of you and your path shall be full of wonders and great discoveries! Do you know that those who search will always find answers in the end?"

Her enigmatic words left me quite speechless, but the best was yet to come. She opened her black handbag and extracted a piece of folded white paper. She placed it directly in my hand, and ordered me to read it only after she had left. Then she rose from the bench with incredible agility for someone her age, and before I could even open my mouth, walked towards the sea, her black silhouette disappearing into thin air, leaving behind the piece of paper as the only proof of our brief encounter.

I opened it at once. There was only one word handwritten in child-like calligraphy: *London.*

I could not contain my emotions and started to cry. *Did I just receive a message from the other side or was this a spiteful joke?* I questioned. The piece of paper was real enough and I had just witnessed with my own eyes the mysterious phenomenon of the lady's disembodiment. Plus, nobody knew where I was because I hadn't planned it myself. I thought again about the glint in her eyes, her strange behavior, and the mysterious words she'd spoken to me in my mother's tongue instead of in French. I was now certain that she knew exactly who I was. *But who was she* I wondered. *Was she an Angel, a messenger from above? Was London to be my future destination?* I slipped the piece of paper into the pocket of my jeans and decided that for once silence was best. This was such an inconceivable story that even my spiritual-minded mother would have doubted it.

That evening when Lorenzo came home he was delighted to find me in much higher spirits. Reunited at last we chatted into the night before exchanging a chaste kiss on the lips and falling asleep in separate beds.

Having fallen into a deep dream, I travelled into a world of Light where many Angels were flying around. After awhile, one of them started to move in my direction with a great flapping of his majestic wings. I looked at the friendly Angel, carefully noticing his cheeky smile first and then immediately afterwards recognized the older lady's black handbag swinging from his arm. I woke up the next morning remembering the dream clearly and feeling so much more at peace.

London was indeed the next destination on my journey. When and how I would get there was still unknown. I left Lorenzo a few days later with a much lighter heart. Even if still mysterious, the future seemed brighter and was pointing north, to a land still ruled by a queen.

Back in Florence I started to attend a number of auditions. Like a fisherman I cast my net, and I did well. I was to dance in a production of *Swan Lake*, starring a famous Italian ballerina. Furthermore, I had won a scholarship to attend a prestigious ballet foundation course that had launched the careers of several well-known dancers. The program would run from the upcoming autumn to spring. I now had a full schedule for the year ahead. My mother was content but I was restless as London was constantly in the back of my mind.

Summer, autumn, winter—the wheel of time was spinning faster then ever and by spring, just before the end of my course, I received a letter from Lorenzo announcing that he was leaving Monte Carlo and moving to London. His words were full of enthusiasm describing the city buzzing with the most extraordinary energy and offering many opportunities. He encouraged me to join him as soon as possible. I was speechless.

The sign had arrived and after reading his letter a number of times, my decision was made. London was truly to be. No extra encouragement was needed and immediately I devised a plan of action. With the small sum of money I already had, plus extra earnings from the approaching summer season, I had now achieved some financial independence and could reach Lorenzo in London soon after in September. Once there, I would have the opportunity to audition for local ballet companies and hopefully secure a job that could give me regular income.

I broke the news to my mother, still singed by my NY bravado, and she wasn't pleased at first. She wanted me to understand that freedom always comes with a price and this price was learning to be responsible for my own actions. Eventually I had to agree.

She already knew the truth that we create our own reality through our actions, thoughts, and words. Yes, I was still very young and still coming to understand and embrace this vital Spiritual Knowledge that allows us to paint upon our own life canvas all that our heart truly loves.

It is especially when we work in co-creation with Spirit that grace will shower us with abundance, removing all obstacles from our path. To recognize that we are often the ones imposing limits on ourselves through illusions, fears, and insecurities would eventually become a powerful step forward towards my awareness of how to create in a new way.

About to take a new step upon my life roadmap, I knew all was fated as after all an Angel in black had shown me the way....

A few weeks before my departure, my mother gifted me with a visit to a special lady, a well-known Tarot card reader. I was excited to receive insights about my future and to have new esoteric experiences. As soon as I met the lady, I sensed that the session was going to be a powerful one. The room, heavily scented with mystical frankincense, was in semidarkness. While she started to shuffle the cards, mystery and anticipation filled the air. I could not ignore the intensity of growing energy that had left me light-headed. I knew in my heart that what I was about to hear would be meaningful, as I believed that those who are gifted can see into the future and give accurate predictions. So many mythical tales of the past mention oracles, and this woman in front of me was just a modern version of one.

Gradually I started to regress in time. The room became a temple and the ordinary looking Tarot card reader became an ancient Greek priestess about to reveal the words of God. Flashes of gold and purple light kept appearing and disappearing around the lady's crown. I was transported elsewhere and automatically chose some cards with my trembling fingers.

After a long unnerving pause, she spoke to me with great purpose. "There is a precise reason, the real unseen motive for why you have been pushed by fate towards London. You lived in that city and in that country previously, in other incarnations, and there you shall meet again those you knew before.

"Seven men,"she stated. "Seven significant men from your past lives shall return to you."

After her opening line I could hardly breath, my eyes transfixed on the cards while her voice, almost fading in the distance, described how all of these seven relationships were to be of a karmic nature, aligned to the path of my destiny.

"You are on a search," she whispered. "You are searching for the one, but it is not as straightforward as you may think. Many souls of men will come to you before you will settle with this one in many years to come. The search will take you around the world and you shall uncover so much more than what you may envisage at present."

I was in a state of semi-trance and all of a sudden, I witnessed the lady's face transform into an Angel's face. The Angel told me that I was searching. *Am I searching for love or what else am I searching for?* I wondered. The Tarot cards revealed that affairs of the heart would guide me towards where I needed to go then and in the future—but love itself would not be easily obtained.

She continued, "In the future, you will forget about all of these predictions and often you will not follow your heart, till one day you will experience such a deep remembrance that it shall lead you down a new path."

At the time I found it difficult to comprehend the exact meaning of those sibylline prophecies. What I did understand though was the mystery of it, this great mystery called *LIFE* that was about to take me on the greatest of adventures. Then the lady spoke again. This time her voice took me right back to the present. She was asking me if I had a final question for her cards. More than one hour must have gone by in what seemed like the space of one minute.

"Yes," I said without much thinking. "Lorenzo. Could you please tell me about him?"

Six more cards were extracted and a triumphant smile appeared on the woman's face. "He is not showing you his real self but it is through him that you will meet an important man, the first one of many fated encounters that will help you shape your destiny." She concluded by stating that London was meant to be and that I should have no fear, as when we are supported by fate all is possible.

I was spellbound and wished to tell her about my previous encounter with the Angel but something held me back. In the meantime, my mother was silent. Dancing had not been mentioned once. After a short pause, the session came to an end.

On the plane to London I felt positively agitated. My mind was loaded with questions but the most pressing ones were about my beloved Lorenzo: *Why was he not who I thought he was? What was he hiding? I know him well and we have kept no secrets from each other.*

Searching for clues in my memories, I suddenly perceived the truth. Lorenzo was always admiring and talking about male body forms but never commented on the beauty of the female body. Again I felt rather frustrated, as in the back of my mind I had always wondered why he had never attempted to kiss me properly. Maybe this was the simple answer. Lorenzo was gay and because of my naivety, I had never noticed it or did not want to admit it to myself, as my tendency was only to see what fit my own desires.

Our passionate friendship could have been just a front to hide his real nature from his family and everyone else. This final thought filled me with dread. Plenty of romantic notions had impregnated my soul and Lorenzo was the scale on which I judged all of those ideals. He was beautiful, noble, and infused with an aura of bygone splendor. Sometimes he was possibly a touch too consumed by his endless fascination with his family history. And we were opposites in a way: he was often projecting himself into the past while I was obsessed with the future.

Nevertheless, I adored him and was scared and sad at the thought of losing him. Next, I put my hand into the deep pocket of my trench coat and extracted the piece of paper given to me by the Angel in Monte Carlo. "London" was clearly written in black ink. I knew there were no coincidences, no mistakes. So I resigned myself to my own fate and closed my eyes, trying to rest a little. Almost two hours later I landed at Heathrow Airport, with a heavy heart and feeling that the closeness between Lorenzo and I would never be the same.

The new center of action, a recently established dance school, was a dark-red and white Victorian building at the edge of Mayfair, close to Oxford Street. At the core of this operation was Nick, a dashing young man filled with charm and artistic sensitivity. He was Lorenzo's new friend, and, Lorenzo's reason for being in London. It didn't take me long to work out their relationship, even if it was played down by both of them. The Tarot cards had spoken the truth. The future was already unfolding as predicted, and with disappointment also came excitement as the thrill of a new love had been promised.

At the very beginning, I received a cold shower as Lorenzo and Nick were sharing a large apartment and I was not invited to join them. I spent the first few nights in a bed and breakfast and soon after, to be fair, they both redeemed themselves by organizing all the practicalities of my life. I was to study with Madame Messerer, a famous Russian teacher who taught both at the dance center and at the Royal Ballet. Cheap and safe accommodations were also found. I was to be a lodger at Madame's best friend's apartment in Barons Court.

Pamela, my new landlady, was a very proper English woman on the surface, but underneath she had a great sense of humor and a big heart. I warmed to her instantly and truly enjoyed spending evenings in her company. Madame also resided in the same building and would often join us for dinner. Both women were wise and had many tales to tell. I was a young person who enjoyed and appreciated the company of my elders. I recognized their value, as this was part of my grandparents' legacy.

Every morning I jumped on the tube and travelled a few stops to the dance school. The center was buzzing with young people from all over the world and in between classes I would kill time in the cafeteria downstairs chatting with the other students and making fast friends.

Then, unexpectedly, a few weeks after my arrival, I was confronted with a very new experience. Infatuation caught me by surprise, coloring each one of my senses in shades of vermillion. That fated day, while on a break after morning class, my eyes fell upon a tall stranger and time stood still for a few seconds, suspended between past and present as my soul knew him well.

He was sitting opposite me occupying the most private spot in the room, a small nook with a single table at the far corner of the cafeteria. His long legs stretched all the way underneath the round white table, his boots peeking out at the other end. He was wearing a dark polo neck under a sharply cut jacket and dark jeans, which complemented his elongated and sharp silhouette, nearly spider-like. He looked rather distinguished against the stark whiteness of the wall. He was a man in command, comfortable in his own skin. His expression, intelligent and inquisitive, radiated from a face that lacked conventional beauty; but beauty often lies in imperfection—his strong features gave him an unmistakable and memorable look.

He was openly looking at me with evident curiosity and an amused smile on his weathered face. I felt shy and withdrew my stare but sensed that he was still focused on me and had no shame in being so direct. There was something compelling about this man, something that shook me deeply as I had never experienced such a powerful attraction towards anyone before. A few moments later, Nick entered the cafeteria and sat beside him. *Well*, I thought, *at least it would not be difficult to find out who he was.*

That same night I told Pamela the brief story of my encounter and while I was describing it to her in every possible detail, we both became so excited as children do when sharing the most significant of their daily discoveries! Pamela had experienced a wonderful marriage. Her husband had unfortunately died a few years previously, but her romantic spirit was far from damaged. Immediately, she was responsive and generous to me, dispensing much advice and sharing her own precious memories of the first encounter with her husband.

"What is life without love?" Pamela murmured at the end of her tale.

"I don't know," I replied. "But I hope to find out before too long."—as soon as I spoke these words, I was overwhelmed with grief.

How painful it must have been for Pamela to go through the loss of her beloved husband. I too had loved and lost in a different way and was still dealing with the wreckage of the emotional consequences. Then fear gripped me tightly. First, there was the fear of rejection, where I would be unable to fully experience intimacy with another. Second, there was the fear of experiencing this love only to lose it later on. *Which one was worse?* I wondered, feeling trapped inside my own anguish....

Dearest reader, I was still a virgin and already memories concerning lost loves, betrayal, and unfinished relationships were coursing through my cells. Sometimes what we want the most terrifies us the most. This can cause self-sabotage and in my case it would prove to be a sorrowful truth. The love of another was my greatest desire and simultaneously also represented my greatest challenge, as it was what I was the least equipped to give or receive because of my karma.

I could not sleep that night while a single thought was hammering inside my brain. *Am I going to see the tall stranger ever again?*

In the following weeks, every time I went down to the cafeteria my heart would pound. The stranger would often be there, sitting at the same table, conducting his meetings with Nick. Each time he would stare at me blatantly, stirring both my senses and curiosity as I had never before been the object of such male attention. I held back a little longer till one day I was desperate to know the identity of my admirer. After taking a deep breath, I finally found the courage to ask Nick about him. You can't imagine my surprise when Nick confessed to me that he had been waiting for me to come forward and ask this question. Merlin had told Nick he wanted to take me out for dinner, and since then Nick had been unsure of how to approach me with his request.

Merlin was not his real name, but for the purpose of privacy, I am renaming each one of the seven key men in my life as the famous characters of the Arthurian legends; each one of them a romantic Knight or wizard who gifted me with many important Spiritual Lessons.

The only other information I got from Nick was that Merlin was his boss. The rest I thought I could find out directly from the horse's mouth as of course my answer to the dinner request was a big YES!

That same evening I shared my news with my two elderly companions. While Pamela was delighted and squeaking with excitement, Madam Messerer was looking rather worried, and repeated several times in her broken English: "He is too old for you. No good. No good." I was learning fast that I couldn't make everybody around me happy. Therefore, I was going to do exactly as I pleased. But what I didn't know was that a painful lesson was about to be learned.

My karma with men was bountiful—I was coming of age and the first repayment was soon due.

Dinner with Merlin was highly entertaining. He was the most interesting human being I had ever met and I could not quite understand why a man with such a brilliant mind would want to spend time with a nineteen-year-old who was filled with complexes and fears. He had made his fortune gambling on innovative ideas that turned out to be extremely lucrative. He was also a divorcee with four children. And funnily enough, he seemed to be as fascinated with me as I was with him. After awhile I felt truly comfortable in his company, forgetting all of my anxieties. Once dinner was over, his behavior was impeccable. He returned me home to Pamela with just a kiss on the cheek.

Many more lunches and dinners followed as the mysterious Merlin became my confident. I didn't know him well but instinctively I felt I could trust him. There was only one thing in our relationship that was not materializing like all the rest, which caused me much disappointment. He would not touch me. I was longing to be held in his arms but I didn't dare make the first move. I had no carnal knowledge of men. Physical love was a great mystery to me and I felt bound by my own ignorance and inexperience, so terrified of being clumsy and unsophisticated. I compared myself to all the other women he might have slept with, and this made me feel inadequate and fearful of being judged for my lack of sexual skills. I was beside myself but still lived in hope that the situation would shift.

One day I confided in him something that was burdening me. I was fast running out of money and was too proud to ask my mother for help, or to go back to Florence with my tail between my legs. What I confessed to him though was only part of a much bigger story. Once again I had lost my passion for dancing. I was trying to come to terms with this reality that I couldn't quite digest yet, and worst of all, I had no clue about what I could possibly do with myself if I was to stop dancing.

As soon as I poured my heart out to him, without hesitation he invited me to move into his mansion. Very generously, he offered me a large bedroom and my own bathroom *en suite*. The bedroom, he told me, was gorgeous. There were large French windows opening up to a beautiful garden where tall ancient trees were home to birds and squirrels. It sounded idyllic and for once I felt real gratitude in my heart. Yet I was unable to express myself—holding back my true feelings of love and affection for him.

Being emotionally crippled was my curse. So much of it was from the fear of showing my vulnerability. I couldn't reveal myself, not even to the man I was passionately in love with. The wall around my heart was so tall and thick that it prevented me from exposing the loving nature that was hidden deeply inside my being.

When I broke the news of my pending move to Lorenzo and Nick the day after, all hell broke loose. Lorenzo threatened to call my mother and tell her that I was about to become the lover of a dubious and much older man. Of course this made me laugh, as the reality couldn't be further from his conclusions. Nick was a little calmer as he told me that Merlin was well-known for his adventures with young girls, and that many had their hearts broken by him. He confessed this was originally the reason why he was hesitant to tell me about Merlin's dinner invitation. Again I dismissed this caution.

Pamela was my only supporter. She calmed me down offering me the safety of her home in case the new arrangement with Merlin didn't work out. She also gave me a little piece of wisdom: "You have to try dearest. You don't want to live a life filled with regrets, so please don't start now." I have met a few fairy godmothers upon my path and Pamela with her fair hair and big blue eyes was certainly one of them. She had no agenda and only cared for my happiness. Because she had lost her own love, she truly wanted me to find mine.

A few days later I was finally ready to move closer to the object of my desire. I arrived at Merlin's gothic mansion in North

London sometime at the beginning of November. Like a real wizard, he dwelt in his luxurious cave, surrounded by his most beloved treasures. His home was filled with art of a particular kind and something was immediately revealed to me: Pre-Raphaelite drawings and paintings depicting images of young women with alabaster skin and long flowing Titian hair hung from every wall. Their physical resemblances to my own persona was what struck me in an instant. In the entrance hall displayed to welcome all visitors, placed in the middle of an imposing antique table, was a marble bust of a girl whose face and profile could have been mine. I was astounded, but as usual pretended to be calm and collected and made no comment. *Was I also part of his collection?* I asked myself while unpacking my few belongings.

But looking around my new surroundings my heart at once softened in gratitude to my benefactor. My bedroom had lovely proportions and the garden was truly enchanting. Outside, a fine mist spread around tall trees creating an air of mystery. I felt like the heroine in a gothic tale living on the edge of a magical forest. Transported by this dreamy atmosphere, I moved closer to the French windows where small droplets of rain were forming an intricate web of liquid lace. Wishing to explore the grounds, I opened the glass door and filled my nostrils with fresh air. The earth, dampened by the rain, had released a musky, woody aroma that took me straight back to childhood. Walking on the soft carpet made of grass and foliage, I briefly caught glimpses of reddish and golden tree branches being swallowed up by fog.

Darkness was fast approaching. In the twilight, birds were singing their last ode to a dying day. My soul, filled with visions of mystical beauty, responded with a great flow of emotions, gradually slowing down my train of thoughts. I remembered how much I loved that time of year; slightly melancholic, as nature prepared herself for a long winter sleep, gifting us with her last burst of life. Inside, a tingling sensation made me shiver. All of a sudden I was certain that I would indeed experience romance in this house. But our minds never see the full picture of events yet to unfold, and fate can at times touch our lives in the most surprising ways.

Merlin was a man about town and endless invitations to functions and parties piled up on his desk each day. He would often ask me to go along with him. In spite of being very shy at first, I slowly started to enjoy the London crowd much more than the one I had previously met in NY. It was somehow more bohemian, more artistic and eclectic than the rich kids' club I had frequented with Lorenzo. It was at one of these parties when I met Arthur.

With his long disheveled dark curly hair and almond-shaped eyes, Arthur had a rock-star's look. The son of a famous musician, he was very funny and a great raconteur. After entertaining us for quite awhile, he received Merlin's stamp of approval in the shape of an invitation to one of his famous Sunday lunches. Our new friend promised to visit us upon his return from a Christmas break in the Caribbean—in retrospect, it is fascinating now to witness how destiny casts its threads, weaving them between our lives and ultimately designing a future, still hidden from us. Something that at the time was utterly unthinkable was secretly already creating its own foundations … for now, Arthur was simply another fun friend, but somewhere deep down I secretly hoped to see him again.

My first Christmas in London was fast approaching. One day Merlin introduced me to his children. They were adorable and very striking, especially the oldest one who was about my age. Gawain resembled a handsome Viking warrior. Like his father, he was tall with longish blonde hair and clear blue eyes. There was something untamed about him that intrigued me and gradually we began to form a beautiful friendship.

Another month passed, and still untouched by Merlin, I was in a deeply frustrating limbo of unfulfilled desires. Was I simply a vision that had walked out of one of his paintings, a human

manifestation of his fantasies that had to remain as such? And yet he was like the father I never had, so generous in every way.

Spending a vast amount of time together, he was teaching me plenty, becoming, in fact, not just my benefactor but also my new mentor. He supported me financially, giving me luxurious rent-free accommodations as well as paying me a weekly sum of money for doing occasional errands for either him or Nick. I had Merlin's devotion, a considerable roof over my head, and enough money to be temporarily independent from my family.

Still, what I sought the most eluded me, and this constant failure to achieve what I wanted bordered on obsession and started to push me over the edge.

Dearest reader, I had yet to learn about projection. If we project all of our wants and desires onto somebody else, we automatically give our power away. Plus, to put anybody else on a pedestal, projecting all of our fantasies upon this individual is unfair to that person, who then has to constantly live up to our expectations. Blinded by an exaggerated form of romanticism that so often distorts the truth, this same lesson has come back to me time after time in different forms over many years in which I have been bound to the wheel of karma in each one of my intimate relationships.

But one fateful evening brought an unforeseen turn of events.

It was almost dark when Gawain arrived unexpectedly at the house. I was pleased to see him, and after consuming a lovely dinner with him and Merlin, his father retired to his quarters and Gawain and I carried on with our conversation.

The night was still. The only noise, the sound of our own voices now reduced to whispers as we didn't want to disturb Merlin. We laid on soft cushions on the floor, gazing up at the stars peaking through the tall trees, reflecting their glow on the large glass window; small wondrous points of light mapping a mysterious path upon the nocturnal sky. We turned off the artificial light and

instead lit a couple of candles so we could have a better view of the starry sky.

Suddenly the atmosphere became intimate, our hands touched and we kissed; at first shy and giggly, then with growing passion. It was simple, natural, and beautiful. All my fear of not being an expert in the art of love dissolved, as I followed my instincts, the knowledge already inside me. This revelation hit me like thunder and I surrendered myself completely to the sexual dance, while our bodies became more and more entwined. After hours of passionate kisses, touching, and stroking, somehow we managed to reach my bed where we fell happily asleep in each other's arms.

I must have slept very little as I woke at dawn to the sound of bird song. Gawain was beside me, still dreaming peacefully. He looked so beautiful, like an Angel fallen from the sky to gift me with pure bliss. Once I became more present and to the full realization of what had happened, I felt very awkward, aware of even more complications piling up in my already messy life. Gosh! I loved the father but had slept with the son. How Shakespearean of me!

Gawain had just shown me the beauty of physical love, gifting me with something very precious and empowering that for whatever reasons his father could not give me. *What was I supposed to do? Wait eternally for Merlin to make his move or keep exploring with his son?* My question was answered shortly by Gawain's passion. As young lovers, from that moment on, my bedroom on the edge of the enchanted forest became our love nest, where we were fed by the magical lotus flower of Calypsos and all was forgotten except our insatiable lust.

He had fallen in love with me. The days and weeks that followed were the most romantic of times. But when winter turned into spring our bubble burst. Gawain was due to travel to Australia for his gap year. The trip had been arranged prior to our encounter and needed to be honored. We were both devastated to leave each other so soon. But the complexity of the situation did not just include the two of us. In those last few months, Merlin had seriously distanced himself from me, and in spite of my decision to be with his son, I felt punished. Still, I missed him terribly—I was in love with Merlin and this uncomfortable truth was the unspoken reality of what I felt within my heart.

One morning after Gawain's departure I was having breakfast alone in the kitchen when I heard a female voice coming from upstairs. *Had Merlin brought a woman home?* Then I saw her, a pretty young thing plastered in makeup and scantily dressed. He quickly introduced us and left the house in a great hurry, taking the blonde girl with him. I was livid, jealousy erupted inside of me with the fury of a volcanic explosion. "How dare he!" I screamed loudly, smashing my empty teacup onto the floor.

Of course it was nonsense. Merlin was a free man and I was having a romance with his son.

But I could not see the situation fairly as I was being influenced, yet again, by a huge female aspect that was insinuating negative thoughts inside my mind about disrespect, betrayal, and rejection.

Only interested in my own version of the story, I had sunk into the illusion that I was practically perfect in contrast to the imperfections of others. Did I ever dare to speak the truth to Merlin? Of course not. I expected everything from others without ever giving away anything of my own. This was my pattern, this absolute resistance that hid the truth of what I felt.

Sadly, this very powerful thought form, my aspect, would be in the driver's seat, controlling the process of each one of my future intimate relationships, bringing upon myself much distress and misunderstanding—I have been unfair to all of my Knights, always and only seeing the situation from my own narrow point of view. I was cursed by all the unresolved deeds of my past lives and had no idea how to disentangle myself from my own karma.

Dearest reader, even so young, I already faced such twisted emotional affairs of the heart.

When I finally calmed down, I started to pick up the many broken pieces of what used to be my favorite teacup, and with tears streaming down my face, remembered God and prayed and prayed to him to help me emerge from this state of great confusion and show me the path ahead.

With Gawain now faraway in Australia, my relationship with Merlin readjusted itself little by little. In reality it could never be the same. I was now his son's girlfriend. Gawain's shadow was constantly between us and neither Merlin nor I could ignore his invisible Presence. Merlin was unreadable and it was very difficult for me to detect his inner thoughts. The notion that I would never find out what those thoughts were created great sadness inside of me. And to make things worse, by a cruel twist of fate, Merlin often confided in me his wish to find a companion for himself. He would often say, "Why can't I find a girl just like you?"

His words kept me awake at night, as endless tears marked the realization that I had created my own punishment for being dishonest about my feelings, not having the courage to speak the truth of my own heart. If I had done so, the situation could have been different, maybe I would have been happy; but it was too late. I had to accept defeat and make the most of the little time I had left alone with him before Gawain's return.

It was around then that Arthur appeared again in my life. First he came to Merlin's famous Sunday lunch, and then I started to see him regularly at the dance center where a craze for fitness classes brought hundreds of people jumping up and down every evening, sweating in the name of perfect bodies. Arthur was very popular with all of my ballet friends, especially the girls. He often invited us to his flat, close to Hyde Park, making us laugh with all of his jokes and storytelling. His apartment was unusual. He was a successful art dealer and collector and his space reflected his wonderful and eclectic taste to perfection. It was filled with African art as well as many amazing and original objects that he sometimes discovered in the most unusual places.

I visited him more and more frequently—his place a safe heaven where I could amuse myself with ease, forgetting all of my heartaches. Our friendship grew quickly. He was funny, kind, and inspiring. I felt I could trust him as much as I trusted Merlin. There was something very solid about Arthur, even though he was a womanizer and I knew of his many affairs. All of my girlfriends were like ripe fruit falling directly from the tree into his lap. I felt sorry for them as it was obvious they were just a bit of fun for Arthur and nothing more. With me, he was different, much more attentive. He would listen with great patience to all of my dramas.

Spring arrived and nature exploded, rich in color, perfume, and texture.

I was feeling the calling of her awakening and loved wandering around London parks witnessing the magic of Mother Earth being reborn. I would walk for hours on the wild grounds of Hampstead Heath, trying to find answers that would bring me some relief.

My emotional state was a mess and so was the rest of my life. I had no direction and felt completely lost. Going back to Florence was not an option. Auditioning for a ballet company could have been a possibility but there was a serious problem. Being swamped with emotional upheaval had resulted in extra kilos on my otherwise light frame. Presenting myself at an audition was not advisable. My mother wasn't around and I lacked the discipline to go on a diet on my own.

But the deeper truth that I could not yet face was that I fully lacked both the discipline and dedication to truly succeed in my dancing career. I was all over the place. A miracle was needed, a sign from the other side to help me find my path again.

Eventually the saddest day of all arrived. Merlin was flying to Los Angeles where he would meet Gawain who had finished his gap year in Australia, and the two would return together. Upon his departure I wanted to tell my beloved wizard how much my heart was his, but not one sound came out of my mouth apart from the usual goodbye.

I knew the end had come. A sensation of finality so like what I had previously felt when I lost both my grandmother and Marika, again spread through me with intensity, making me feel sick. Our love was never to be and I was devastated, harshly blaming myself for failing.

Afterwards I fell into a vortex of depression that isolated me. For a while I didn't want to see anybody. I was mourning Merlin and the death of a dream that was never to come true. A few weeks went by till at last I received a sign I was so desperately waiting for.

Gifted with a new vision of things to come, it was time to see Arthur. Destiny was pointing in his direction.

London was in the middle of a wave of magnificent weather. Hundreds of people were out and about, sunning themselves in the parks, filling up pubs and restaurants. The English, usually so reserved, were smiling and laughing, and this infectious gaiety broke through my gloominess making me feel much lighter. On one of these beautiful days, Arthur and I were returning from the park when we kissed. I knew in that instant that we were meant to be together. Just a few nights previously I had dreamt that he was coming towards me with open arms. He was the miracle I had asked for. Once again I felt touched by God, as love is a miracle in itself. Almost immediately Arthur asked me to live with him. I was very nervous and unsure of what to do so I told him that I could not leave Merlin till he had returned from his American journey.

I felt a tinge of deep melancholy at the idea of leaving Merlin and also pure dread as I needed to break the bad news to Gawain who had been sending me the most romantic love letters which I could not answer in kind. Anticipating their return was sheer agony, but finally the wait was over. I pulled myself together and approached the confrontation in the most grown-up manner I could manage.

The wizard was first. To my great relief, Merlin's reaction was positive. At last I understood how uncomfortable he had felt in the situation, as much as I had, if not more. Yet he was a truly generous friend. He sensed that I was anxious about moving in with Arthur, and like Pamela had done before, also promised me that his home would always be open in case things didn't work out. These simple words relieved my many fears, and tears rolled down my cheeks. In that moment I finally realized that Merlin deeply cared for me in his own way.

After I left he fell gravely ill for quite awhile. Of course it could have been a coincidence but something told me otherwise. For many years afterwards I often thought about him, seeing him occasionally here and there, but it was never the same; and as time moved on our lives became more and more distant till we completely lost touch.

Gawain was a different story. He didn't take it well at all. It was harrowing for me to say I was leaving him for another man after all of our passionate and intimate moments together, including my first discovery of the pleasures of lovemaking.

There is something very bonding about a first love and I felt as much pain in delivering the blow of separation as he did in losing me. I wished I could have told him the whole truth, that I needed to go in order to free us all from the unhealthy dynamics that would eventually damage us even further.

I left Merlin's cave on a glorious summer day never to return again, or so I believed. My life on the edge of the enchanted forest was short-lived, yet intense. It will never be forgotten and will always be cherished as that was the temple of my first sweet love.

The honeymoon with Arthur was over pretty fast, causing me to suddenly enroll in a crash course to learn the mechanisms of that particular relationship. For a start, to live in his home was the equivalent of living inside his own creation, designed and controlled by Arthur in every single detail. There was not much space for my own self- expression as every inch of the apartment was blueprinted with his very distinctive taste.

I soon realized that I had not just entered a relationship with somebody, again much older then me, but that in fact I had entered an entire world, a microcosm where Arthur was the sun and everything rotated around him. My saving grace was my complete lack of interest in anything remotely domestic including interior decorating as he was the master of the house and I simply the guest.

In a peculiar way, Arthur and I complemented each other rather well; certainly we shared an abundance of positive traits, but we also verged on the unhealthy. He was an impressive, multitalented man, and had a certain genius with things. I say things because he was a fanatical collector and loved objects, all kinds of objects that resonated with his unique point of view. Furthermore, he possessed a natural instinct to foresee what people wanted before they knew it themselves. To be the girlfriend of a tastemaker was not an easy task as Arthur could be so kind, as well as incredibly critical—I often felt I was the target of his disapproval, as my own taste was still undeveloped and quite unremarkable compared to his. His negative comments fueled my illusion of not being enough.

I quickly realized that if I wanted to stay in the relationship I needed to pull myself together and have a complete makeover. First, all my extra weight had to go. I was in need of discipline, not for the love of dancing but simply because I was fed up feeling like an ugly duckling, often left alone in a corner at the many parties that we would attend together.

Invited everywhere, my boyfriend was a social animal deeply skilled at interacting perfectly with others. Arthur enjoyed great popularity with men and women alike and knew many famous and interesting people, as he himself came from a glamorous showbiz background.

I, however, was shy and overweight, poorly dressed and lacking direction in life. I felt badly about myself when invited to all of those glamorous parties filled with gorgeous women dressed to the hilt and with bodies to die for. It was absolute torture with so many parts of my consciousness being triggered all at once. Consumed with jealousy, I would watch Arthur flirt madly with other women as if I didn't exist. I was also constantly hurt by the behavior of most of his friends, who in the beginning could never remember my name. To them I was simply another on an endless list of his girlfriends.

My illusion of not feeling enough expanded at great speed, giving me a sense of a total loss of identity and unworthiness even beyond what I had previously experienced. So dearest reader, in an odd way history was repeating itself. I had been more or less ignored by my father, sexually ignored by Merlin, and now again I was hitting a wall with Arthur.

Out of desperation, I found the strength to go on an insanely strict diet, determined to transform myself into an exotic creature people would want to know and remember. I was resolute that nobody would ignore me ever again. To be thin was a start, but not enough. A new look was needed, but how? I hardly had any money, and while Arthur was paying for everything, his generosity did not stretch to spoiling me with too many presents.

It was around that time that I started to religiously buy fashion magazines. I would gaze upon each page with lust, taking in every detail, and study all the names of the designers and the seasonal trends. Inspired by the elegance and sophisticated beauty of the models, I started to develop this insane desire to replicate that look in my own life. I so wanted to transform myself into one of those wonderful looking young women, to wear those amazing outfits, and to be admired by others.

The previous pilgrimages to the fashion stores in NY had been just a timid start, a seed compared to the obsession that was exploding inside of me; a compulsive desire for exquisite clothes and accessories. Having come from a theatrical background, I had learned the power of appearance very earlier on and fully understood that with fashion the same principles could be easily applied. That fashion itself could become the right platform to express myself in a creative way. After all, I could be who I wanted to be....

One day I had a revelation, but not of the spiritual kind.

My first true friends in London were Leila and Dariush, stunning and wonderful Persian siblings. I used to spend much time in their elegant home and one afternoon I was introduced to their auntie visiting from Paris. I couldn't take my eyes off of her. She was a very pretty woman, however that was not quite the reason for my fascination. I was enthralled by what she was wearing as I had never before seen such a perfect and sharp outfit. It gave her body the most graceful of shapes. Casually, she told me the name of the designer, somebody I had never heard of called Azzedine Alaia.

A few months later, in *Vogue*, I read the first article ever written on Alaia, and understood that not only had I found what I wanted to wear, but also that I possessed a natural instinct for what could become fashionable as the magazine was heralding this designer as the next big thing.

In truth I grew up with my grandmothers wearing couture clothes and also my mother who had her own original personal style. Fashion was in my genes but not until then did it become so completely relevant to me. At the very start it was my love for Arthur, and equally my fear of losing him, that fully brought fashion into my life as I wished to be beautiful for him. He was an esthete and indirectly taught me something very useful that eventually would turn my life around in the most astonishing way.

It took me one year to lose all my extra weight. By Christmas, after days of arguing, I finally convinced Arthur to buy me my first Alaia dress; an elegant chocolate-brown acetate bondage number that did not leave much to the imagination, showing my new figure to its best advantage ... there I was standing in the middle of a crowded cocktail party, tall in my new satin electric blue heels, looking as slim and alluring as those other women I used to envy. I could feel the burning eyes of men on me.

The dress was my armor and I felt invincible in it. Of course it was all an act. Nothing had changed. Underneath, I was still a troubled, shy, and insecure young woman, but no one needed to know the truth. In fact, I believed that people were not at all interested in the real me, too complex, too sensitive, too dreamy.

But the other version of myself, this new creature of my own invention, had great potential to be successful in the harsh world. The building of a new identity takes military planning and this, beloved reader is what I did.

Little by little I constructed another being on top of my real being, and the original me got pushed so far back that she became a distant shadow while the new me took over like a whirlwind that left me spoiled, cold, selfish, snobbish, narcissistic, and mainly interested in the pursuit of all of my wants and desires.

So, at twenty-one years of age I became a new fully-fledged member of "The Program" There is nothing sinister about The Program dearest reader. It is simply an educational system based on a set of old beliefs taught to us from childhood. It denies the Synchronicity of Universal Flow and the power of living in co-creation with Spirit, and the ability to recognize our own divinity and the divinity in all there is.

This transformation of mine was about to bring me some success but the cost was high as both Arthur and I struggled to endure the long-lasting effects of my new persona.

Even in the deepest of winter, flowers are born under the snow ... in a time where my Shadow grew bigger than my Light, I was lucky enough to receive a wonderful gift from the Heavens in the form of friends, as one after the other members of my Soul Family started to pop up from all directions becoming the future pillars of my existence. They were the few who saw beyond my masquerade. Many of them are still standing strong around me today, as the passing of time has not decayed but strengthened our affection for each other.

I owed them so much as they gave me the most precious of gifts, their unconditional love, accepting my Darkness as much as my Light.

But the unfortunate effect on my relationship with Arthur was like a butterfly in a spider's web—I was caught up in a net of glamour, fun, and superficiality. From the shores of the South of France to those of Ibiza and Barbados, he and I were often on the move and life was a never-ending party.

My interest in dancing was slowing down rapidly, till one day, after a very bad injury, I made the decision to stop altogether. And that was it. Dancing was no more. Everybody around me was shocked as I had talent, but my passion for classical ballet had been suffering a slow death for a while. It was time to put an end to the past and carry on with my own metamorphosis.

Arthur truly loved me in his own way, but sexually we were not compatible. With Gawain I had experienced something that was magical. We were the same age, both quite inexperienced and starting our journey together. This made us equal in bed. Arthur though was much older, extremely experienced, and a product of the sixties culture of free love.

Prior to our relationship, he had slept with hundreds of women and sex was no longer at the center of his life, at least not at home. Many times I felt rejected. From my side, making love was still a novelty and I was constantly hungry for it while Arthur was rarely interested. There was an imbalance between us that ultimately wasn't our fault. We just came from different perspectives and a wide age gap was not helping. I was incapable of fully understanding this at the time and so frustration took over as I was left constantly unfulfilled.

One day, about two years into our relationship, hidden inside a book I discovered by pure chance a love letter written to Arthur by a girl I vaguely knew. Arthur owned a beautiful house in Ibiza and usually spent most of the summer there while I would only join him for a few weeks, as I liked to visit my parents in Italy around then. The letter was written with the ink of passion, the girl madly in love with him. Every word, every sentence, was an ode to their summer of love and the possibility of seeing each other again.

It was hard to describe the betrayal I felt. I was a true believer in romantic love and the sudden fall from my pink cloud hurt me badly. I had to confront him, which I did while rage still boiled in my veins. Arthur faced my fury with great calm and the answer I received was even more shocking than his betrayal.

Of course he was not pleased to be found out, but in a very composed and matter-of-fact manner, he explained to me that I was the one he truly loved, the one he chose as his companion. However, it was normal for him to be attracted to other women and that his recent affair was probably not going to be his last one. "The nature of men is different," he carried on, "but you have nothing to worry about as you are my chosen partner and no other."

I was speechless, my ego bruised beyond repair and my heart frozen. Afterwards I cried for days, ruminating over *What am I to do? I am in love with Arthur and don't want to let go of him, but how could I cope with such a situation?*

The solution eventually arrived. It was not planned but simply sprang from the seeds of rejection.

A huge void had grown inside me. The void was caused by many different things: there was the loneliness I constantly felt, there were Arthur's many affairs that fed my insecurities and sense of unworthiness, there was the unclarity of being without direction while surrounded by a multitude of successful people who made me feel even more inadequate.

On top of all of this, I had temporarily lost my mother's friendship. Giovanna was upset with me since I had confessed to her that my dancing was over, while I was making nothing out of myself apart from being a professional party girl.

It was difficult for me to feel centered—I was restless and in a state of constant agitation. My reaction to pain and discomfort was usually to wander around the city in order to distract myself. During the day I would scout all of the fashion shops for inspiration, maybe buying something inexpensive to wear at night. And every evening, without fail, with or without Arthur, I would go out.

Apart from Lorenzo and the Persian siblings, I didn't have many close friends but I still knew a lot of people and was never short of invitations. It was during my nocturnal wanderings that I met countless attractive young men and started to indulge in numerous affairs. *If Arthur could do it so could I.* Without a trace of guilt, I went on a rampage of sweet revenge.

I learned fast, but unfortunately it was not a healthy lesson. I was on the edge of becoming the youngest and most cynical person who ever lived. My affairs and Arthur's affairs became the talk of the town, vastly entertaining our friends and beyond. While gossip flew, strangely enough at home, he and I were getting on splendidly. He realized that he had met his match and it was now his turn to fear losing me.

This game made me heartless, and while I was hurting many around me, I didn't realize the emotional harm that I was also inflicting on myself. In the meantime, I had developed sophisticated social skills, a fashionable style, and some lethal charm that I dispensed right, left, and center in order to get exactly what I wanted. The aim: Have as much fun as possible while forgetting all my real issues. And what better way to distract myself than with an endless string of love affairs?

Soon I started to frequent the house of a well-known songwriter and his eccentric wife. Night became day and day my night. It was a turning point in the wrong direction. My new friends' place was often crowded with many well-known musicians and extravagant characters. It was a hedonistic version of Ali Baba's cave that offered potential sexual encounters, food, drink, and all sorts of drugs, all night long to a decadent group of misfits. Our host and hostess were very generous. How could I resist such temptation? Well, I couldn't and one fateful night I touched cocaine for the first time and received a memorable hit that led me to want much more.

I was trapped in a downward spiral. Abusing myself with different substances became an almost daily ritual. For me it was all a bit of fun, something to fill my internal void because being stoned and high desensitized me, altered my perception and distorted the truth about my life. A total eclipse of my Light obscured my being while I slipped deeper and deeper into Darkness without any awareness of what was truly happening.

Addiction surged full force through my genes as it had previously with many other members of my family. I was already addicted to all my wants and desires, and now to drugs as well. I had also confused true love with lust, creating many energetically unclear chords between all my lovers and myself, plunging into a vortex of deceit. But of course I was totally convinced that I was in control of my own actions, as all addicts believe, because it is almost impossible to find an honest addict who recognizes the truth of their state of being.

I had forgotten all about the Angels and my special experiences. Those memories faded away like images of old pictures eroded by time. Instead, I started to see myself as a glamorous *Vampire*, a dark creature, stalking the night in search of forbidden pleasure and unexpected highs. Luckily, all my invisible friends in Higher Places had not forgotten about me and a very unusual group of

Angels arrived to my rescue. Earth, not Heaven, was their home. These Angels had human bodies and complex personalities. Once I started to recognize them, Light flooded back into my life and danger was averted, at least for the time being.

I first encountered one of these Angels in the most unlikely of places. Like me, she was a frequent guest at the House of Darkness, also searching for a way to fill her own void.

Sometimes pearls can be hidden in the mud, concealed by the grit and grime, till we take a deeper look and a glimpse of something very precious suddenly is reveled to us.

This is exactly what happened when I first met Lella. In the beginning, I didn't even like her. I looked down on her, as I believed her to be even more lost than I was. It took me awhile before I recognized this rather original Angel who eventually became one of my greatest friends and teachers.

The second Angel was also veiled from me in her initial visitations. I was quick to judge her, thought she was far too complex, and not enough fun for my liking. But Donatella was also another hidden gem and from the first day I saw her Light I have never let her go.

My next Angel, Crispin, came in masculine form. An Oxford graduate, he was eccentric, intellectual, and daring. Possessing a heart of gold and a wonderful sense of humor, I adored him. My companion on so many adventures, he also became my night Angel and guide. Together we explored the club, fashion, and art scenes that were exploding in London, helping me to expand my future vision.

My Persian Angels Leila and Dariush also were always supporting me in every moment with kind smiles on their faces. Another Angel, Freya, would join the Angel Squad a bit later on and became one of my most loyal friends; her helping hand a godsend from the very start.

The Angel Squad grew in size through the years but in the beginning these were the ones who took me by the hand and supported my return to the Light.

Lifted up from my druggy torpor, my beautiful friends started to show me that there was so much potential inside my being and that the time was ripe to direct my energies into building a life for myself. Freed from drugs, I started to dream again, and to contemplate that clothes could possibly become more than just a personal obsession. Through my social scene, I mixed with many individuals involved in the fashion business, and secretly aspired to be part of this exclusive, creative, and colorful world. On the other hand, I was also suffering from great insecurities, my illusions of not being enough blocked me from truly believing that I could succeed.

One day I was given the opportunity to work at a very exclusive boutique called Joseph. For a while the designer shop had been the perfect training ground for many girls who afterwards ended up working at top fashion magazines. This path appealed to me, although as a snob with a growing ego, I hated the idea of being a shop assistant and felt it was rather beneath me.

But to learn some humility was exactly the medicine I needed and after many discussions with Arthur and my Angels I was convinced to try. After all, I needed to start from somewhere, and to be on the shop floor offered me the perfect opportunity to learn more about clothes, fabrics, shapes, and cuts. Plus, all day long I would be surrounded by what I loved the most; an amazing collection of designer clothes. So I entered the glamorous world of fashion through the back door but I was not destined to stay there long.

My friend Lella was working in a nearby jewelry shop on Fulham Road. We often met during our lunch break, repeatedly telling each other how tedious life was as shop assistants. I dutifully worked, first at Joseph, and then at the boutique of a well-known

British designer for almost a year. The novelty had faded away and only the paycheck was still keeping me going as I enjoyed being financially independent from Arthur. In my mind, everything was measured and judged, and to be a shop assistant rated very low on the scale of my own values around success and glamour.

One day, during one of our lunches, Lella said something to me that got my attention: "Why don't you try to work for a magazine? Most days, many Fashion Editors come to borrow jewelry from our store and I believe that you could easily become one of them." Immediately, small negative voices whispered in my ear that *I couldn't possibly be a Fashion Editor and that no one was going to give me the chance to enter this door.*

But for all my doubts, Lella was unshakable in her faith in me. Offering to help further, she gave me a list with all the names and numbers of people working in the fashion departments of all the top magazines so that I could find out if there were any jobs or work placements available.

After weeks of holding back because of my fear of failure, at last I found the courage to call those people. It was not belief in myself that pushed me forward, but the even bigger fear of not achieving anything important in my life.

At first I was confronted by many rejections that made me feel smaller and smaller. Till one day I called a top newspaper Fashion Director, who to my complete astonishment not only answered her phone, but invited me for an interview so we could discuss a possible work placement. When we finally met, the connection was instant and one month later I was sitting at a desk in the offices of the legendary *The Sunday Times*. My new boss, a very well-respected editor, was at the time one of the best in the business. I could hardly believe that I had been given this incredible opportunity, because the energy of being less than others was sitting deeply in my consciousness, blinding me to my true potential.

Yes dearest reader, every time we put ourselves down, believing that we are not as good as everyone else, we are in truth becoming more and more severed from our own Light, failing to realize that we fully have this infinite potential within us. But once we give our power away to illusions such as this, limitations are sealed inside our minds, blocking the Universal Flow of our own spark of Creation.

My personality was filled with contradictions. I desperately wanted to be recognized but simultaneously lacked the self-confidence needed to gain such recognition. My saving grace was to encounter beautiful beings along the way who saw the Light in me, in my potential, as I was incapable of recognizing it in myself. So after awhile, under the loving guidance of my first Fashion Angel, I became much more confidant. I truly adored my work, feeling a deep sense of belonging in my new position. Finally, after many years of searching I had discovered what I truly wanted to be, and could see the full picture of my dreaming.

Striving to become a Fashion Editor was the perfect fit for the new me, my new identity. I wanted to wear the best clothes, create beautiful fashion shoots, and travel the world scouting for perfect locations. I wanted to stay in luxurious hotels, go to fashion shows, meet and be friends with all the designers, be invited to all the most exclusive parties, and eat in the best restaurants.

My wants were not just about wishing to have this particular job, but to fully embody being a Fashion Editor and the alluring life that would go along with the role. Still, in the midst of constructing my new identity, this was a major puzzle piece I needed to both complete my metamorphosis and to satisfy my craving for glamour. But in the midst of this transformation, the exposure to the realm of all wants and desires would damage me as I believed the tricky illusion that happiness would only be achieved through material possessions.

A new chapter of my life was about to begin. The joy of expressing my Power of Creation was deeply felt by my soul, as was the great loss of

innocence brought about by my yearning to possess everything I wanted and desired. But you see dearest reader, in the end we come to learn that there is no right or wrong, because all is one and all is needed in order to grow our wisdom so that we may keep evolving.

I have no regrets about my life in the Fashion World … only infinite gratefulness as creativity can be expressed on this earth in so many ways and the ephemeral beauty of fashion is but one of those expressions of pure creation.

While still in my early days at *The Sunday Times*, I had been invited for dinner by my Angel friend Donatella and her pop star boyfriend. I was told briefly on the phone about the other guest, somebody important in the music business, but I certainly had no idea that I was about to meet one of the greatest loves of my life.

I was smitten with Lancelot the second I saw him across the table in a crowded restaurant.

That fated night, when I arrived late flustered and disheveled from having run all the way to the restaurant, I came face-to-face with a devilishly handsome man with a compelling and electrifying personality. Lancelot was a force of nature, and immediately I felt caught in a whirlwind of emotional and sexual craving that was hard to control.

My new object of desire was a romantic character straight out of a book, embodying at once two very distinctive personality aspects. There was the city Lancelot, dressed in expensive, sharply-cut designer suits, looking every inch the super successful businessman with matching lifestyle. And then there was Lancelot, the cowboy, the horse rider galloping recklessly through the red barren landscape of the Australian Outback. Passionate about Mother Earth, he loved being surrounded by nature in its wildest forms and undoubtedly it was the raw energy of that virgin land that had gifted him with the strength and resilience of his unique character.

His soul was indeed bound to his native land. And this is where I went fundamentally wrong from the very beginning, because I had no understanding of the real nature of his being. It was difficult for me to see deep within him or others as I did not know how to see deep within myself, preferring to be like a butterfly poised lightly on flower after flower.

In spite of these misunderstandings of the soul, a magnetic attraction between Lancelot and I threw us immediately into the vortex of a wild and tumultuous affair. In the following days we met again and again, till I felt truly burned by the intensity of our encounters, knowing perfectly well that our time together was limited, bound by the diversity of our life's arrangements. When he left London I felt an intense sense of abandonment, as yet again, our connection was an ancient one, leaving me to experience the loss of a piece of my heart.

But a week after his departure, I received a surprise telephone call that confronted me with the meaning of love marked by deep unsolved karma. Being a daring risk-taker, Lancelot asked me to join him in Australia. Since he had gone I'd thought about him incessantly, missing him like I had never missed anyone before. My body and heart ached for him, and yet for a few seconds I remained utterly speechless, frozen by the opportunity to manifest this dream of love in my reality.

Immediately my mind was reminding me that *I hardly know him, that this is just a temporary crush and nothing more. But is this the truth? My soul knows him well, I am sure of that.* Still I was unable to give him an answer. Gripped by fear, I lacked the readiness of heart to take such a step forward. Lancelot telephoned me a few more times until only the sound of silence was left between us.

A few months later, I woke from a dream in a state of great agitation. I had dreamed of Lancelot with another woman. That same afternoon I received a call from Donatella. She wanted me to know that Lancelot had just married. Pushing back the tears, I pretended I did not care, when in fact I felt broken inside.

But it was far from over … for the next twenty years Lancelot and I would find and loose one another, time after time in an endless circle designed by karma. I never again had full access to him or was allowed to explore the strong soul connection that we shared from the very beginning. Ours was to be a doomed affair based on stolen moments, fugitive instants scattered here and there across the fabric of time and sealed by the deepest karma from many lifetimes ago….

After this episode, my disillusionment with men grew stronger. I felt alone in my relationship with Arthur and decided to put all of my focus and energy into building a successful career, something that I could fully control and that could never let me down.

Ruled by karma and by many aspects, I was bound by my self-imposed limitations of how I thought my life should be, but still persevered and slowly started to ascend the mountain of my ambition. I remembered a dream of so long ago where alone, I climbed a high wall in an enchanted garden. *Trust the dream* I said to myself. *Just trust the dream and don't look back.*

As a result of my experience at *The Sunday Times*, *Elle* magazine recruited me for the next work placement. On the day I arrived at the cool headquarters of this illustrious international publication, I would never have guessed that it was to become my fashion temple for the next twelve years. Through a series of good fortune, I was soon able to secure a job as a Fashion Assistant. Funnily enough, Jackie, the Fashion Editor who gave me the position, was also Australian. This faraway land had come to my attention every so often since childhood, reminding me that I had a strong connection to it.

But at that time all I could think of was my fashion career and how I was going to move ahead in order to become a Fashion Editor myself. My life journey was finally back on track and I was now certain that step-by-step, I would achieve the success and recognition that I so wanted.

Determined no longer to be distracted by painful love affairs, I created a new illusion to never fully believe in love for another, as my career was far more important then any affairs of the heart.

I associated love with pain because every time I loved I experienced loss. So how could I trust love?

Yet, despite my closed heart, thoughts of God and all the wonderful beings of Light suddenly resurfaced from the depths of my consciousness. Undeniably I was still being offered so much support from the Heavens. For brief moments the fog would clear, and there was gratefulness in my heart together with an understanding that if we truly follow the sign posts on the road map of our destiny, the right direction will always unfold in front of us in a magical and mysterious way.

My mother was relieved that I had found a new vocation and this brought us closer together after all of our previous disagreements. Yes, peace with Giovanna was made, but in truth this was also a time marked by both physical and energetic separation from my genetic family. Especially with my father and sister, who were almost strangers to me; with none of us making any particular effort to reverse the rather distant relationships we had created. I did not have much understanding or compassion for either my father or sister as my heart was firmly closed and my profound issues with both of them ran too deep for me to be able to resolve them.

I was not equipped with Love and Light then, and it was indeed my lower state of awareness that forced me to sit in the unresolved energies of my family karma for many years to come.

At *Elle* my work was going extremely well. My gypsy life had begun. I moved from one location to the next, discovering the traveler within.

To be an explorer was always my destiny. But only later on I became aware of how our Spirit mirrors our human personality. I started to travel the earth without realizing that I could travel beyond this planet to so many different dimensions and realities.

Globe-trotting around five continents showed me that so many different realities already exist here on earth, even if many people choose to live in only one of them. It was quite trippy to be shooting ball gowns in a warehouse in NY one day, and the next capturing the lightness of summer dresses on a Caribbean beach, and a week later photographing winter coats in Paris.

The idea that we could have all these different lives according to which place we visited was utterly fascinating to me and as "The Masked Lady" I had plenty of new locations to play my many roles. Hopping earthly realities was wonderful therapy for my restless state of mind. And yet it was my reality in London that now urgently needed my full attention as Arthur and I were running out of time....

Arthur had been an amazing companion, truly loving and supportive through all of my troubles and victories. He had been my Pygmalion, supporting my transformation from awkward teenager to sophisticated young woman. But I was twenty-five years old living in an open relationship that was emotionally unhealthy and denying me the freedom to fall in love with anyone else. The cocktail party-years, the social training, had gifted me with tremendous knowledge on how to deal with all sorts of people, at least on a superficial level. My life with Arthur could only have been described as the most brilliant preparation I could possibly have received to help me towards my next steps.

Despite my fear of love, it was romantic love that I most wanted, even if I was not really contemplating a life of marriage and children. I had never forgotten my dream of finding the one, the other side of

myself, but I had masterfully buried it, or so I thought. In a strange way this compulsive search for love was what made me feel the most alive. And the most disappointed too as I could not truly open myself up to anybody.

I knew in my heart that Arthur was not the one. But at the same time I was struggling to leave as I cared so much for him and felt protected by how he truly knew the ways of the world and that I could trust him implicitly. But in the end, the call for freedom was what I sided with.

Lella, the Angel, came swiftly to my rescue and offered me a room in her lovely apartment. To know that there was a secure new roof over my head finally gave me the courage to reveal my own truth to Arthur.

To tell him of our separation was horribly painful. I was filled with unbearable sadness and guilt but sensed that it was best for both of us in the long-term. At once, he offered to marry me; but it was too late. So much in life is about timing. If Arthur had asked me at the beginning of our relationship I would have happily said yes, but seven years had passed and the erosion of our most intimate connection, the sexual connection, had become a huge chasm between us.

Afterwards, I prayed to God to make that the last time I would have to tell somebody I loved that I was leaving them. And dearest reader, my wish was granted. Soon it was my turn to be the one left behind. And yet unconsciously I was still the first to reject, if only through my fear of love, or my uncaring and superficial behavior; the perfect mask to hide my inability to express the hidden tenderness of my heart.

In time, Arthur and I became close friends and our affection for each other grew steadily. He is still a shining member of my Soul Family, loved and appreciated by me beyond measure.

Moving in with Lella marked the real beginning of my adult life. No longer protected by either Merlin or Arthur, I was just my own creation taking full responsibility for all the actions in my life. I felt as light as a feather, even if occasionally a tinge of panic shook me as there were fewer safety nets. But to take up the challenge of being completely independent was very exciting and I never looked back.

Lella and I both represented the epitome of cool London girls. I had a glamorous job in media and she had just embarked on a new career as a talented jewelry designer. Our lifestyle was bohemian and carefree with plenty of social opportunities that greatly entertained us, bringing a constant flow of new people through the revolving door of our apartment. Our charming West London house was situated not too far from Portobello Market, our favorite place to hunt weekly for vintage treasures and inspiring ideas.

Our time together passed fast and furiously until one day I discovered that my Angel sister was hiding a dark secret. To my great shock, Lella revealed to me that she was HIV positive. At the time AIDS was the equivalent of a death sentence with many departing the planet because no effective therapy was yet in place. This unsettling truth brought me an unbearable sense of anguish, though Lella reassured me that she already had a plan in place. With the help of a formidable Chinese doctor, she would cure herself in an alternative way, without taking any of the normal medications with their dangerous side effects.

Still affected from this revelation and wondering why I was cursed with the possible loss of everyone I loved, from that moment on, I became incredibly protective of Lella, instantly forgiving her bad moods and sometimes arrogant behavior. I so admired her courage and felt very attracted to her strong spiritual side—she taught me more than I could recognize at the time.

Her philosophy was that everything needed to be appreciated. Every sunset, small flower, well-cooked dinner, all, in her view were as precious as works of art. She was often my eyes when I was blind to what occurred inside and around me. And further, she knew my heart, seeing through my selfishness, my coldness, my fake superiority, and all of the other constructions of my mind. Being suspended between life and death gave her deep gratitude and an acute sense of perception which allowed her to cut through the superficial, and get straight to the heart of any matter.

My friend could see Light when Darkness was upon me, she could see my suffering when I pretended everything was perfect. Like a caring mother, she fed me with the most delicious food, and when necessary, told me exactly how it was while many others wouldn't have dared. She believed in me, and was a source of constant encouragement and sound advise. She touched my heart in very special ways. Similar to me, she was also supported by invisible forces, which, through dreams or a sense of knowing, would always direct her towards the right choices.

But living with someone who could potentially pass away at any given moment also reinforced my own belief in living life exactly how I wanted with no compromises and very few concessions to others.

Thus, my selfishness was often rampant with my ego in the driver's seat of the vehicle of my being, directing my mind to disconnect more and more from my heart. My awareness that life was fragile, strangely enough, cemented within me a total lack of consciousness about the feelings of others. My thoughts, my feelings, my way of being, all were calculated by a cold mind to perceive that everything revolved around me.

Lella was the opposite: all emotions and no mind. Somehow the key to our relationship was in balancing each other out.

Despite the situation, laughter and not tears resounded in our home where plenty of stories about boys would often distract us from more painful matters. A veiled sadness, only slightly perceptible, was occasionally felt by us both but was immediately washed away by the next party, the next fashion trip, the next lover, the next beautiful necklace.

One other member of our magic circle was the stunning Donatella, a complicated being who could not see her own worth and could not easily speak of her own truth, yet had an immense talent for seeing the potential and truth in others. She was introspective and had killer instincts. She was the one who rescued Lella and I from the House of Darkness—she was the one, who like Cassandra, told me many truths. Donatella was often the voice of my consciousness, one I was not always ready to listen to. Like me, my darling friend was not religious; but unlike me then, she had great faith in God and recognized the power of prayer.

My own prayers had gotten shorter and shorter and were not recited from the heart, but only out of fear as I was convinced that if I stopped praying I would be unable to obtain from God what I was asking for. I had been used to bargaining with the Almighty since I was a child, and at that point Lella's life was a very important subject between God and I.

Tata Anna had recently passed away too, and with the loss of her spiritual fervor parts of my childhood had also passed away—I had changed so much and had lost *The Way of the Light*, more interested in the material and more guided by my wants and desires instead of my heart and soul. The beautiful child within me was buried underneath the thick crustaceous armor that had fully encased my being.

My quest for clothes, shoes, and handbags gifted me with only briefs moments of pleasure. I was quickly bored with everything, including some of my lovers who were coming and going on a merry-go-round of emptiness and superficiality. The only things I truly believed in were my creativity, my friends, and occasionally myself.

But sometimes in the midst of my frenetic life, I would meet some-body special; somebody who would touch my heart and soul only to then quickly disappear. This was the karma I had been bound to by my closed heart. This karma that I could not undo or understand pulsed through my reality with a relentless beat.

One morning I was sent on a shoot. I had been asked to gather together some clothes in order to style a young artist named Per-cival who was on the brink of stardom and the focal point of the shoot. The Features Editor was going to interview him and could hardly contain her excitement—though it was slightly tinged by the fact that this rising star already had a girlfriend.

We arrived at the studio quite early on so we would have plenty of time to set up. My mood was rather gloomy. I was not interested in the artist and had no interest in dressing him either. I thought the whole exercise was a waste of time. But fate didn't share my point of view as something mysterious was at work....

Finally, when he made his entrance, and to everybody's as-tonishment, Percival walked straight towards me and never left my side for the duration of the shoot. His behavior caught me by surprise and pushed me to reconsider.

I saw an indefinable quality in this charismatic young man that made him very attractive beyond his good looks. Strength and vulnerability, fire and ice, bright mind and delicate sensibility, all were equally present in his complex personality already layered over with opposites. Percival was a one of a kind and there was no doubt that he was destined for stardom.

By the end of the shoot he overheard me asking the photog-rapher's assistant to call me a taxi. Percival immediately offered to take me home in his car. I knew he lived in the opposite direction, so my heart smiled while I took up his kind offer with a certain curiosity.

It was only after I was in his car during the long ride home that I felt a profound sense of remembrance of the mysterious force of our soul connection. Percival was not the best of drivers and talked nonstop, his deep voice wonderfully articulating his love of music. A cascade of beautifully chosen words unfolded into lyrical prose, while he recounted to perfection all of the emotions he felt while listening to a particular piece of music. There was such poetry in the way he delivered his ode, the whole of his being animated with nervous energy, his sensitivity and intensity exposed. I was intrigued listening to him with great fascination, losing myself in his marvelous blue eyes.

For the first time ever, I was perfectly happy to sit in the worst London traffic because I wanted to be in his company for as long as possible. In the back of my mind though I knew he had a girlfriend, and that I might never see him again; a thought that brought up in me an inexplicable sadness. When the ride unfortunately came to an end, we said our goodbyes and went our separate ways.

That weekend I travelled to Paris for a fashion shoot. But in the "City of Lights" all I could think of was Percival, with a growing feeling that our souls knew each other well and for longer than we could possibly remember.

Upon my return to London, the Features Editor summoned me to her office. She was convinced I had made an impression on the young artist and therefore was the best person to deal with him: "Could you please phone him to discuss his pictures for the upcoming article?" I couldn't believe this twist of fate after I had surrendered myself to the idea that I would never see him again.

After a short telephone call, Percival and I agreed to meet close to my home that evening at a fashionable café-restaurant in Holland Park where we would have a drink and look through the photos. In actuality it took us just five minutes to choose pictures. But drinks turned into dinner, and five hours later we were still talking, deep in a conversation that encompassed the histories of our young lives.

He was akin to a young lion, eager to make his mark on the world. So much hope was in his heart! There was a certain purity of thought in his mind, his dreams, and ideas—his personality still undamaged by life.

Whereas I was the cynical one, the one who had lost the *Way of the Light*, and although I was touched profoundly by the remembrance of his soul, I didn't dare tell him. There was also something else that we shared deeply, a profound love for our respective mothers. That magical summer night, Percival lit a spark inside of me. I seldom felt alive. But with him, in that moment, I felt exactly that: alive.

When he drove me home, I invited him to come upstairs. I promised to give him a book but before I knew it, we were passionately kissing, losing our clothes on the apartment floor until finally reaching my bed. A long night of pleasure was in front of us, too late to have regrets, too late to worry about his girlfriend who he never mentioned once—a subject I decided to avoid as much as he obviously had.

Morning came and he left quite early, with guilt painted all over his handsome face. He promised to call me soon and disappeared into the daylight while I was left lingering in bed, his sweet smell all over my naked body and the shadow of disappointment upon my heart.

Then the truth sank in. I was wrong to believe that to go with a man who wasn't free was something I could just avoid.

A few days later, as promised, Percival called me with a grave voice, asking me if we could meet. Riddled with remorse, he sat opposite me in a crowded bar, pouring his heart out about his girlfriend. As he described their rapport, I knew that nothing was going to save their relationship. I felt awkward and out of place, quickly realizing that I could not share this insight with him. So I stayed in silence and listened to him unravel all of his unresolved heart energies.

I wanted to tell him that he had touched my soul in a special way, though of course nothing of the kind came out of my mouth. He seemed quite tormented and I was unable to give him any peace or much support, wrapped up in my own unhappy thoughts and incapacity to speak my own truth. I had to accept that he was with someone else and most probably I had been just a distraction for him, nothing more. This realization made me sad, and in that moment I felt my usual pattern of not being enough. I felt unwanted.

But despite my negative internal mechanisms, when he called me again a few weeks later, I did not have the strength to refuse and saw him a few more times, sabotaging my self-esteem even more.

I had not yet learned that I had no respect towards the woman he lived with, and to mirror that, I had no respect for myself either. My sense of unworthiness and my desire prevented me from seeing this truth, while I sugarcoated the whole affair with romanticism. This disrespectful way of being towards other women, the sisterhood in spiritual terms, brought more karma to me and I would certainly pay the price for my wrongdoings.

But there was another undercurrent between Percival and I yet to be discovered. One night after making love he shyly asked if I ever thought that we could have met before in a past life. I was astonished by his question, but instead of speaking my own truth and sharing with him what I felt all along, I froze and cut him off. Soon after, he vanished without a word and I felt another unexplainable sense of loss. I heard that he had married his girlfriend only to divorce shortly later. I also heard that his mother had died—I felt his heartbreak as I was well aware of their closeness.

Then there was a void, a blank space between us lasting over ten years, till the day I had a dream and knew that Percival would come back into my life.

A very clear pattern was emerging in regards to my intimate relationships. I was unable to express my feelings, unable to show myself to another; as I was so trapped inside my own construction of being repressed and forgotten. Chained to my fears I lived in terror of appearing weak, being rejected, and simultaneously suffering a tremendous sense of loss. Every time a story finished, I was consumed with pain and anxiety and could not stop loneliness from overtaking me, like an icy wind deeply penetrating my heart, it produced an internal chill that I couldn't thaw.

The only alternative I knew of was to focus even more on my career. My work was a great source of inspiration, and as before with dancing, I was truly dedicated to it. I felt protected amongst all those beautiful clothes, all those precious inanimate objects. Nothing could hurt me there. Fashion was my safe haven. I adored the creative process of choosing and gathering all the apparel for a shoot, and couldn't wait to become a Fashion Editor myself, to be able to express my own point of view in the pages of the magazine.

But I lost myself in fashion so much that I became consumed with possessing all the clothes and accessories I was constantly exposed to. My obsession to own also sometimes extended to human beings, as I could be rather possessive of my friends and lovers too.

To have the illusion of owning anyone outside of ourselves is a negative energy that will only bring us hard lessons as it did for me.

The sovereignty of each of us is sacred and therefore needs to be respected as such. To interfere with the energy of another individual through any form of manipulation, such as to take the power of another by imposing our will on them, only diminishes our own power through the Universal Law of Creation. Instead, to empower others with love increases our own power. And dearest reader, what is this great power inside of us all but the almighty power of our own heart....

One day I was asked by my Fashion Director to accompany her to Milano on a very special project. She had been asked to style the Prada fashion show that season—one of the jewels in the Fashion World crown—and so I went along to help her out. I felt a great synergy with the Prada style and with the lovely people working there. Soon, a strong friendship was forged between all of us. I immediately liked and respected the owner Miuccia, a distinguished woman and quite a character. Her point of view on fashion was individualistic and very particular. I was like a sponge, absorbing everything she said, down to the smallest detail.

Showtime was a very exciting and high-pressure moment in which the designer had ten to fifteen minutes to convince press, buyers, and consumers that what they saw on the catwalk was exactly what they all wanted. So much was at stake and to be able to work on the creation of the fashion show and to witness Prada making history was thrilling. That show and others soon to follow marked the beginning of the incredible success of the label. Part of my own reward was the gift of a full wardrobe of Prada clothes. Now that I looked like a Fashion Editor, I knew I would become one.

It was around that same time when I started to smoke cigarettes, one of the most enduring of all of my addictions. Aesthetically, I had always liked the look of smoking from having observed my grandmother Maroussia elegantly inhaling and exhaling. Memories of how she would bring with such elegance the cigarette to her lips had been visually imprinted in my mind, and ever since I was a teenager I had tried to emulate her, hoping to give myself an air of greater sophistication. But in truth I detested the taste of cigarettes and was rather disappointed that smoking did not give the extra oomph to my personality I had hoped for. Actually, I viewed cigarettes as a fashion accessory without any understanding of the hidden dangers and a few years later finally managed to find a luxury brand of cigarettes with a delicious blend of fine tobaccos. I was hooked, literally puffing my way through life when sometimes a pack a day was not enough....

Screening me behind a cloud of smoke, cigarettes became my new best friend, always available in helping me to be less shy and reducing feeling under pressure. Smoking came to represent a very special ritual that I could not live without, a further layer of separation between my being and all others by repressing even more of my feelings; an illusion as dangerous as the poisonous substances that I was inhaling and exhaling exactly like my grandmother had done before me.

The following season I returned to Prada, though assisted a different person. The new stylist, a famous name in the Fashion World, was rather mean to people he viewed as inferior or of no particular use to him. In return, I started to judge this stylist very harshly.

Dearest reader, I was unaware then that sometimes when we judge others we should look more deeply inside ourselves as we may carry exactly the same faulty seeds. We all go through very similar patterns of being judgmental as this is part of an old program that affects our consciousness in very specific ways.

Usually this common pattern is triggered by self-criticism as often we are judging our own being without love or compassion and then reflecting this unresolved energy on to others. I was also unaware that it is only when we learn to be kinder to ourselves that we feel kinder towards others, and recognize the divinity that is unquestionably in each one of us.

On this second visit to the Prada headquarters I was blessed with a very special encounter. Meeting my fashion fairy godmother, an authentic muse of style, was a key moment that helped me shift to the next level in my career. As Marika was my true mentor while I was a dancer, the inimitable Manuela Pavesi became my true mentor in the Fashion World, teaching me what I needed to know and much more.

After having spent many years as one of the most recognized Fashion Editors on the planet, Manuela had just begun a new phase of her creative expression as a photographer, and was often on the look out for young talent to collaborate with. When Miuccia, Manuela's best friend introduced us, the connection was instant and my fashion career went into overdrive. My fairy godmother touched my life with her magic wand and soon after I was made a Fashion Editor, manifesting at last one of my biggest desires. Swinging her wand in all the right directions, Manuela also recommended me to another fashion legend, the photographer Helmut Newton who for several uninterrupted years invited me to join him in Monte Carlo to collaborate on major advertising campaigns.

To be back in Monte Carlo in my new incarnation as a *fashionista* made me feel even more empowered. I was a success and this was the sweetest revenge on Marika.

While Marika was descending towards the twilight of her existence, I was entering the golden dawn of mine. My unforgiving nature had been an aspect of the Darker side of my soul, the Shadow perpetually following me around, often obscuring my Light. I should have forgiven her and simply remembered with gratitude all that she had given me. After all, I was the one who had left her without a second glance. But I wasn't ready to see this truth as I was still blinded by pride and could seldom admit that I was wrong. I was wrong about holding on to harsh unforgiving energy, not knowing it only creates a heavy burden of separation upon our hearts, dragging us into a vortex of negativity, bleakness, and imprisonment. To forgive is simply the key to the freedom of our heart. This lesson would be one of the hardest to integrate, for my soul had experienced many previous lives encapsulated in an unforgiving state of being.

By all appearances the glamorous fashion life that I had dreamt about for so long was at last fully manifesting. I embodied my role to perfection, forgetting more and more that being a Fashion Editor was simply an aspect of myself and not the whole of my being. Armed with a new title, a growing designer wardrobe, and regular pages in the magazine stamped with my personal ideas, I felt invincible and in control.

That is until love was about to touch me again and consequently my deepest fears were about to be exposed even more. It was February 14th, Valentine's Day. Dressed in all white, I was walking on a street not too far from Merlin's house, the house of my first love in North London.

That evening, love was on my mind, like the sweet promise of something precious that all of a sudden might be gifted back to me. I felt uplifted while I moved uphill towards an art gallery. It was opening night for a photographic exhibition appropriately called "The Kiss." My friend, Donatella, a talented fine art photographer, had one of her pictures showing in the exhibition and all of our closest friends were gathering there to celebrate our dear Angel.

When I finally arrived, the room was incredibly crowded; I could hardly spot my friends. Then in the distance I saw Lella talking to a tall stranger and my heart stopped beating for a moment. His figure was still slightly out of focus, but the closer I got, the more my breath slowed down. I saw a ghost, the ghost of someone I must have loved a long time ago. Standing still for a moment amongst the noisy crowd, I travelled somewhere else, travelled through time in a sequence of very fast images flashing through my mind depicting the past life that I once shared with this stranger. While lost in this new esoteric experience, Donatella's voice brought me back to reality. She took my hand and led me towards him.

Tristan was his name, a gift of love and sorrow, wrapped up in a box with an expiration date.

My time with Tristan was without a doubt the most harmonious I have ever had with any of my lovers. To this day, I fully recollect a collage of many wonderful moments, precious tiny speckles of Light still holding together against the passage of time.

The sharing of the simple things in life was the present that he brought to my life. Endless walks in nature, classical music concerts, cool small bars, museums—everything was so simple and enchanting. Tristan would give me wonderful books to read. There was one in particular that I adored, a twisted love story, according to him, in which the female protagonist and I shared many similarities. The novel was a tragic account of the impossibility of perfect love, a doomed prophecy that would soon be reflected in our own relationship.

Tristan would sometimes laugh at my extravagant outfits, a bit out-there for somebody who grew up with the strict code of conduct of an upper-class European family. Despite my superficial over-the-top appearance, he accepted me for who I was. Our intellectual and spiritual exchanges were profound—a golden thread that bound us tightly to one another. With Tristan I received a glimpse of how magnificent it is to be able to share everything with your lover. Those first few months together were the equivalent of living in Arcadia, our own "Arcadia of Love."

Even the British weather was in synchronicity with our love story, gifting us with an unusually bright and warm spring and summer. I felt radiant but was in denial of a truth that I had known from the very beginning. Tristan was only in London temporarily while he finished his important laws studies. Afterwards, he had already accepted an offer to go to Russia and then back to Berlin, his permanent residence.

September was to be the month of our separation, the expiration date of our romance. In September I was also due to travel to Venice with Manuela on a photographic assignment for *Elle*. Tristan decided to join me once the shoot was over so that we could spend our last few days together in that magical city before his departure to Russia.

One day, just before my trip to Venice, he asked if I would ever consider following him abroad. My mind was quick to tell me that it would be impossible: *My career has just started to take off. How could I possibly give it up now? And what am I going to do in Moscow or Berlin anyway?* I was madly in love but still unable to give myself to him—my mind had already worked out that to trust love was absolute madness. So I said no to love yet again, preferring to retain the illusion of being in control, limited by my ever-growing fears. The disappointment and hurt on Tristan's face were evident.

Our time in Venice was pure agony, the swan song of our love story dying amongst the decaying palaces and churches eroded by water and time. The city at the beginning of fall was tinged with melancholy, the perfect setting for the end of our affair. We were both trying not to deal with it, clinging to every minute that we had left together, lingering upon the last breath of our quivering emotions. The course of time though is irreversible and he left me behind in Venice with the most terrible sense of loss that I had ever inflicted upon myself.

My return to London was a miserable one. I was numb with pain and could not eat or sleep properly for days. In the end I did what I knew best and threw myself back into work, pushing my feelings as far down as I could, all the way into the deepest recesses of my being. Tristan and I carried on maybe for another year or so, but by then it was a diluted version of what we had shared before. We met occasionally in Berlin, or in Estonia, a truly beautiful Northern European country where Tristan had bought back some land that once upon a time had belonged to his noble family. And it was in Estonia, in the deepest of winter, when amidst a fairy-tale landscape covered by the whitest snow, my story with Tristan truly reached the end and I had to let him go forever.

But it was not over yet as fate had in store for me another great loss.

A couple of months after my last trip to Estonia, I attended the International Fashion Shows in Milano. The shows were one of my favorite things. They were a time for high glamour and I always carefully prepared myself for this fashion marathon with its expensive dinners and flamboyant parties. It was also nourishment, fuel for my work as all my ideas for the magazine derived from what I witnessed on the catwalks. I would watch the shows with great pleasure, imagining through the clothes all the different women I would portray in various fashion shoots.

My creative process was so much fun that I would take it to the extreme not just in my work, but also in myself. I wanted to be one those imaginary women dressed in a certain way, having a certain attitude. My narcissistic side that I had cultivated since childhood had emerge even more. I spent hours thinking about what to wear and who I wanted to impersonate by wearing certain clothing. My choice of accessories was key, the proportions of my outfit, vital. After struggling with weight through my teenage years, I had become very slim and well-proportioned; my body still toned by dance, I could wear whatever I wanted.

I had put all of my energy into dressing myself in my own unique style and gradually my peers started noticing me more and more. As a result, I received regular presents from designers and PR companies, exquisite new additions to my ever-expanding wardrobe. Immortalized by hoards of Japanese photographers who would follow me around various shows, I decided to cultivate my image even more, taking my self-obsession to a new level, each day pushing Tristan a little bit more of out of my mind.

The morning of my arrival in Milano I was confronted with severe bleeding. At first I thought it was just a very heavy menstruation cycle. But by midday the flow of blood was increasing in intensity. I had gone to the washroom during one of our showroom appointments, and while I was pulling my knickers down, an unusually large blood clot fell on the turquoise floor of the bathroom. With all of my lack of self-awareness, I picked it up and flushed it down the toilet. Only a few hours later, when forced to go to hospital as my bleeding was getting out of control, I found out the shocking truth: I had just lost a child, the one and only child I would ever carry.

The doctor advised me to see a specialist upon my return to London in order to receive further analysis. When I did so, I was told that I was unable to carry children. The reasons were not completely clear, but drug abuse certainly was an important factor as the chemicals in certain substances were known to increase the risk of women becoming infertile. The news had a profound impact on my feminine spirit, wounding my womanhood to its core.

When my friends asked out of concern, I told them I was fine and that I never wanted children anyway. But in private I could not stop weeping as I was certain that I would never gift a child to the one man I would love in the future. I was barren, and this knowledge expanded my level of emptiness and sense of unworthiness already living in my being.

I broke the news to Tristan over the telephone and heard infinite sadness in his broken voice. At times the birth of a child can change the outcome of a relationship in a very positive way. In our case, it sealed our irrevocable separation. About one year after, he married a French girl from his university days.

Only many years later did we see each other again. We met one late night in Paris on the eve of the birth of his first child. I was so happy for him and his wife. He was besotted with the idea of becoming a father, and was genuinely excited that he could share this with me. At least one of us was going to be touched by this magical act of creation.

In that moment, I suddenly realized that fate always has a perfect way of working things out. And that often we are just the observers of our own lives, as many invisible threads move around us in mysterious ways. So much faith and patience is required to have an understanding that everything is always in Divine Order, even when we may not think it is.

After this painful double loss, my own existence became more and more entwined with my career, the line so blurred that there was no longer a distinction between the two. In order to forget, I started to travel extensively, spending long periods of time in exotic locations as far away from home as possible. Escaping to different terrestrial realities distracted me, gifted me with a temporary form of healing. Superficially I lived in a way that many could easily envy, but this was only the gilded façade that did not reflect the eroded interior of my being. I had dreamt of this glamorous life and a part of me knew clearly that I was privileged to be in my position. And yet, a life of such external beauty and luxury was not resolving any of my internal issues or supporting me to open my closed heart.

The pace of my work was relentless with constant deadlines to be met. There was never time to reflect on my state of being, and in truth I preferred it that way. Everything in my life revolved around fashion and my encasement in it created protection from the external world, and above all, from my feelings, as by then, my own feelings made me more and more uncomfortable.

I held tightly to the false credo that showing emotions was just for weak people, and felt safe only when barricaded inside my own self-ishness. Being a control freak became a rather predominant aspect of my personality. And to live a life projected six months in advance was my normal way of being, as this was the nature of how fashion magazines worked. So to live in the present was a very remote concept, as I constantly projected myself into the future, clueless about the power of the now. Unaware of the binding ropes of my many illusions, I sought everything from outside my own Source, carefully avoiding looking too deeply into my wounded soul. Cigarettes, alcohol, and occasional drugs were the finishing touches that numbed me to perfection. My Light was dimming and my heart firmly shut. But in my illusion, my mind was still strong and in charge.

Then one day my worst nightmare suddenly materialized.

Lella, till that point the picture of health despite being HIV positive, fell gravely ill with pneumonia. It pushed her to the brink of death. The thought of death always had the power to shake me deeply, reminding me of my own mortality and therefore showing me that time was slipping away. While Lella was fighting for her life, and in the aftermath of this grave event, something slowly started to shift inside of me, almost unnoticeable at first:

I received the precise sensation of being in a Waiting Room where the life I was presently living was ultimately only a temporary form of entertainment while something else was being prepared for me. I had no inclination of what could possibly happen next, just that it would be very different. How this came into my awareness, I can't explain … it was suddenly there, a golden seed planted in my heart, a memory from a distant time and a sign of things to come....

It was around this period when a magical dream also came to me. I saw an island surrounded by tempestuous waters. The island was shaped as a tall ragged cliff, battered by high waves crashing violently against its ancient rocks. I was walking uphill towards the top, moving slowly and battling against the fury of winds that were trying to push me back at every step. Finally I reached the peak—a flat space where a mysterious stone circle made of mono-lithic-shaped crystals stood. I took my place in the center of the circle and waited.

A strange stillness was in the air. The wind had vanished, the sound of the crashing waves reduced to a faint whisper. Then, one by one, a group of tall sages appeared, encircling me in complete silence. I knew in that moment I had met them before in my childhood dreams and that I could trust them. They were all dressed the same way, wearing long white tunics, shining as pure Light. An infinite look of love and goodness was expressed through their amazingly bright eyes, while their bodies radiated laser beams of rainbow-colored rays. No words were exchanged, only the telepathic message that this mysterious *Brotherhood of Light* was highly protective of me and that one day soon all would make sense in my life....

From that moment on, the knowledge that I was simply in the *Waiting Room* began to slowly grow. But I could not see what was next. I could only perceive that the bewildering world of the unseen would soon reclaim me.

Witnessing Lella's illness in full bloom was not for the faint of heart. My beautiful friend was reduced to the shadow of her former self and I was plagued day and night by gloomy thoughts of losing her. I started to pray once more to God with great fervor, asking him to spare her life; to for once be fair, as I had never forgiven God for having taken from me my beloved grandmother Rita.

At last, God answered my prayers and Lella slowly got better. Her recovery brought her and all of us who unconditionally loved her great relief.

I needed distractions from that harrowing experience so was looking forward to attending a glamorous summer wedding I had been invited to. Crispin's brother was getting married to a South American beauty.

The day of the ceremony, dressed in a vintage white and silver sequin dress and sporting a large pale-cream satin hat, I made my

way towards the registry office situated off Kings Road. Arriving almost last, I took my seat in a corner towards the back so I could have a good view of the elegant guests from all corners of the globe convened inside the registry office's large room—this was a very international wedding.

Semi-hidden by my large hat, I had fun scanning the crowd and taking mental notes on what the other girls were wearing. Suddenly I noticed a masculine, handsome face that was unknown to me. Unaware that I was staring at him with intensity, the young man was completely absorbed in the ceremony. There was a depth of spirit in his beautiful eyes, the same one that I had seen before in all the eyes of my other Knights. Then I recognized him at once from a past life and knew he was to be my next knight....

The wedding lunch was held at the magically romantic country property of my Angel friend Crispin and I was to be seated next to the beautiful stranger. This was simply how Galahad entered my life. Scion of one of the grandest European aristocratic families, he had an elegance of the soul, physical beauty, and above all, an unshakable faith in God. What impressed me at once was the vastness of his heart, which, unlike anyone else I had met before, was wide open. What I found difficult to accept was that he was a devoted Catholic and a purist, while I had resolved never to set foot inside a church. In addition, my lifestyle was bohemian and at times possibly a touch decadent. Despite these profound differences, Galahad and I shared a deep soul connection that supported us as we daily surmounted our many disagreements.

On holiday in Ibiza that same summer, I took a huge single portion of pure Ecstasy in powder form. The hit was so powerful that for about ten minutes I thought I was going to die. But once the drug settled in my system, I began to experience the most wondrous multidimensional trip. I believed that the copious amount of the drug had opened the gateways of my perception to a new level as I could now see more clearly through the veils. I could also hear people's thoughts and was able to go on a very deep journey within that led me to some powerful new insights. I experienced a different reality that was not of this earth. I was fascinated by my new discoveries, feeling like the real version of *Alice in Wonderland*.

Back in London, my new way of being kept expanding even without the help of chemicals. And soon after I began to fall into trances, connecting with spirits of dead people such as my grandmother Rita.

In the midst of all these new activities, I received a call from a top fashion scout proposing a dream job at Chanel, the venerable French fashion house. Working at *Elle* was still wonderful and fun but I had been there for a long time and was in need of a new challenge. Over the next several months I travelled to Paris in order to meet key people at Chanel—the owner, the designer, the perfume nose, the CEO, and so on. Part of me was incredibly excited by this potential opportunity but the idea of moving to Paris did not appeal to me as I loved my life in London.

Then, one day another offer fell into my lap that truly felt right. *The Sunday Times Style Magazine* was looking for a new *Fashion Director*. Commanding a readership of one million weekly, at the time this was one of the most prestigious jobs in fashion; not just in London, but worldwide. The new editor, Tiffany, a super bright Cambridge graduate, was not so knowledgeable about fashion. Therefore, she offered me something rather precious called artistic freedom. I sensed that this was a golden opportunity, a new step towards achieving an even higher profile in the industry. So I accepted and became *Fashion Director* of *The Sunday Times*. What thrilled me the most was that more than a decade before, I had started my fashion journey in this same place as a humble assistant on a work placement, and now I was returning in full glory to occupy one of the top positions.

The launch of our first new issue was to be celebrated at the Serpentine Gallery with a grand party attended by all the "Fashion Gotha" and plenty of celebrities. That night I felt that all the energy I had put into my career had at last been rewarded with my realization of so many of my wants and desires. Though a big one was still absent.

My growing ego had blinded me from seeing that Galahad was dissatisfied with our relationship. At the beginning of our love story, we shared plenty of quality time together. We would journey around the world to so many wonderful places, not just discovering new landscapes, but also the landscapes inside ourselves, those of our souls. Being in motion with Galahad was very special and I loved my travelling companion. He was also my teacher of the heart, showing me the strength of his open heart, something that was truly foreign to me, as was his faith in God. At times we also had heated confrontations about our differences, but the beauty of reconciliation was never far away as we both recognized that each one of us had different ideals. In doing so, we always found respect for each other.

But with the growth of my success, Galahad became even unhappier; splitting up with me several times and then coming back—experiences that were draining for both of us. I should have understood straightaway that I could not give him what he needed the most, instead of pretending to be able to do so. I was not honest with myself and therefore I was not honest with him. Completely sucked in by the fashion vortex, I was hardly around and too tired to even make love to him when I was present.

Galahad's dreams were different from mine. He wished to have a family but I could not bear him children. This was a source of great sadness for me. And yet I was so attached to him, I could not give him up as my wants were not just material, but often extended to wanting certain people. For selfish reasons, I wanted Galahad to stay very much in my life on my own terms.

Dearest reader, to be in denial of our own truth or the truth of others is not advisable, as it will never bring us happiness or peace.

When he finally left me for good, I went into a state of deep despair, feeling the loss and abandonment to such a degree that I thought I

would never recover from it. All my success, my glamorous life, seemed completely worthless compared to feeling unable to truly love and to be loved by another. For the very first time I saw the emptiness of my existence with new eyes and asked myself: Is this it? Is this all there is to life? Without yet having full knowledge of the bigger picture, I started to realize that life without love was a pretty sad reality.

What I could not understand though was that love is something so much more vast than just being in the experience of love with another in a romantic relationship. In leaving me, Galahad planted a seed of truth in my consciousness that with time would grow into something rather large and all-encompassing. I will always be grateful to him for showing me that it was possible to live in open heart and to possess unshakable Spiritual Faith.

Feeling much stronger, Lella was in need of a very long holiday; as was I. The opportunity came through our Angel friend Donatella who was soon off to Australia with her boyfriend for Christmas. Lella was adamant that we should join them, as the idea of winter sun was indeed very appealing and restorative for our tired bodies and minds.

The sound of the word "Australia" jolted inside my being. Soon I had a vision of walking with my grandfather along that country lane of so long ago. I had listened to his tales and dreamed of those faraway countries. And Australia, being the furthest of all, had been the most fascinating to me. *Where is that child now? Where is the dream?* I asked then suddenly realized that I had stopped dreaming—my fashion dream had manifested but a blank space still laid in front of me. Then in my vision the blank space became a white room. *Was this the Waiting Room? A reality simply contained in a much larger reality that I have yet to discover?*

When the vision left me, I immediately telephoned Lancelot. With a tremor in my voice I told him of our imminent arrival. He was speechless, but once he recovered he invited us to his country property, saying that we could stay with him for as long as we wanted. A few days later, he called back. The flame that we carried for each other had never been extinguished—our passion had kept it alive throughout all those years, both of us often uncaring of our commitments to other relationships. But in the wake of the news that I was travelling to his land, he felt rather emotional and confused. Particularly because he was not single at that moment in time.

In my selfishness, I was not remotely concerned for his girlfriend or for his feelings. I only knew my own wants, still faraway from learning this vital lesson of love and respect. All that I could think about was that maybe my own lasting love would be realized with Lancelot as my knight in shining armor.

Australia awaited me and a new set of dreams would soon be conceived in the womb of this powerful and ancient land that held for me the biggest surprise of all. My life was about to expand as I took a new mysterious journey, leading me towards an entirely new reality.

AWAKENING— SYDNEY

I landed in Sydney on a gorgeous summer's day with Lella at my side. We were to join Donatella and her boyfriend Leo for a few days in town, and all fly inland to celebrate Christmas with Lancelot at his country property.

I fell in love with Sydney at first sight. There was something unique about this city set on the edge of one of the most spectacular harbors in the world. Facing the aquamarine waters of the Pacific, Sydney embodies an interesting combination of exoticism and modernity in which unruly nature harmoniously fuses with human progress. What truly touched my heart was the wild beauty of the ocean kept at bay by tall and impervious cliffs. Every morning I walked for miles along those cliffs, just staring out at the deep-blue skies and water, seemingly blending into one. Being utterly spellbound by my surroundings, I felt as if I had been transported to another planet in which all colors were enhanced and everything seemed to be bigger and brighter.

Often during those long walks I rested for a little while on one of the many rocks scattered along the way, wondering what life had in store for me. Deeply breathing in the unusual fragrance lingering in the air, a mixture of sea salt and the sweet aroma of frangipani, I dreamed with open eyes gazing out at sea, entirely lost in my thoughts. *Will my impending encounter with Lancelot bring me the romance that I am so frantically searching for? Or will I fail again?* I often felt cursed because as soon as I found love I quickly lost it again, one lover after another. The final result was always similar, leaving me with an unbearable sense of loss that I had to replace with something else—cigarettes, shoes, drugs, handbags—however the emptiness grew more profound each time.

It was during these reflective moments when I came to realize fully that despite my successful career, I was not so happy after all. My extensive collection of the most exquisite clothes and accessories, while pretty to look at and great to possess, could not replace love.

What I did not yet know was that each one of us has a great source of Love and Light, an eternal flame that burns inside every one of our hearts with no exception. Taught since childhood to look for love outside of my own source, I was unaware that it already existed inside of me; that we have all we need within us, as the Love, Light, and Power of Creation dwells in that very flame of our hearts.

To meditate, to explore the infinite internal landscape of my being was not my way at the time, so instead, everything was processed by my mind alone with all the limitations attached to it. In that moment Lancelot became my only hope for love and therefore my obsession, as he and only he embodied what I was looking for according to the illusion created by my mind.

But something else became even more apparent during each one of my walks—the knowledge that my soul was already acquainted with this foreign land. I had experienced a similar feeling when twenty years earlier I had arrived in England—a sense of familiarity with a previously unknown country that was illogical but utterly real. Once again I was trying to work out whether the strange familiarity was just connected to the memories of my grandfather's childhood tales of Australia or to something much more ancient, maybe a past life. I did not have any of the answers then, only memories slowly re-emerging from the depths of my consciousness which would eventually steer me towards future choices.

We soon left Sydney, and after a short flight and a long car journey up a dusty road we finally arrived at our destination, Lancelot's kingdom. At last, so many years after our original encounter, it was a rather surreal experience. During that long period of time filled with endless reunions and painful separations, I had often tried to imagine this place that was so dear to my lover's heart. And now his land made of red earth, giant trees, and spectacular wide-open spaces ,had just materialized in front of my eyes in all of its splendor.

Almost incredulous, I could hardly talk when Lancelot suddenly appeared out of nowhere to greet us. But sadly he was not alone. His current girlfriend was standing close to him, spoiling the romanticism of that special moment. Choked with emotions I pretended to be indifferent when in truth behind my mask I was bursting with both desire and disappointment. I knew that I had to accept Lancelot was just a friend, while I also knew perfectly well that I would strike once his girlfriend was out of the picture. My Angel friends, Donatella and Lella, warned me to refrain from acting foolishly, so I waited.

That same night, on another walk illuminated by the bright light of a giant silver moon, I again experienced the full power of the amazing energy of nature in its purest form. I felt the bond between the Australian land and my soul even more profoundly. In that remote corner of the world all else seemed so far away, almost insignificant compared to the life force that emanated directly from the earth itself. Drunk on the fullness of everything that surrounded me, I overflowed with an immense desire to be with Lancelot, ultimately rejecting any form of common sense. Charged with those strong emotions, I ignored that he was already with someone else.

Once again I had chosen to disrespect the sisterhood by interfering in full consciousness with an energetic dynamic that had already been established between him and his current girlfriend,

In those days, I often saw other women as rivals and not as sisters, especially those too close to the men I wanted for myself. Jealousy, vengefulness, competitiveness, and a lack of compassion were what I often secretly felt towards these women.

But I could never fully admit to my negative feelings because of pride, preferring to hide behind a mask of superiority and distance. This was a potent aspect of my consciousness that needed as much healing as the other contrasting aspect that reflected rejection and abandonment.

The morning after my nocturnal walk, I woke up to the wondrous sight of a flowery carpet of delicate rose petals scattered on my hair, and on the bedroom floor, leaving a pink trail all the way around the bed. I knew immediately that only Lancelot could be the author of such a gesture. *Is this a sign? A sign for action* I wondered. In that moment I sighed with relief, sure that he wanted me.

Over the following days, the sexual tension between us grew in intensity till finally, just after Christmas, his girlfriend left to return to Sydney. Finally I had him all to myself. The days that followed were magical, the ragged beauty of the Australian outback exotically framing many of the passionate moments shared in the company of my Knight. I was so overtaken by my desire for him that not a trace of guilt touched my consciousness, and I had no second thoughts regarding the hurt that I was possibly causing, not just to his girlfriend but also to us both.

At that moment in time, blinded by desire, I could not see that misusing our sexual power would produce a great imbalance in everyone concerned. I lacked the full awareness that we are indeed the creators of our own reality, responsible for each one of our own actions. The wheel of karma always brings us back to similar unresolved circumstances, till the lessons are deeply learned—clearly, I had yet to learn them. I was stuck in a pattern of wants and desires that overruled my heart, leading me into conflicts instead of resolutions. This was the real reason why my love stories never endured. I was not cursed, but instead it was simply the karma accumulated during many past lives that bound me to unhappiness. In this case it would be through my obsession with Lancelot.

One day during my holiday a copy of the Australian edition of *Harper's Bazaar* appeared on the table by the swimming pool. I picked up the magazine and while I was going through its glossy and well-designed pages I suddenly had an insight. *What was preventing me from moving to Australia? I could easily work for a magazine like Harper's and finally be with Lancelot.*

I expressed my new intention to Lella and Donatella. My Angels did not really take me seriously, but in my mind the seeds of change were expanding daily, creating a lovely dream where I was employed by an Australian publication and living happily ever after with my true love. But my fear of rejection prevented me from investigating more deeply the level of truth regarding our possible relationship.

Could it truly work? Could we make each other happy? Could I cope with his numerous children, and with the type of life he is living? All of these serious matters had hardly been taken into consideration as I only saw life from my own narrow point of view, embellished through the pink tinted lenses of romance. I simply decided that everything was possible, even giving up my glamorous life and prestigious career for the love of a man. I believed that if I didn't jump, I would regret it. Too many times I had been left to wonder about different outcomes that some of my relationships might have had if I had said yes to love. This brave new idea of mine was rather thrilling, bringing a breath of fresh air to a life that no longer satisfied me.

The call of this land, the inexplicable pull towards the nature of this wild and sometimes inhospitable continent, touched me so profoundly. My newfound connection with Australia sincerely sprang directly from my heart and soul, while my wanting Lancelot was an obsession born from the mind and infused with deep karma.

Armed with this rather extravagant new idea, I returned to Europe a month later pretty determined to manifest my new dream and therefore to once again shift my present reality to a different one that I believed would suit me better.

A couple of weeks passed and I was away in Paris attending the couture shows, missing my lover deeply. One late night there, I had a drink with a colleague in the hotel's bar and felt inspired by some mysterious force. I felt guided to express to her my desire to move to Australia. To my absolute astonishment, she casually told me that one of her best friends was the editor of *Harper's Bazaar Australia*, the very same magazine that had inspired my new dream. If I wanted, she could easily put me in touch with her.

From that moment on things moved rapidly. A couple of months later I met the editor, Alison, during the fashion shows in Milan and was instantly offered the job. Soon after in May, I briefly returned to Sydney to sign my new contract. I was the future *Fashion Director* of *Harper's Bazaar Australia*, due to start my new job at the end of August.

In the meantime the situation with Lancelot had shown some signs of improvement. To my utter delight, his current relationship was slowly dissolving, and after another one of our passionate encounters while I was in Sydney, I convinced myself that all was proceeding according to plan: *Obviously I was meant to live on*

this magical continent across so many lands and so many seas. Obviously I was meant to be with Lancelot and experience happiness in love.

The next number of weeks were like a roller coaster. To leave behind twenty years of life in London was rather stressful even if it was my decision. My dearest friends and family initially were shocked, reacting to the news as if I was planning to vanish from the face of the earth. But eventually they all came round, accepting my decision with much love and grace.

The fashion community was also in disbelief that I was giving up my prestigious position for life in such a remote place. Moving to Australia was certainly not a good career move in the snobbish world of fashion. The usual comment was how somebody as sophisticated as I could possibly cope with a very different lifestyle— but this was exactly the point because my wish was to live in a fresh way and also to experience something that was opposite to what I already knew.

For once, I was determined to find out if I could also obtain this gift of intimate love with another, a gift that seemed so easily given to many but not to me....

Many were the vivid dreams that accompanied me till the day of my departure. One in particular deeply impressed me.

All around me was a barren landscape of rocks and red earth, a deserted and hostile place where I felt in great danger. How was I going to survive? But then I saw in the distance a group of Aboriginal men coming towards me. I was in fear at first as I didn't know their intentions. But after awhile it became obvious that they wanted to help me, so I followed them until we arrived at a deep crack between two massive white rocks, a secret passageway to a very surprising new reality.

Once on the other side, the most luscious of oases awaited us. I couldn't believe it as I gazed in astonishment at the untouched beauty of my new surroundings where trees, lakes, and waterfalls had replaced the desolate landscape from a second ago.

Then one member of the group, an Aboriginal elder spoke to me. "Dear friend, you must learn to open your Spiritual Eyes. There are many hidden realities all around you, doorways to other worlds. One day you shall receive the key to access these magical worlds and in return you will give the key to others so they may also experience something so precious." While he was sharing his wisdom with me, a tall Being of Light entered my dream, emerging from behind the crystalline waterfalls. He was incredibly radiant to the point that everything began to shimmer brightly until my dream faded, leaving me rather besotted and with a deep sense of mystery ... something important was going to happen to me in that faraway land, but what could it be?

So beloved reader, with this invisible force propelling me towards the shores of a new future, I simply had to trust the signs and travel alone the current of fate that always moves us in such mysterious ways ...

But I was also dreaming of love, to love a man with a wild heart....

Once I settled in my new reality, nothing was as I had imagined it. The first contact with my new life in Australia was comparable to an earthquake that shook me to the foundation of my being.

In a very superficial way, my arrival in Sydney was a great success. Heralded as the new queen of fashion, I was constantly appearing in the gossip pages of all the local newspapers and attending the most exclusive social events. Part of me did not welcome this newfound fame as I was a very private person and the intrusive curiosity about my persona made me feel rather exposed. But then again my ego was rather pleased to stare at my pictures and read articles about me.

At work I also had to deal with a new kind of experience that was rather confrontational. As soon as I set foot in the *Harper's Bazaar* office, many members of the original team resented me. They viewed me as somebody with a hard-core personality who was going to turn their lives into a fashion hell. Maybe they were not so far from the truth as I was wearing by then a well-constructed protective armor, and was often used to getting my own way. Yet, I was being paid a high salary to imprint new life on the fashion pages of the magazine, and with the support of my editor Alison, and our amazing CEO John, the task had to be achieved.

While I was battling in the fashion field, my relationship with Lancelot went from bad to worse. Since my arrival, a strange defense mechanism had arisen within me that had forced me to go into refusal mode, causing a total shutdown of my emotions. I wasn't able to express any kind of love or affection towards my Knight. Paralyzed by fear, I became cold and could not receive him in anyway; not with words, not with any form of physical expression. He had fully separated from his previous girlfriend and must have felt rather confused. But being a man of action, he did not waste much time trying to cope with my incomprehensible behavior and promptly found himself a new lover.

I was left broken inside, not at all understanding myself. The reason I had moved all the way across the world was to be with this man and yet I could hardly go near him!!! I felt the loneliness of my soul more then ever while my heart remained firmly closed.

My Angel Squad was not there to support me either, and I missed them tremendously. Every single day the same questions troubled my mind, but I was far too proud to admit things were more dark than rosy.

So I carried on and hoped for a shift by reverting to my usual *modus operandi*, fully focusing on my career. Creating a wonderful magazine and getting to know well the whole Australian fashion business community were to be my next primary objectives. The distraction from my failures at love was badly needed.

Something peculiar happened during the first month of my new life in Sydney, something that hid a far greater meaning. One day wondering the city in the company of Andrew, a dear friend and gifted photographer, we both became intrigued by the masterful creations displayed in the beautifully designed window of a jewelry store. We decided to enter and find out more....

The shop had a magical atmosphere, each one of the jewels designed as if they were precious talismans with many mystical symbols inscribed on them.

I was immediately inspired to choose some pieces for an upcoming shoot.

Only a few months later I learned more about the man behind those exquisite creations. At first it was just a picture of him that left me stunned because as soon as I saw his face, I not only recognized him but I also perceived that this stranger held an important key to my future life.

Three more years were to pass, till one day, from many lives ago, Giovanni, the mysterious jeweler fully materialized in my life, bringing with him the winds of change and the most unexpected of all surprised....

In the midst of all this upheaval, something very special held me together—a charming apartment overlooking the dramatic cliffs of Tamarama and the Pacific Ocean. Originally, it had been Lancelot's apartment, and to this day I am so grateful to him for giving me the opportunity to live in such a manner, exposed to the power of nature, to the roaring sound of crashing waves that soothed me no matter how desperate and sad I felt. As a result, the ocean became an infinite embrace and my home a temple of transformation.

Dearest reader, I must tell you that was actually the very first time I had ever lived on my own. I was not used to being in my own company—a combination of a frantic life and avoiding going too deep had always prevented me from truly stopping and taking a good look inside my damaged soul. But because at the start of my Australian adventure I had hardly any close friends, I was forced to be on my own.

Lancelot's daughter, a wonderful girl very close to my heart, had decorated the apartment in the most delightful way. Every day, cocooned by fine white cotton veils over a romantic four-poster bed, I went to sleep and woke up facing the ocean. The magnificent view sprawled in front of my eyes was never the same. The perpetual motion of the waves, and the ever-changing color of the seawater, from palest aquamarine to a deep cobalt blue, were incredibly comforting to my heart and soul. After twenty years in urban London, to be touched so closely by the raw beauty of nature was indeed a very special experience, that unbeknownst to me had already started an alchemical process of change within.

The apartment had a TV that did not work because of weak signals. So stripped of distractions, most evenings I sat for hours reading, or pondering about my life in a sort of semi-meditative state. One evening I received a very clear insight. Suddenly I felt out of place with my carefully constructed image that looked almost old-fashioned in this new land where hiding behind an aristocratic background and an ultra-sophisticated mannerism meant nothing to the locals. Sydney society was utterly different from that in London, as Australians were free of the strict class system that still governed England. Their general approach to life was far more simple and direct, influenced by the powerful nature that they seemed to understand so well. If I wanted to succeed in my new environment, I needed to change and embrace a new attitude that would support me bonding with Australians, making them realize that I appreciated who they were.

I understood that since my arrival I had judged an awful lot instead of embracing my new environment and therefore my new reality. Even at work, I had to become much more loving towards my team because it is very possible to firmly lead and still recognize the equality of others.

Empowered by these new understandings, I felt ready to carve out my own place amongst the Sydney-siders, not in separation but in union with them. Even my personal style needed a make-over. My designer clothes looked rather stiff and out of place on the shores of Tamarama, where barefoot surfers were the emblem of the Australian way of life. More lightness was needed. So funkier casual wear was introduced, reshaping my wardrobe and making me feel more at ease in my new situation.

My next big realization arrived as a surprise when my new keyword became "youth." It was only on the brink of my turning forty that I came to understand how important it was to look after our young. I had never experienced motherhood, but maybe, just maybe, instead of being the mother of a couple of children I could be the mother of many—a new gang of cool kids was taking over the Australian fashion scene gifting me with the inspiration to access something still unexplored in my being ... the maternal instinct, the nourishing side of my feminine spirit. Part mentor and part friend, I gave to this new generation of talent the editorial support they needed, as well as my friendship.

To be in the company of the young also opened up something inside of me, creating a crack in my selfishness. I had discovered that to pass on my knowledge and reveal a bit more of myself to others was actually very rewarding indeed. And so a first breach into my armor was made at last!

Following that opening, I began to witness something very unusual. Several brightly-colored Aboriginal totems made of wood, adorning the white walls of my apartment, were my silent companions on many lonely nights. I stared at them quite often, especially at one in particular—a round one standing above the fireplace and opposite the white sofa where I normally sat. I knew the totems were rather old and valuable because Lancelot was an avid collector of Aboriginal art and chose his pieces well.

One late night after endless cigarettes and cups of tea, I was about to go to bed when suddenly I saw all of the Aboriginal totems moving around the room, or rather their Light forms zigzag across the space in a spectacular display. It felt like a fusion between the fantastical worlds of *Alice in Wonderland* and *Harry Potter*. When I finally reached my bed, I made a mental note to ask Lancelot about these works of art that seemed to have lives of their own.

From that night onwards, every evening I witnessed a wonderful Light display. I came to see it as a form of welcoming me back home, a sign from the other side that I was not alone. In truth, I was being activated by powerful Light technologies in preparation for things to come. But at that time I had not one drop of awareness regarding this, just the sense that the world of the unseen was getting back in touch with me in a strong way.

When Lancelot finally answered my question, all he knew was that the provenance was tied to a tribe in the Kimberley. When I decided to investigate more I goggled the name of this tribe and discovered that they claimed to descend directly from the stars. It was the first time I had ever heard of the concept that humans could descend from the stars. Yet it resonated inside of my heart as I remembered the strange dream with the Aboriginals and the luminous Being of Light that had suddenly appeared from behind the waterfall.

Not knowing what the ultimate truth would turn out to be, every night in my home I watched a supernatural phenomenon that was indeed not of human nature. And my fascination with the other side was about to assume an even deeper meaning.

In the meantime, at work the situation greatly improved and the team I wanted was finally in place. My young Fashion Editors Kate and Christine were incredibly gifted and clearly it was my time to continue mentoring. It was fulfilling to help emerging talented individuals reach their full potential, and between young editors, photographers, and designers, I truly gave a helping hand to develop the next generation of Australian *fashionistas*. I taught them that how they styled themselves was vital to moving ahead in their fashion careers. Even to this day, both Kate and Christine are among the most photographed girls on fashion websites with hundreds of thousands of followers, proving exactly my theory.

A great improvement in the friendship department was also on the way as not one but two fairies were about to enter my life. The first came in the shape of the wife of John, my CEO and protector. Alice is an ethereal being who emanates Light and love. In the very beginning, our friendship was based exclusively on our fashion collaborations. She is a talented fine art photographer, sharing a very similar sense of aesthetics to mine. But soon enough, I discovered that my new friend also had a rich and mysterious spiritual life. . It was hard for me to grasp the full meaning of what she was doing. I knew that it involved a lot of meditation and that she had a teacher guiding her, but that was my limited understanding of a much bigger truth—although I did notice every time I was with her that I would mysteriously calm down from my usual state of perpetual agitation.

Her Presence was enough to make me feel better and so much lighter. Alice had Light—a very soft but potent frequency of Light emanated from her being into mine, producing this immediate release of negative thought forms and infusing me with a new sensation of wellness. I was so happy to have found a new special friend, somebody I could share everything with, including my sadness about Lancelot.

My first two years in Australia were difficult and tumultuous. Lancelot was a thorn inside my heart, and my lack of awareness of his true needs, my worst form of blindness as without this key it was impossible to find the door to his heart.

One day he asked if he could pass by as he had something important to tell me. For a brief moment I was excited, but that was quickly replaced by a churning sensation in my gut sensing gloomy news. I was hardly spending any time with him. He used to tell me that he was too busy with work, but of course I knew that a different lover had already replaced me. Trying to carry on as usual, I could not forgive myself for having created only distance between us since my arrival in Sydney. And yet, I was still hoping that he was going to return to me.

Dearest reader, Lancelot came to break the news of his impending marriage to a much younger girl; the final blow to our already complex affair. I was so stunned all that came out of my mouth was a feeble "But I love you." To which he promptly replied "You need to see things for what they truly are and accept that on a day-to-day basis we are not made for each other." The woman he wished to share his life with was no fashion goddess but a simpler woman who would be fulfilled just being at his side; cooking, looking after his children, and appreciating the country life and land that he felt so connected to.

He loved me too, but if we were to marry, after the honeymoon period the fastest divorce in history was more or less guaranteed— he knew in his heart that I was not wife material, at least not for him. In his opinion I could not cope with his chaotic family life. And he reminded me that my romantic view of love had blinded me from seeing the reality of what having a proper relationship with him would truly mean.

I was flabbergasted. The way in which he described our Love Story was so hurtful, bordering on cruelty. But in retrospect, Lancelot was probably much more honest that I ever was.

I was well aware that I was not a practical person, especially in the kitchen as he wanted. Thoughts raced through my mind: *But what about love? Was marriage just a convenient arrangement for you? And if this is your view of women, I don't want you anyway!*

What I also kept to myself was the direct knowledge that came through me like thunder while he carried on talking about his future bride, a bit too perfect to be true. In the message that I received from somewhere else, I was told his marriage was going to be short-lived, leaving him with a high price to pay for his choice. If I had said this out loud I would have sounded like a jilted woman, and I had far too much pride to reveal that.

After all, each one of us is entitled to their own experiences, even the negative ones, for the purpose of our learnings and the burning of our karma. And he had plenty of karma with this young woman just as I had plenty of karma with him

At the end of our challenging conversation, Lancelot left rather flustered while I descended into the worst spiral of depression I had ever endured.

Over the next few months I practically stopped eating. Most days I had no will to leave my bed and carry on living. I felt utterly rejected because there was no understanding in my heart about my own nature versus Lancelot's nature, and furthermore no understanding of the karma that bound our love. I had been obsessed and blinded with wanting him at all costs and did not see that I was the creator of my own drama. I had been so tightly wrapped up in a spider web of illusions that I had convinced myself I was indeed his ideal woman and he would come to this realization one day. When in fact he was not my future husband, but simply my teacher. The subject of my lesson was to learn to let go of all the wants and desires that were limiting other possible offerings.

Stuck in a pool of stagnant energy, saturated in negative thought forms regarding others and myself, my Light was dimmed by all the negativity and absence of a real dream of the heart. It would not be much longer though for the veils to lift so that I could see the truth—often the darkest hours are the ones before dawn in which our beautiful Light is still hidden from us, and our mighty hearts are still closed by unspeakable fears.

ᴀWᴀKENING–
ULURU

Feeling bleak and uninspired, I was grateful when an unexpected journey brought an escape from all my sorrows.

Since my arrival in Sydney, I had more than once expressed the wish to do an epic fashion shoot at Ayers Rock, the heart center of Australia. To my delight, a deal was signed between *Harper's Bazaar* and a luxurious resort located just opposite the famous red rock. That financial agreement made the shoot possible. And as soon as everything was organized, I left Sydney for the remote location, travelling in the company of my photographer Alice, and a small team, including the usual models, assistants, and hair and make-up people.

Uluru, one of the most sacred of all Aboriginal sites, represented in my eyes the perfect backdrop for our fantasy fashion shoot. But I could not see the truth of why I was directed there as I had not yet realized there are many layers to our existence. There is the surface that makes

circumstances appear in a certain way, while underneath there are hidden reasons, sometimes difficult to grasp in the moment but may later on reveal to us a very different reality. We can call it the Jigsaw Puzzle Effect where one piece after another gets put in place to slowly complete the greater picture that represents a new understanding, a new lesson that will ultimately lead us step-by-step along this wondrous journey called LIFE.

The full picture, had I been able to see it, would have shown me an overview of what had happened to me since childhood; the collection of all of the unusual mystical phenomenons that were not accidental but instead had been beautifully crafted by a specific Higher Plan. I knew for example that the magical Aboriginal totems were encoded with mysterious powers of Light and yet I could not see the link between these unusual objects and my trip to Ayers Rock. And so dearest reader, there was indeed a specific Higher Purpose to this journey but I was still under the illusion that I was simply visiting the ideal location for my fashion shoot.

When I finally gazed upon the mystical rock from the plane's window, it suddenly emerged in front of my eyes in deep contrast to the surrounding flatness of a vast deserted land. I felt an indescribable emotion that invaded my soul with a surge of forgotten memories. I was utterly surprised to be touched in such a way by the stark landscape stripped of any kind of prettiness or embellishment, and yet so majestic in its pure primordial state.

But above all, I had no idea that I was about to land in one of the prime keystone portals on earth, an energetic power point where the inter-dimensional veils were extremely thin and so much Light was grounded for our entire planet. In the next few days I was to experience some profound truths about reality, an intriguing subject that had already showed me more than one facet of its many dimensions.

One early morning at the very beginning of our trip, we were trekking around Uluru in search of the right spot to take the first

couple of pictures, when I suddenly and very distinctly heard a chorus of female voices singing a sweet melody that filled the stillness in the air. I looked around but there was nobody. I asked the others if they had also heard women's voices, but everyone in my team, apart from Alice, stared at me as if I was crazy. Mystified by this experience and slightly annoyed that they didn't believe me, I decided to keep private any further esoteric experiences.

There were quite a few more. For instance, on another early morning just across from the sandy trail around the rock, I was gifted with a very clear vision. With open eyes I saw a group of Aboriginal women performing a ceremony around a fire. I could hear their incomprehensible language, while in wonder I watched their hypnotic dance around flames that were as red as the earth beneath my feet.

I knew that I could sometimes glimpse into the unseen, but what I saw in that moment was so real and detailed, it left me feeling rather startled. Already possessing a little bit of an understanding about the concept that our planet is but one dimension in a world of multidimensional realities, the vision was simply proof of this theory. What I observed totally existed, but only in an alternative realm that was parallel to our earthly reality, and obviously could not be seen by everyone.

While lost in my observations, I was also presented with a picture of my own family that instantly reminded me that I shared this gift with my parents and my sister. Evidently we were an unusual family—that thought made me feel less alone and much closer to them, especially to my father and sister, giving me a rare moment of happiness where I understood that what we had in common, this gift of sight, was indeed rather special.

Growing up with the many tales of ghosts, fairies, and strange visions that each member of my family had experienced on a regular basis, I was under the impression that it was normal for everyone to pierce the veils of the unseen. But in time I discovered that this was not the case and that many did not believe or see these other worlds—furthermore, the nonbelievers mostly condemned with arrogance those who held the gift of sight.

I have no judgment regarding this now, but it can be pretty isolating to possess certain gifts and not be able to express them when others make fun of you or put you down because of your gifts.

This message, dearest reader, is especially aimed to parents who have children that can see, so please learn to listen to these young ones with love and tender care, and without dismissing their sacred gift because if the gift is not received and recognized as sacred it will close down eventually, never to return during their lifetime. Yes, there are many people on earth who still believe only in what is tangible, and if they cannot see or experience something, it simply does not exist for them. I guess this is fair enough although it is also important to keep an open mind at all times because there is infinite potential within our beings. Judgmental minds can often prevent us from believing truth, and instead let old programs inside of our consciousness continue to influence us.

On the last day, after the fashion shoot was successfully wrapped, we decided as a team to go and visit the Olgas, another sacred rock formation close to Uluru. But at the very start of our walk I literally became lost in a time warp. Suddenly I was alone, unsure of where I was or how I had been separated from the rest of the team. It was as if I had jumped dimensions with the whole of my body for a few seconds. Feeling disoriented, I grew concerned as the landscape around me immediately reminded me of the beginning of a strange dream I once had back in London. I was pondering what to do next when out of nowhere a booming voice as powerful as thunder spoke to me.

"Sit on that rock close to you!" the voice commanded. "Don't be afraid, just wait there and in a little while the only male member of your group will come back to collect you. Then, you must walk behind the others with your friend Alice so that she can be a witness to what occurs. At a certain point, you will be asked again to sit in a special place where you will receive your next instructions." The voice was so clear and authoritative that without any doubt I did exactly as I was told.

Ten minutes later, exactly as predicted, Alice's male assistant came back to get me. Nobody understood how I had broken away from the others, but there was no time for me to waste in trying to figure out exactly what had taken place because I was on a mission to follow the mysterious Entity's orders. I explained to Alice the situation, and without batting an eyelid my dearest friend immediately backed me up, making sure that we indeed lingered behind in order to purposely lose the others.

Soon after, Alice and I came upon a rock formation made into the shape of a wave. It was then that I started to speak and sing in a language that I did not know. Then I heard the same booming voice asking us to stop at the very top of the wavy ridge. From there the view was stunning. The redness of the land and the intense blue of the immense Australian sky dramatically converged upon an endless horizon, a landscape of bare beauty and ancient mysteries that infused us with an initiation steeped in deep spirituality.

There was a sense of stillness and purity in the air. Being completely on our own, surrounded by the vastness of the infinite desert so sacred to the Aboriginals for hundreds of thousands of years, was profound. And in that moment, tiny speckles of sacredness came through me as I felt invaded by Spirit. I dropped to the ground unable to stand anymore, such was the power coming through my being. Again I spoke, though in a much lower tone and in a mixture of the strange language plus English. I channeled information about past lives in that land, and about how my life would soon involve traveling in an unexpected new direction, leading me eventually on a deeper Spiritual Path.

So it was true!!! I was Aboriginal in a different incarnation and this insight finally explained my profound soul connection with the Australian land. But while I was trying to come to my own conclusions on several other points, I was told again by the booming voice to get up and keep moving. "Soon," the voice bellowed, "Spirit shall touch you both, as he will gift you with a deep blessing."

I was shaking, but with Alice's help we started to walk the final part of the trail wondering what would happen next. Then, out of thin air, a huge white kangaroo materialized in front of us; after touching us both with the lightness of a feather, the apparition dematerialized just as quickly. We were both stunned, hugging each other and feeling that indeed a great blessing had been dispensed upon us even if we could not quite understand the full meaning of our experience.

Both nervous about being judged by others, Alice and I made a promise never to talk to anyone else about our supernatural encounter. I was so glad that my friend was part of this great adventure, as later on we could reassure each other that it did truly happen and it was not a figment of our imaginations. Not long after, I returned twice more to the portal, each time receiving Spiritual Gifts and keys that were still beyond my full understanding.

When I got back to Sydney, I received a further surprise. My relationship with the Aboriginal totems had transformed; especially with the round one above the fireplace, which unexpectedly turned into a doorway, a bridge between realities. If I stared at it long enough, I entered a wheel of time, a vortex where several images appeared in front of me in rapid succession. Sometimes what I saw made no sense to my mind as I was travelling back and forth between past and future, causing a certain degree of confusion. But other times the people and situations that I knew well emerged from this wheel giving me very clear insights. In truth, what I received in Uluru was a Spiritual Initiation which opened me up more deeply to one of my natural gifts, the gift of seership, meaning the ability to see through different dimensions.

And one night inside the Aboriginal vortex, I first witnessed Lancelot fighting with his wife. Soon after, I also saw a child, their child. My heart sank as I knew this had to be true. A few days after, a friend rang me up and confirmed that Lancelot was about to become a father yet again. I let myself go and cried all of my tears. Not only could I not be with the man I wanted, but I was also unable to compete with other women because I could not have children.

Viewing myself as an absolute failure and feeling wounded to the core of my being, I looked again at the Aboriginal totems and wondered if maybe something else entirely was planned for me; something truly different that could help me somehow release all the pain that I had been carrying in the depth of my being. I remembered the lucid dream before I left London and the words of the Aboriginal elder, then the prophecy of the Olgas, and again wondered what Spirit meant when he spoke of a change of life direction. *What could happen to allow such a radical shift to take place in my life?*

That night I went to bed filled with sadness, thinking that I would never experience love with another—that a life of eternal solitude was my destiny. I felt so utterly defeated not knowing that soon, dearest reader, the love I wanted so much was to come back to me because love is everywhere and love is in everything.

AWAKENING–
BALI

Feeling the crushing burden of loneliness upon my soul, my attempt to love and to be loved had failed miserably because I could not open my heart. Not being able to let go of my mask or express my emotions in their pure essence without pride or fear, seemed to me an impossible task. Pretending to always be in control and devoid of any weakness was my standard pattern, no matter the circumstances. Hiding my pain, terrible loneliness, and frustration at my inability to shift my patterns, I never bothered to explain myself to anyone, preferring instead to present an impeccably edited version where everything visible to others was close to perfection and self-sufficiency.

This fake identity that I had originally created to shield myself from others ultimately proved to also create profound hardships in my most important relationship—the one with myself. My personal relationship with the Self wasn't either loving or honest. Therefore, everything else

was a consequence of my lack of consciousness that pushed me into the shadow of my ego and blinded me from seeing my own Light and the Light of others.

This was a lesson that I could not seem to learn. Therefore, the repetition of one unsuccessful love affair after another was simply the manifestation of unresolved karma that had been blocking the flow of love in my heart. But as usual, instead of trying to find a positive resolution, I ran away, searching for distractions in order to avoid having to look inside myself.

Next I sought refuge in the Sydney nightlife. Disguised by glamour, a darker reality thrived under the glitter of the endless social occasions I attended where drugs and alcohol were plentiful. And yet again I fell into the drug trap, sabotaging myself with a potent cocktail of Ecstasy, grass, and cigarettes, hoping to obliterate from my life Lancelot and all of my other lost loves once and for all. But in the process I was dragged down deeper into the Darkness.

So dearest reader, if you suffer from any kind of addiction, with all of my love, I suggest that you carefully read what I am about to share with you.

At the time, I didn't realize that the regular consumption of drugs or alcohol could open portals, interdimensional doorways allowing in beings that are not of the Light to interfere with our own energy field. As a consequence, this reinforces our co-dependency with the vast spectrum of human addictions. Addictions are simply reflections of the diseases of our souls, ones mainly caused by unresolved energies in our genetics or past incarnations. They are what fill up for a brief moment the internal void created by the veils of illusions in our consciousness and lack of self love in our hearts. But they will never truly fill our void in a satisfying way, only our illusions.

During that bleak period, on an evening like many others, I was at home chatting with two girlfriends. One of my friends was sitting in a comfortable armchair across from me and the other was next to me on the sofa. Suddenly, I noticed a fluorescent-green being of rather large proportions attached to my friend sitting opposite me. She was totally unaware of being encapsulated inside this strange apparition and worst of all, the disturbing vision was not budging an inch. Half-fascinated and half-horrified, I observed the fluorescent-green creature with more attention, while pretending to my friends that nothing was happening.

What impressed me the most were its eyes, reddish and malefic. There was no love in those wicked eyes, only the greediness of sucking from its victims all of their Light, weakening them, and ultimately enslaving their souls in even deeper addictions. While I was starting to feel rather uncomfortable about whether to confront the Darkness, my friend decided to leave, and with great relief I accompanied her to the door. But just before she went, I saw the strange being fully reflected in her eyes. Despite the balmy temperature of a fine summer evening, a chill rose up my spine and quickly spread through my entire being, leaving me feeling completely unsettled.

When I refocused my attention towards my other girlfriend, I could see from her expression that she was rather puzzled by something. Without wasting one more minute, I was guided to share with her what I had seen. The incredible thing was that she had had exactly the same experience, also witnessing the evil looking being superimposed upon our friend. Having in common the gift of sight, we both knew straightaway that whatever we had seen was of a Dark Nature. Our younger friend was into addiction deeply and had probably inadvertently opened the portal to the Darkness exactly because of her drug abuse.

After this unpleasant episode, many more occurred where I kept seeing disturbing attachments within others, not realizing that the real reason I was being shown these unpleasant spectacles was because I had also opened an interdimensional doorway to Darkness.

Then one night I went a step further into the Dark. I began to soul travel in the astral planes, a reality between the Earthly Dimension and the Realms of Light, meeting the Dark Lords and many other malevolent beings who were chanting my name endlessly, promising me the manifestation of all of my wants and desires if I joined them and learned the ways of the Dark Arts. As with the period of my childhood nightmares, night after night, falling asleep became an ordeal because I knew that as soon as I closed my eyes I would be delivered into the tight grip of these sinister creatures.

As night fell I would begin to sense them, their ominous Presence dancing around me; a highly disturbing sensation that filled me with dread. The Aboriginal totems had stopped generating their magical Light display and I felt an even greater overall lack of positive energy inside my home. But despite all these signs, I was still taking drugs, and in doing so was responsible for both the facilitation and escalation of those negative and daunting experiences.

More than a month had passed when one evening, as usual, I fell into the Darkness. I became lost inside a large empty house filled with strange malicious cartoonish beings. I pretended to be friendly with them so I could buy myself time and find an escape as the creatures continued chanting my name louder and louder. When I finally managed to get away, I ran out the door and straight into a celestial vision of great beauty.

Painted with strokes of the brightest Light, I found myself in the middle of a magnificent garden where at last I felt deeply peaceful. Behind me, a wall filled with fluorescent-pink roses gave off a powerful aroma that I could actually smell. A crystalline golden temple encircled me in its full majesty. Supported by several pillars and topped with a large round dome, the temple was not just an apparition, but had itself become part of the room.

Wide-awake and crying uncontrollably, I felt I was sitting inside the central room of such a temple, as a holographic vision that had temporarily shifted the reality inside my bedroom then transformed into a magnificent luminescent realm. *How could this be possible?* Feeling suspended between worlds, I started to calm down, enveloped by such a strong surge of energy that made my breath slow down considerably until I saw him.

This great Presence that I had only met once before when I was a little girl in a long-ago dream, was youthful in appearance; his golden hair and sapphire eyes emanated the same powerful Light as the rest of his imposing figure.

"Do you remember me?" He asked with a powerful but loving voice.

I could not speak but nodded my head slightly as the energy was so intense that I was unable to move.

"Claudia, dearest one, it is time to know where you are going from now on. Are you choosing the Darkness or are you choosing the Light? Both equally reclaim you as their own, but the choice is yours because you have free will, beloved, like all other human beings."

Somehow I managed to whisper, "Please help me. I choose the Light. Please liberate me from these evil visitations."

The Entity continued, "We welcome you fully back into the Light as is your wish, but you must promise to give up all drugs right now. This is vitally important so that these portals of Darkness can be sealed off straightaway. We will fully protect you from this day on, but you must be much more aware of your own actions. This is the first lesson that we are bringing to you, a lesson of responsibility. We will not be able to support you if you cannot take care of this very simple step."

At first I murmured almost to myself, "I am never going to touch drugs ever again." Then I affirmed louder, "I solemnly promise this to God and to the Entity in front of me."

Dawn broke through the night, the first rays of the morning sun slowly spread upon the ocean while my bedroom magically shape-shifted back to its original state of reality. In that precise moment I knew that a new day had not just arisen above the sea, but had also emerged from the depths of my being. I thanked God and the mysterious Entity, then prayed with the same fervor that was once in my heart, when my prayers were still pure and innocent.

Amidst a rainfall of tears, I swore to myself to find my way back towards all that I had pushed away during my relentless chase after the chimeras of wants and desires. I had spent so much time hiding behind veils that I could not even remember who I was, and yet what had just happened was very significant, showing me once more that my earthly reality was not my only one. So much more existed beyond veils just as so much more of my own Self existed beyond my own veils.

And so the doorway to a new awareness was unlocked. I chose the Light and a wondrous new world opened up. This was no dream—I was fully awake when my reality shifted around me. I had smelled the roses, bared witness to the temple grounding, and spoken with the mysterious Entity. Yet, I still had no understanding of why all of this had happened to me. *Is this a gift from the Heavens because I am so heartbroken? A sign that I could eventually be happy?* I had to accept that time would be key to understanding all of my unanswered questions. But at last I was safe from the Darkness, or so I thought.

A month later I made my choice to step into the Light—a trip to Bali was organized for my next fashion shoot and Alice, our crew, and I were soon off to this exotic location. My dear friend warned me that Bali was an Island of the Spirits and that many strange manifestations could happen there. But I was convinced nothing could quite displace me after my latest experience. Yet, my mind held limitations as the lush surroundings of the Indonesian island were soon to become the stage of a new powerful initiation.

I often wondered where I was heading and how all of the supernatural events I experienced fit into my daily life. Since that fateful night, I maintained my promise of never touching drugs ever again, such was my fear created by those encounters with the Darkness. I could no longer sleep without the light of a candle next to me, but as long as I was close to some Source of Light, I felt safer. And as a reminiscence of my Catholic upbringing, I also carried with me everywhere I went my great-grandmother's precious diamond cross as a symbol of protection against evil.

Once we arrived in Bali, I immediately put my great-grandmother's diamond cross on the bedside table as a warning against all bad spirits, and hoped for the best. But on the first night in the beautiful villa I immediately felt a powerful Presence in my bedroom. Feeling rather nervous, I tried to ignore the sensation and force myself to go to sleep. Then suddenly three glass shelves on the wall closest to the bed exploded in a thousands pieces, one after the other, producing a tremendous noise followed by a shower of glass as several other objects tumbled to the floor. I jumped out of bed and ran towards Alice's bedroom, while she also had heard the commotion and was running in my direction.

I took refuge for a while in her bedroom. Still shaking with fear, I told her that a powerful Entity must have done this. But as soon as I calmed down I knew that I had to return to my own bedroom and face the situation on my own. For some mysterious reason that Presence wanted my full attention, and its energy did not seem to be of a negative nature. So Alice escorted me back to my room, and once we'd both confirmed that the energy was indeed positive, she left me on my own.

I settled back in and started to converse with this unknown Spirit. I simply told the Spirit that I came in peace and was hoping to be able to communicate with it. In that precise moment, the lights in the room began to switch on and off as by magic and suddenly I clearly saw a tall being made of Light standing right in front of me. He appeared as a male golden figure wearing traditional Balinese clothes. An intricate headpiece completed his ghostly look.

He presented himself as Dalem, an ancient and wise king of Bali, and asked me to forgive him for his rather flamboyant entrance, and that in fact he had been sent to give guidance and protection; that I had nothing to fear about him. In that instant I began to feel incredible loving energy emanating from Dalem, and sensed that this Spirit was telling the truth. I was overcome by emotions, and thinking to myself: *Somebody truly loves me up there. I mean, how extraordinary to have a Spirit as a friend.*

From that night on, Dalem waited for me to return to my bedroom at the end of each day and wonderful conversations took place between us. It was a staggering experience to be able to interact with an Entity from another realm on a daily basis. He shared with me his simple wisdom, with great love and patience. He often told me that my approach to life needed to change and that I needed to understand the bigger picture and the truth beyond all things—not just my own version of the truth as many things are not what they seem on the surface or as I imagined them or wanted them to be.

The subject Dalem was most severe with me about was my obsession with Lancelot. My Spirit friend advised me over and over to let go, as Lancelot was not part of my destiny in this life. He explained that my obsession and much of the karma I had with Lancelot sprang from ancient memories that needed to be cleared and had nothing to do with the reality of my present life. While I listened with great interest to everything else he had to say, I was not ready to hear the truth regarding Lancelot and completely shut down when his name was even mentioned.

My mind was stubborn and believed it always knew best, even better than the ancient king of Bali. But Spirit doesn't know judgment, only love, and Dalem, with great serenity, was always at my side no matter what I decided to do with his wisdom.

Towards the end of our trip, he warned that at the location of our next fashion story, an elegant villa belonging to a well-known Australian writer, I would meet a man extremely well-versed in the Dark Arts. "He will try to seduce your ego—but do not worry, you will be protected."

The next morning, as we settled in at the Australian writer's villa and prepared for the shoot, I was introduced to a mysterious stranger who took an immediate interest in me. Of course I already knew exactly who he was and my guard was up, but my distant behavior did not deter the magician from pursuing me all day long. The stranger had a perfectly shaved head and was dressed in the manner of an Indian guru. But it was his large ruby ring that immediately caught my attention, not because of the ring itself, but because of the strange energy that emanated from it.

After awhile, things started to get weird. Alice's camera suddenly was not functioning, and neither of us felt well, almost gasping for air while a negative energy built up around us. Then the magician began to tell me that I had very unusual Spiritual Gifts and they could be developed and flourish in powerful ways. Somehow this piece of information caught my attention and without even realizing it, I started to engage in conversation, asking him many questions as if in a trance. He pulled me in more and more, suggesting that I could become a student of his master, the most powerful teacher of the Dark Arts in Indonesia who lived on the island of Java. He said his ruby ring was a gift from this teacher.

While I listened in fascination to all of his stories, I felt weaker and weaker. The stranger continued making offers of all kinds in his mellifluous tone until at one point he leaned in and whispered "Somebody as gifted as you could acquire so much power with the right knowledge. You could manifest all desires as is common practice within the Dark Arts."

I wondered *why has Dalem never mentioned that I could have all this power, that I could manifest my wants, instead of preaching about truth and letting go of the only man I love.* But just as all these negative thoughts ran through my mind, I was shown through the veils and witnessed a highly disturbing vision. Ugly little devilish monsters floated around us, weaving Dark filaments of energy between my heart and the heart of the magician. I was shocked at first, but recovered quite quickly, and at once sent an internal cry for help to God, Dalem, and all other Angels and Saints I knew.

A few minutes later, I came out of that Dark incantation and looked straight in the magician's eyes. "I choose the Light and am not interested at all in what you have to offer." With those words I took back my power, and as if by magic, the negative energy started to dissolve. Alice's camera began to work again, and our feelings of nausea disappeared.

I was not afraid of the Darkness anymore and had learned at least one lesson. The magician, taken aback by my simple but potent answer, never talked to me again. Yet, that same night I received some visions of disturbing rituals that belonged to the Dark Side. Immediately I called upon Dalem again to support Alice and me. Using a sponge of Light, he wiped away any residue from that other world that sadly still influences many with its fake promises of lust, power, and riches. Though I also learned from Dalem that everyone has their own destiny here on earth and it is not my place or anyone else's to judge the Darkness, as it is the marriage of the Light with the Darkness that ultimately balances all things.

My trip to the Island of the Spirits was coming to an end and my sadness over leaving Dalem behind deeply affected me. But once on the plane, on my way back to Sydney, I suddenly felt Dalem's unmistakable Presence. He confirmed that it was not yet the moment for him to leave my side. Tears of joy filled my eyes as I was deeply relieved to know that my invisible friend could easily follow me wherever I went—Spirit is not bound by matter. And in that precise moment, I received a powerful insight: I had proof that all the beautiful Spirits of the ones we love are with us at all times.

Upon death, we all become free from our physical bodies, with no more frontiers between realities, no geographical limitations of any kind. And death only parts us from our loved ones temporarily—they are just a Bridge of Light away that co-exists parallel to our own. We can see them, hear them, and even communicate with them, if we learn to expand our consciousness beyond the limitations of the old programs of the mind that see everything in separateness instead of in Oneness. And with time, moving higher up into the Light, they become our Angels always protecting us and our families.

The ancient king of Bali was to become my Guardian Angel, my protector, and my first Spiritual Guide. It was almost time to understand the real reason why I had left London and travelled all the way to Australia. Dalem was right—the answer was not what it seemed but far more than my mind could imagine or comprehend.

AWAKENING–
BYRON BAY

My return to Sydney was marked by my friendship with Dalem; he was invisible to everyone but me. In the next year he was an integral part of my daily existence, dispensing his wisdom and generally guiding me towards both a more holistic approach to life and a better understanding of myself. Despite my general improvement, Lancelot remained my weakness, a burden that I could not shift. Still a slave to my obsession, my spiritual progress seemed to regress as soon as the thought of him entered my mind.

Dalem was there to help me better understand that to be obsessed with somebody or something is a mechanism that can be compared to an energetic drilling of the mind. With any obsession there is always a want, a negative attachment that will never bring us peace or resolution. The more we want something, the more we trick ourselves into the illusion that if we can't get what we want our happiness will be in jeopardy.

He also revealed to me that obsession is like a disease that eats away at the truth, blinding us from seeing the substantial difference between what we want and what we might really need. In fewer words, dearest reader, what we need and what life serves us with are not necessarily what we may wish for. Wants and desires are simply obstacles to our evolution, blocking us from receiving that which is the Highest Good, even if we might not recognize this at the time.

And Dalem told me straightaway that wanting to be with Lancelot was not for my Highest Good, and my obsession was indeed eating away at the truth.

But still I held on. Then one day he gave me a piece of information that I had been longing to hear. Lancelot's marriage would soon be over. Though Dalem had advised me to stay away and to be extremely careful in how I handled myself in that complex situation—in particular, even if Lancelot was on the brink of divorcing, he was still a married man and the father of a newborn—I immediately contacted him.

By ignoring Dalem's warning, I repeated my usual mistakes of being blind to the bigger picture. Our affair proceeded through Lancelot's devastating divorce, and once more my selfishness and lack of compassion prevented me from feeling my lover's pain, as I could only feel my own. Lancelot would often disappear for weeks at a time, leaving me eternally suspended between the agony of loss and the ecstasy of being reunited once more.

My emotional swings and obsessions devoured me. My friends were seriously concerned about the state of my health. I was not taking drugs anymore, but I smoked a huge number of cigarettes daily, hardly ate anything, and could not find peace day or night.

On my way to self-destruction, I was still deaf to Dalem's wisdom, listening instead only to those unresolved aspects of my consciousness that ultimately led me to the same dead end. Karma was repeating itself. Time after time, I fell flat on my face feeling more and more

disempowered and lacking in the awareness that I was indeed the creator of my unsustainable situation.

In the middle of that emotional hurricane, Australian Fashion Week started; it was a welcome distraction from my daily anxieties. And it was then that I had a fated encounter with another man. After having briefly met Giovanni the year before, the mysterious jeweler suddenly reappeared in my life. A mutual friend who knew of our shared interest in spiritual matters introduced us and a deep bond forged.

There was something that intrigued me about this man since the very first time I had set eyes on his photograph at the very beginning of my life in Sydney. I had been sure that I would eventually meet him simply because I recognized his soul from another lifetime, and more likely because he'd been sent to me for a special reason. *But what reason? Is it a romantic one?* I wondered as I looked at his attractive face with growing interest. Always ready to listen to his stories, I perceived him to be open-minded and curious about everything in life—our connection always sparked such interesting conversations between us.

One magical evening on the panoramic terrace of the fashion show venue suspended above the Sydney Opera House, Giovanni told me a fascinating tale. Earlier that year he had met a woman called Qala, a channeler and Spiritual Teacher who lived close to him in the hills above Byron Bay. A few months after their introduction, he said he followed her to Hawaii where she taught at a spiritual retreat. Not quite knowing what to expect in the beginning, he told me he was blown away by her surprising teachings which carried a lot of wisdom and much new information for humanity; including for the newborn children arriving on earth with a much Higher Level of Consciousness. He also added that he had never experienced such extraordinary energy before—a kind that made everyone feel as if they were high on drugs, without actually taking any.

His story immediately reminded me of the energy I had felt in my bedroom the night when I chose to stand in the Light. I wondered if my experience could have held a similar kind of energy to the one he was talking about. Giovanni also tried to explain the meaning of being in a state of super-consciousness, achieved through meditation and specific spiritual studies. Since returning from the retreat, he had rearranged his life completely by following the guidance of this Higher State of Consciousness and said he had incredible clarity about transformations occurring inside of himself; thus various external situations were also automatically and positively shifting for him as well.

With an obvious and genuine enthusiasm for his recent experience, he further revealed to me that we all have a Higher Self; a part of us in a different dimension that holds all knowledge and understanding. At this point, I stared at him in disbelief, my mind judging every one of his words. And when he added that his Higher Self was a golden Being of Light coming from the star Sirius, I could not contain myself any longer and started to laugh. It was too much even for me to accept!

That same night, once back at home, I was watching the Aboriginal totems generating magnificent fireworks as usual, and remembered that those who had created them also believed to be of a starry descent. So I decided to ask Dalem what he thought of the strange story about Giovanni's Higher Self. The Spirit simply replied, "Many are the Dimensions of Consciousness of our being and soon you will receive more understanding of this."

His answer made me think more deeply, *yes, there was more than one reality. I know this truth by now but still don't understand how the dimensions are related to our consciousness.* Reading my mind, Dalem continued, "Many are the Spiritual Mysteries and sooner than you think you will be shown interesting new truths." Then he whispered enigmatically, "The time is almost here" before going back to his own dimension. *Time for what* I repeated to myself wishing I could find the answer right then. *Time for what?*

Over the next few months, Giovanni and I became closer till one day he invited me to stay at Coorabella, his beautiful property in the hills of Byron, and then to go with him to one of Qala's workshops. And dearest reader, you already know that a couple of days before my journey, I was visited by an Angel who revealed to me a new prophecy that left me utterly confused and unable to take in its magnitude. The same day I met this Angel, Dalem disappeared. His mission was complete. *Was it time to exit the Waiting Room?* I wondered … filled with apprehension, I boarded the plane for Byron Bay knowing in my heart that nothing would ever be the same….

Coorabella was Heaven on earth! The sweetness of the rolling hills, the magnificence of the ancient trees, the perfume of the earth and air combined, the purity of the water springs. I had landed in Middle Earth. Set on high ground amidst the lusciousness of nature, stood Giovanni's Queenslander house with a wrapped veranda embracing a magical view of the valley. The interior of his home perfectly reflected the style of an old gothic mansion, complete with four-poster beds in almost every bedroom and luxurious velvet curtains elegantly draped around some of the larger windows. Big silver candelabras sitting on top of antique furniture were displayed around the house, There was even an old suit of steel armor guarding the entrance. Giovanni is a romantic at heart. Influenced by medieval tales, those ancient legends had inspired him to create his jewels, precious talismans from a bygone era.

It was exiting to be surrounded by such beauty and to meet my friend in a more personal way, a much needed break from my constant craving for Lancelot. Giovanni, behaving like an old-fashioned gentleman, offered me his bedroom, a luxurious and inviting room. Standing opposite a massive four-poster bed was a small table on which various objects such as crystals, bird feathers, religious icons, and jewels were randomly arranged.

When I inquired if there was a meaning behind this strange combination of things, his reply surprised me. "This is my altar." My mind stood to attention. *I thought that altars existed only in churches. Is he a pagan?* I mean, I was already aware that he had some rather peculiar ideas. *Maybe he thinks of himself as a kind of Druid and he also really believes he has a golden Higher Self from Sirius.* I wondered too *why am I questioning others' spiritual beliefs when I also experience all sorts of supernatural manifestations?* So I finally decided to relax and enjoy whatever was coming next without any particular expectation.

After a magical day together, nightfall came, spreading over Coorabella a starry mantle of such luminescent beauty that the property emitted an even more mystical aura. Retiring to Giovanni's bedroom, I tried to fall asleep, looking forward to Qala's workshop starting early the next morning.

Suddenly a great flash of Light came from the altar and revealed a few Presences I had never met before—a team of beings of pure white light hovered over me. Without Dalem, I instantly felt alone to fend for myself in this other dimension, but soon after , I heard a telepathic message coming from these unknown Spirits. I needed to not worry—they were just preparing me for the next day with Qala. Immediately my mind went in overdrive: *Am I actually being prepared for the workshop? How organized is that? But what is going to happen to me at this workshop?* Then the same strong energy of the Light that had come to me before enveloped me completely again. I could not move, but knew clearly this was the work of Spirit and so I finally let go and fell into a dreamless sleep.

Morning came. Dressed in a comfortable gym outfit, I felt quite ready to meet Qala, even though a part of me would have loved for us to have stayed back at Coorabella and explored both the friendship with Giovanni and the stunning property.

On the way over to the workshop I told Giovanni what had happened during the night. But my friend was silent for what seemed like an eternity, until finally the only words that came out of his mouth were: "Everyone experiences spirituality in their own way and you have to wait and see what your way is." I hoped that Qala would be more helpful than him, because one thing I was certain of was something was about to happen. Being a control freak, I detested not knowing what was in front of me.

The retreat center was a simple building with a lovely ocean view. Once we arrived, I was immediately confronted with a rather unusual group of people, at least by my standards at that time. I was used to being surrounded by a crowd who, like me, wore masks and possessed attitudes. But instead I observed something of a very different nature that my mind instantly judged as rather ridiculous.

These people all hugged each other for long periods, with their peaceful smiles on their serene faces. Immediately, I hoped that nobody was going to hug me as I felt rather reticent towards any form of physical affection apart from the sexual kind. You must remember dearest reader that I had grown up never being touched, and that had left its mark on me. I felt already so challenged and the workshop hadn't even started!!!

After a short while, we were asked to sit in a circle where I kept observing and judging. One detail really struck me: the brilliant Light in the eyes of these strangers. All those shining eyes and an expression of genuine love seemed to be painted on their faces and somehow touched me despite my surging worries and anxieties. While I sensed Giovanni was comfortable and relaxed, I felt rather uptight.

I was definitely out of my comfort zone, and on top of that had convinced myself things were about to get a lot worse. *Why did I said yes?* I asked myself while staring at the arrangement of crystals and strange drawings adorning the middle of the circle. *Is this conglomeration another altar?*

Then silence fell until at last one of the women in the circle began to speak in a clear voice. As soon as she spoke, I calmed down. Looking straight at her, I immediately sensed that she was Qala. She had that certain Presence of one who knows exactly what they are doing, and as if by magic, I felt reassured that I was in good hands. I trusted Qala from the moment I set eyes on her.

Qala introduced herself and welcomed me with a radiant smile, telling me that I was stepping into the middle of an advanced spiritual program called "Ease." She had a simplicity and directness that I found refreshing, and I smiled back at her straightaway. She continued, "You should not worry if you can not understand everything I am going to channel, so just relax and receive the Light and Love on offer." I bowed my head in a sign of understanding and said thank you, very shyly as I felt I was not really part of this circle, just more of an observer.

Then the first channeling started and the energy engulfed us like a wave of delicious frequencies. This blew away my mind. In a split-second I understood exactly what Giovanni had meant when he told me the story of his first encounter with her.

Qala's words held truth. Even if I could not comprehend every single concept, I felt inside my being a deep resonance with what she was saying . It was as if I had heard it all before across many lifetimes. The wisdom was not new to me but it was profound to hear it all over again as my soul was utterly in harmony with each one of her teachings, with my mind out of the way.

After about two hours into the workshop, my third eye, which until then had been pulsing like crazy, suddenly cracked open and I began to see everything that Qala was describing in detail. She took us on a journey into alternative dimensions where Angels and other beings offered us dispensations, Gifts of Light. I was tripping as if I was high on LSD but there were no drugs involved, only Qala's vibrant voice; I was witnessing the truth of this other reality as if I was there. Afterwards, this experience left me feeling utterly astounded, and to Giovanni's absolute delight, when the workshop was over I could not wait to come back the next day in order to receive a further dose of this magic.

That night Giovanni and I had dinner at the house of mutual friends. Sitting under the moonlight as Qala had advised us to do, I wondered about this extraordinary woman: *how did she know so much?* It was clear to me that she knew many secrets of the Universe and that I could learn some incredible stuff from her. *Could she really be my teacher announced by the Angel?* I was miles away when Giovanni asked if I was ready to leave.

"Yes," I answered. I could not wait to be on my own, lost in this other world that was closer to us than I had ever imagined. That night I understood that to be an explorer of realities was going to be a very significant part of my future and that I had just tasted a little bit more of the infinite landscape of alternative dimensions. I thought of all of the magical dreams that had come to me since I was a child, and for the first time in so long, fell asleep with a smile upon my face.

Back in the circle the next day, I was exposed to a very powerful experience. A clear vision appeared to me, exactly as if I was watching a film. I saw a woman on horseback dressed in medieval clothes. It was winter, the landscape around her bare and rugged with encircling high mountains. The woman came out of a castle in the company of one man. Then she commanded her companion, a warrior dressed in full armor, to take her to the battlefield so that she could witness victory. But after a short ride, a deep valley stood in front of them covered in corpses; men, women, children, horses, all brutally killed during a ferocious battle. They were lying across the land semicovered by the snow with vermilion strokes of blood painted all over the white mantle. It was a sight I could not erase from my mind. But the woman was unmoved, coldly observing the scene with an expressionless face. At that point, I started to cry uncontrollably in front of the circle, not caring what others thought of me, as a terrible realization had suddenly hit me with the power of thunder: I was that heartless woman and she was one of my past lives.

A beautiful lady called Illumina came to my rescue. I was convulsing, feeling inside the deep pain of shame. She held me with much love and explained in a soft voice: "These are soul memories. When you or any individual starts to walk on a deeper Spiritual Path, the most unresolved of our past lives come up swiftly so that we may forgive ourselves and everyone involved, and start a purification period for the soul."

When I finally calmed down, I made a feeble attempt to forgive myself because all I could think of was *how could I truly forgive myself?* What I understood deeply though in that moment was the reason for my uncompassionate heart, as I knew very well that I had never felt compassion for others or for myself; that my heart was firmly closed and that the undeniable cause of all my suffering was my inability to express love. I was deeply shocked by the unveiling of this past life, and realized then that my Spiritual Journey would not only hold many magical surprises but also be highly confrontive.

That afternoon I also experienced Spiritual Surgery for the first time. Qala briefly explained that along with our physical bodies we are also equipped with a "Light Body." And just as we live in a multidimensional world, we are also multidimensional beings with plenty of consciousness distributed in each one of these different realities. Spiritual Surgery was done at all levels of our beings where cellular memory, fear, blockages, old patterns, and programs were removed layer after layer, by skilled Doctors of Light, Master Healer Angels and Archangels.

I was blessed to witness the truth of this amazing experience. Again I was tripping, high on spiritual LSD, while I could clearly see all the Beings of Light operating on those of us in the circle. Some of their Light technologies were shaped in similar ways to the Light produced by the Aboriginal totems. Feeling the extraction of plenty of stuff from my being physically, I felt fearless and trusted that what was happening

would be truly liberating and that we can all heal ourselves with the active help from the other side.

At the end of the workshop I had a short conversation with Qala, and Amaya—the two seemed very close. The wise women let me know that they would be coming to Sydney regularly in the next few months just in case I was interested in carrying on with the training. Then Qala hugged me for the very first time and I melted into her embrace, so stunned by the wave of love that went directly from her heart into mine. Those hugs were so much more than I could understand then—the whole experience of her teachings was so much more that what I could perceive in that instant. This was quite a realization because obviously a part of my being had shifted beyond the limits of only what my mind could grasp so that I could receive truth, and with that awareness I knew that I could obtain incredible help from this revolutionary way of teaching.

That same evening back at Coorabella everything started to unfold in a rather fantastical way. All of a sudden many veils were lifted and many different dimensions became simultaneously accessible to my being. While Giovanni was busy in the kitchen cooking dinner, I took his advice and went outside to admire the sunset. It was a special time of day in the hills of Byron and he didn't want me to miss it.

I sat on the still warm steps from the heat of the day with a nice glass of wine. In front of me, close to the edge of the vegetable garden, was a medium-sized statue of a naked Venus; and while I was lost in the beauty and stillness of that moment, Venus started to spin at great speed, finally revealing to my incredulous eyes a very tall Angel with immense silvery wings. Wearing a lilac tunic of Light, the angelic vision smiled at me, radiating its aura in vast concentric luminous circles that framed him as if it was inside a magnificent old painting.

Then the Presence spoke. "I am Archangel Uriel and come to you beloved one to let you know that all is starting and all is perfect. You are awakening to the Spiritual Truth of your being. You are awakening to the Worlds of Light. It will take some time for you to adjust to these changes dearest one, but do not worry, much support is on the way. You have met your teacher—go back to her soon. She is the one who can guide you. She is the map reader that you need to safely explore your multidimensional Self."

Archangel Uriel stepped towards me. Shocked, I ran as fast as I could back to the kitchen screaming to Giovanni "Venus has become a talking Angel!" But as soon as I reached the kitchen I saw Giovanni surrounded by ghosts—more freaked out than before, I ran back to Uriel, while Giovanni, alarmed by my behavior, chased after me.

Uriel was still there in the same position—probably quite amused by all the commotion as I later learned all members of the *Family of Light* have a great sense of humor. I stood in front of Uriel with Giovanni by my side when I suddenly realized that my friend could not see the Archangel. Giovanni, unaware of this celestial Presence, gently took me by the hand and invited me to go back inside to have dinner. I telepathically said goodbye to Uriel, knowing that I would see him again later, and that something massive had just happened to me.

Dinner was delicious and for a little while I forgot the unseen. But just before dessert, I saw a golden being standing right behind Giovanni. I knew there and then that he was the Higher Self from Sirius. With my mouth open, I apologized to my friend because when he had originally told me the story I hadn't believed him. Giovanni was uncertain of what was going on and told me that an early night would help me to settle, as it seemed obvious to him that I was not myself. Though it was obvious to me that he could not see what I saw, and that I was on my own to experience reality with no veils.

Soon after, Giovanni retired. But I could not go to bed and so decided instead to smoke a cigarette on the veranda. I first prepared a cup of tea with plenty of honey—ignoring the innocuous ghosts still hanging around the kitchen. Nighttime at Coorabella was magical. The endless starry sky and the bright full moon's light reflected a silvery glow upon the land, a spectral landscape that in its stillness invited me to go inside myself. *What is happening to me? What is awakening in the deepest recesses of my soul?* Those last couple of days with Qala had revealed to me some very intriguing aspects of myself. Embraced by the nocturnal silence, I became fully conscious of the fact that I knew so very little about myself, as my soul, the true nature of my being, was still wrapped in mystery.

When I emerged from this deep state of reflection, I received another visual surprise. The ancient tree that stood a small distance from where I sat showed me its true essence. Golden and blue nymphs ran through its trunk and branches while its roots dug into Mother Earth, receiving from her the nourishment needed. And many fine Rays of Light seemed to connect the tree to all other trees, to the stars in the sky, and to the earth below. A spider web of Light surrounded me, interconnecting everything.

I was mesmerized, thinking: Consciousness is in all things. How arrogant humanity's behavior is towards nature, believing that we can do as we please, ravaging her with our ignorance. I wished in that moment that everyone could be graced with second-sight, that everyone could see nature in its essence, that all could witness Angels and the colorful dimensions and different Beings of Light. How lucky was I to be able to see beyond the veils, to look at all this Spiritual Richness!!!

Uplifted by my feelings of gratitude, I eventually made my way to bed. But as soon as I rested my head on the soft pillows, Uriel reappeared. The Archangel bid me goodnight, warning me that a very intense period was ahead where great changes would occur inside of me, and that one day soon, in Divine Time, a great shift would eventually also affect my outer reality. Too tired to work out the exact meaning of the Archangel's words, I closed my eyes and fell deeply into a dream world of Temples of Light—the same as the childhood dreams of a long time ago....

In the following weeks after I returned to Sydney, I experienced a huge loss of memory. I could only remember what was strictly necessary while all the trivial bits of information disappeared from my mind, including the loss of entire chunks of periods of my life. I still knew the outlines, but all details were gone. Suddenly I felt so free, almost weightless, and I did not need food or sleep; only water. This was to last for almost three months. A few times a day I received an internal Light Shower of ice-cold energy that according to Uriel was flushing my body of a lot of unnecessary cellular memories, blockages, and patterns accumulated in many previous lifetimes.

But the most difficult part of this stage of my metamorphosis was a complete disinterest in my work or anything of a practical nature. It was as if I had become one with the Spirit World and looked at everything else with a strong sense of detachment. At night this other world came to visit me through very clear visions and visitations. More horrific past lives were shown to me like movies that I could not switch off. Slowly I learned to forgive myself and all those involved, feeling each time the karmic dissolving of that particular lifetime. Other times I visited Temples of Light in different dimensions, always accompanied by a winged golden lion. Yes, the same lion I had met when I was a child. In those temples I connected with very tall Beings of Light. They introduced themselves as the *Enlightened Masters*.

I remembered them too from a long time ago as they were the same beings I had dreamed of during my childhood, and had met again, in a more recent soul journey, around the crystal circle on top of a magical island surrounded by tempestuous waters. I could clearly feel their love towards me while they explained with great patience that they had always been my teachers and would continue to teach me during this lifetime. I was fascinated by the *Masters* but also nervous to receive their teachings—I found the idea of confronting many new truths daunting, especially those deeply buried in my unconscious..

I also dreamed of living a parallel life somewhere else in the Universe—a place where nature could grow giant trees and giant flowers of spectacular beauty. In that magical environment, I lived with others in a compound shaped a bit like a castle, a fort on top of a hill. Everything was made of the purest Light, and this Light was our source for everything we needed in that life. Once, I saw myself dressed in armor of white Light, like a futuristic Joan of Arc, leading my companions downhill from our castle. We were all riding on winged horses and I was holding something that looked like a white flag but it was in fact a piece of Light Technology. We traveled great distances on those flying horses, and I often witnessed my group galloping across galaxies, suns, moons, and stars. The Universe was our home as much as the earth is my home in this human body.

A door had slowly opened and I was now journeying far inside, moving between dimensions of my own consciousness, without yet understanding the true meaning of it all.

While I was navigating amidst the tsunami of my Spiritual Awakening, many people also started to notice the great difference in my being, wondering what had happened to me in Byron Bay. I was so taken with the other world that my character traits were indeed morphing into something else. While I was trying to share a bit about what was going on with those closest to me, I felt utterly misunderstood to the point of sometimes not wanting to bother giving any explanations at all.

In the meantime, my Angel friend Donatella from London had just relocated to Australia a few months before. Along with

Alice, my editor Alison, and a few more friends, she was part of an "investigative team" sent to find answers on my inexplicable shift. According to them, an intervention was absolutely needed. When confronted by a barrage of questions I was not sure whether to laugh or cry.

How was I to explain that I could never go back to my previous state of being and that something irreversible was happening to me called Spiritual Awakening?

Soon the news also reached European shores, such was the commotion created by all my friends. Only afterwards I understood that they purely acted in this way because they loved me and felt protective of me. But to be exposed to a mini-witch hunt hurt me and made me feel even more vulnerable at a time when I was so unsure of what was happening to my being, let alone trying to explain it to others. In the end, my friends judged Giovanni and Qala as the culprits of the whole affair and it took awhile till all came back into balance.

You see dearest reader, there always has to be someone to break the mold so that others can also see their own Light. Despite all the hardship in the very beginning of my Spiritual Awakening, I have no regrets and only one piece of advice to share with you. Follow your heart without fear, follow your destiny without hesitation, as they will always lead you in the right direction to where you are truly meant to be.

Eventually the day came when I realized it was time to get in touch with Qala. My Awakening was massive and I could not deal with it alone. I needed her help.

The evening I joined her and Amaya at a restaurant on the North Shore, I was filled with apprehension regarding the truth of my Awakening. But somehow I knew that Qala had all the answers. In her wonderful way of explaining the most far-out things as if they were indeed extremely normal, she revealed that my new state of being was in fact my original state of being. I had simply forgotten it because this is what happens when we travel to earth and enter a human body.

We are all born with veils on this planet, initially unaware of the truth about who we truly are or the real nature of our soul.

To receive Spiritual Awakening is simply to remember this hidden truth, not just our human reality which is the most transient of all of our realities.

Qala also explained that in addition to my other yet to be discovered Spiritual Gifts, I already held the gift of seership and that I had possessed it through many lifetimes. It is a wonderful gift that allows seeing through different realities, and she said that one day I would be able to help others with it. I looked at Qala stunned, not really understanding how my interdimensional journeys could possibly help others.

Next I asked her the question that had been on my mind from the very beginning of our conversation: "Who are the *Enlightened Masters?*"

Qala and Amaya exchanged knowing glances while I felt the heat of my impatience rising. *What's going on now?* I wondered. But instead of answering my question, Qala asked me about my relationship with the *Enlightened Masters.* How had they come to me? What did they say? Where had I met them? Was I alone when I met them? So I told her the story from the very beginning, from my dreams as a child. I strongly felt that Qala and Amaya were holding something back and that it was not the right time for them to disclose more.

Qala then turned the conversation to what she called "Mystery Schools." She explained these were where students could learn about the deeper meaning of universal mysteries and reveal the truth of our own beings. Qala, through channelling, was bringing this system of New Education directly to the students from the Worlds of Light, the Inner Planes. "Would you like to join this school?" she asked.

I could not believe what I had just heard. I had known all about *Mystery Schools* since I was young and had often wondered what happened to those famous and sacred places of old civilizations where gifted people trained and learned to develop their Higher Consciousness. Her invitation was an offer to support the growth of the infinite potential of transformation that we all have. Yes dearest reader, we all have this infinite potential, each one of you as much as I.

I accepted her offer to enroll in a one-year training at the *Mystery School*, and in that same moment chose Qala as my teacher. She was the one. I knew it with every fiber of my being.

At first I thought it was funny that as a girl I had left school so early, and now I was going back to school as a grown woman. But then I wondered more seriously about my busy life and job at *Harper's Bazaar. When will I find time to study?* But God always has methods of arranging things, and I needed not worry as my new way was pointing up towards the stars and down towards the heart of Gaia. Indeed, a different system of travelling on my life journey was about to surge from a wave of great remembrance.

One day, soon after my visit with Qala and Amaya, the precious parcel I was so eagerly waiting for finally arrived. The box was superbly wrapped in golden paper and tied with a rainbow of ribbons. And I must confess that while staring at the magical package sent by Qala's office, I felt very much like Harry Potter on his first day at Hogwarts.

Emanating from it was a wave of intense energy that immediately awakened all of my senses. Enclosed was the material for my first *Mystery Schools* named The Makira Pod—every manual was encoded with special Light Frequencies. I opened the parcel in slow motion, being deliberately extra careful as it was something holy to me. I began to extract from the box all of the school material. Then came upon a small piece of paper. Written in bold purple was: *My Divine Presence Name: Ishkah Jzaniya Christos,* and underneath that was the word: *Keepership;* followed by the cryptic phrase: *The Rays of Creation.*

Dearest reader please let me explain a little bit more....

When we become students of the Mystery Schools, the Masters reveal to us both the name of our Divine Presence, our sacred name and our Keepership. The Keepership refers to the mastery of our own Presence, and potentially when fully activated, our greatest gift to the world. It would take me many initiations to finally understand what truly was the purpose of my Keepership and how it could transform my life and the life of others through its sacred power.

The Divine Presence is the ultimate spiritual umbrella of our whole being, holding all of our different Bodies of Light as we are multidimensional beings and the physical body is only one of our many forms. When we give ourselves permission to study the Spiritual Mystery, we start to understand that our Divine Presence holds the super-consciousness; meaning the all-encompassing Light, Truth, Wisdom, Love, and Power that our being and soul have accumulated during endless lifetimes.

The Light is pure consciousness. When the Light is fed by the energy of Love, the Love of an open heart, our consciousness begins to expand, creating in time our infinite potential. The source of our own Power resides inside us, though we often believe the opposite—that everything needs to be sourced from the outside.

The truth is that by focusing on the inner, life transformation will occur in ways that we could never imagine. The keyword that encapsulates this new reality is "Ascension." Yes, beloved reader, each of our souls can ascend while we are still in our human body, as we no longer need to die to achieve this amazing state of Lightness and liberation from duality. To be able to live our daily life in such a High State of Consciousness is the ultimate purpose of ascending.

In many ancient civilizations this was common knowledge till the old ways got lost and religion bound humanity to a new set of belief systems. We have re-entered an era though when it is again possible to study the old ways through this New Education system. The school would teach me how to powerfully revert my attention back inside my-self, giving me the knowledge to understand that we each have a Light Body which is the key to Spiritual Metamorphosis.

There was also another revolutionary aspect to this New Education schooling system.. All students of the Mystery Schools entered a pod, meaning we would be held in group consciousness to help us shift in a much more powerful way that if it was done individually. In the Realms of Light, the Angels and all other beings work together in group con-sciousness. The Enlightened Masters, for example, are an enlightened group consciousness serving all beings in the Universe with their mastery of Love, Light, and Power.

At the beginning my mind didn't grasp the meaning of this all. But being in the pod was my saving grace as in the end I didn't have the discipline to study that much but still received plenty because the other students did their sacred work which supported my consciousness to move forward regardless.

As a result, my relationship with the *Enlightened Masters* grew to a new level and they truly became my new friends in Higher Places.

Travelling around the Universe in a series of wondrous soul journeys to various portals and Cities of Light was my favorite pastime. Indeed, the school had a pink manual that taught us where to go to retrieve gifts and parts of ourselves in these magical otherworldly places. I jokingly started calling myself "Claudia in Wonderland," with my seership showing me the best movies ever.

The evolution of my consciousness was in full swing as the first stage of my Awakening was that of the Light. But the way of the heart was still to be found.

During my first year at the school I received a puzzling dream. After almost a thirteen-year gap, I dreamed of Percival. In the dream I found myself in a house surrounded by water, when all of a sudden I saw my old lover swimming across the blue sea, heading in my direction, moving closer and closer until he emerged from the water and entered my home. I woke up that morning remembering the dream perfectly and feeling rather unsettled by it. I knew that my story with Percival was unfinished and questioned myself: *Are the wheels of karma turning again in our direction?*

A few weeks later I received an extraordinary piece of news. Percival was soon to be travelling to Australia to attend an art festival. My friend Linda, an unlikely messenger, had received this information from someone who was collaborating with Percival on the event. The festival was still a few months away, so after a couple of days of wondering whether there was any further meaning to my dream, I grew distracted by my busy life and reverted my attention to more pressing matters.

My Awakening was slowly grounding inside my cellular and DNA structure and the school was helping me to integrate all of that knowledge into my whole way of being. In time I felt more stable, as much was shifting within me and already affecting parts of my outer reality. So while my Spiritual Life was growing, interest in my fashion life was diminishing. Gone was my passion for it, now replaced by a multidimensional adventure that was constantly opening new doors of my consciousness and changing my perceptions; in particular about other people.

For many years, apart from my very close friends or those I was doing business with, I didn't have much interest in the rest of humanity. My selfishness, critical judgments of others, and uncompassionate heart were all barriers for me. But with the slow deconstruction of my previous being, I became more open to others and by the *Universal Law of Reflection* others grew more open towards me.

I became popular; not just because I held an influential position in fashion, but because I withheld much less of myself and acted generally with more unconditional acceptance. I saw this as a great accomplishment. I was very slowly opening my heart. I say very slowly as it was still surrounded by a fortress.

My work with Qala began extending way beyond the school too. I regularly attended each of her workshops in Sydney and also received private sessions from her. I learned I was one of those souls that liked to come back to earth on a regular basis—and while I was considered to be an old soul, I had accumulated enough unresolved energy to last me a few more lifetimes.

Qala gifted me with readings from the Akashic Records, the records of the soul that reveal ancient unresolved lives that may negatively influence our present lives. She was also consistently clearing me, giving me the understanding of why I behaved a certain way, why I carried certain fears, and why I felt the way I did. All of this helped me put Light into so many aspects of my being, each one representing an old pattern within my consciousness.

When I attended her workshops, in spite of my newfound openness with people, I was not yet truly openhearted enough to continually see the divinity and equality in others; largely because I was not yet truly accepting of these qualities in myself. For example, though I could not wait to receive a hug from Qala, I would freeze if somebody else not of my choosing wanted to hug me. My mind was still overly selective about giving and receiving.

Also, physically, I feared intimacy. Starved of this since childhood I had developed a very unbalanced, even ironic view. What I mean is I loved to be touched during sex and had frequently sought that out earlier in my life, but I detested physical contact in all other cases, including simple exchanges of affection with my closest friends.

So while my being was a work in progress, a building site where so much was still unfinished, another teacher of the heart was about to land in Sydney.

After enjoying a dance performance on the opening night of the art festival, Linda and I were about to leave when, as if in a dream, I saw Percival walking up the side of the large hall. My heart skipped a beat. I was not expecting to see him and yet it was the way he looked that shocked me the most.

Gone was his young lion-like aura, his youthfulness; the man I saw appeared to have been deeply consumed by something, almost as if life had been unkind to him. With his image imprinted on my mind, I made my way to the bathroom, asking Linda to wait for me just outside the theater. But when I came out, she was nowhere to be found. I went back inside and saw her in the foyer chatting to Percival and another person who must have been her friend. So I braced myself and moved slowly towards them as I had no other choice but to confront Percival.

As I approached, he looked straight at me, opened his arms and moved in my direction. After thirteen years it was simply beautiful to fall into each other's arms once again, his warm embrace instantly dissolving any awkwardness.

For the next few weeks he and I were inseparable, spending a lot of time rediscovering each other. I came to realize that I liked the new Percival much more than his younger version, even though he had become rather cynical. But clearly his cynicism was one of his masks just as one of mine was aloofness. Occasionally, I was a bit hurt by some of his skeptical remarks, above all the ones on the subject of love. I wondered what circumstances had built those high walls of protection around his heart—despite their height, his internal suffering and sensitive nature still were quite apparent to me.

Another peculiarity was that while he was in Sydney I developed a relationship with the Spirit of his deceased mother. She was using my channel to send messages to him so I often obliged and passed on whatever she wanted me to tell him. This channeled connection with her was profound—at times she also appeared to me through dreams.

Apart from some complex character traits, Percival also possessed a wonderful depth of soul that came from his understanding of human nature. He was an acute and insightful observer, an intellectual with heart; a beautiful heart even if it was closed. So we both had closed hearts, but somehow the connection of our souls was powerful enough to overcome that barrier. When he left Sydney, I missed his Presence, his companionship, and our wonderful stimulating conversations.

With Percival, I truly experienced a special exchange at all levels: spiritual, mental, and physical; something not so easily found with another.

But again my happiness was short-lived because as soon as I found him, I just as quickly lost him once more. We managed to keep in close contact for a while, and then silence fell between us, till one day another dream came.

Soon after Percival's departure, my enduring situation, my obsession with Lancelot brought some bad news. His ex-wife had managed to win a huge divorce settlement, so he was forced to sell the apartment that had been my beloved home. Immediately I saw this as a very clear example of karma at work. Because of my previous unfair behavior, I was now losing something that was so precious to me.

The apartment represented my temple of transformation, a magical place where, surrounded by the Light of the Aboriginal totems, I undertook many new challenges that brought me all the way to my Awakening.

Losing it felt like severe punishment, but for the first time, instead of believing that I was the victim of external circumstances, I accepted that I had also helped to create the situation. And maybe there was a Higher Reason for my leaving. Detaching myself from Lancelot was most probably that reason.

One day, not long after I was told I had to find a new apartment, I ended up at a spectacular location; the backdrop for one of my fashion shoots. We were shooting in a luxurious apartment located inside a new skyscraper designed by a famous British architect. A giant of glass and steel, the modern tower had only been recently completed, standing proudly in the heart of Sydney. I fell in love straightaway with the idea of a life suspended over the city, surrounded by the immense and ever-changing Australian sky.

To live by the ocean was absolutely special, but I knew that instead of trying to replicate what I was leaving, it would be so much better to find a completely different accommodation, one that I could never compare to my previous home.

The skyscraper was called Lumiere, "light" in French. Just the name was a sign. So without wasting any time, I left the ocean for the sky to be closer to the Heavens. Moving apartments helped me shift many old energies and brought a fresh start. I finally let go of Lancelot. And even though I made a few more attempts here and there, my attraction to him waned as more Light grounded within me, supporting the expansion of my consciousness and many new understandings.

During that time I also lost Linda as a friend in an intricate story involving a lack of truth. My new life did not allow for the survival of anything that was not aligned with my path. And in the next few years I would experience the shedding of many more people, things, and situations to make space for more Spirit.

Someone left and someone else arrived ... it was around that time when a second fairy unexpectedly appeared in my life. Alethea, simply renamed by me as The Fairy, is one of the purest and most openhearted people I have ever encountered in my life. The red-headed beauty endlessly devotes her time to helping others, especially children. Married to Eli, a Divine Man who loves her unconditionally, she freely flies wherever she wants in order to touch as many souls as she can with her magic wand. Friends had always been the most precious of all my treasures, and once again I was supported by a full Angel Squad and Fairies that have reincarnated on earth. Giovanni had also joined the ranks of my close friends, and I often spent many wonderful weekends at Coorabella with him and his new girlfriend. After a few tumultuous years it finally seemed that my life in Sydney had become much more stable.

I was still careful though to keep my spirituality and my everyday life separate. Qala often mentioned I was getting ready to focus more on my Spiritual Evolution, but I had not felt yet that urge to let go of the life I had created. Even if I lacked my previous ambition and drive to achieve more in my career, I was still rather attached to my glamorous position. It allowed me to live in an expensive apartment, be the center of attention, wear beautiful clothes, and eat out every night in the most fashionable restaurants. Despite my strong Spiritual Awakening, I was still attached to many superficialities—particularly to money; fearing poverty even though I was earning a high salary. I came from a family that lost so much financially, so my fear of scarcity was deeply imprinted in my belief system and old programs had yet to be dissolved.

Other resistance arose too. Yes, I felt a great difference in my being and was very grateful for my Awakening, but in truth I was not yet truly committed to my Spiritual Discipline. Every time Qala told me that ultimately my life was going to evolve in a different way, I felt triggered and denied that could actually be the truth.

It was like being split in two. I loved to travel in the other dimensions, meeting the Masters and other beautiful beings, but they were up there and I was down here feeling separate from them while still trying to control every aspect of my life. Because of my own fears, I distrusted Spirit and the process of co-creation with the Family of Light. I had zero understanding of Oneness—it was just a concept in my mind that had no real resonance within my core even after all I had been through.

Then one day, something happened that shook me deeply.

During one of my private sessions with Qala, an aspect of such power was finally exposed. Even Qala was unable to put this aspect of my consciousness into the Light. To my complete dismay, she explained very clearly that I had lived many lives in Egypt where I had abused my own Spiritual Power. Without going into too many details, she continued: "You are still bound by your Egyptian karma. You have to walk again in that ancient land if you wish to truly liberate yourself from those aspects that are blocking you from trusting your Spiritual Path." She added, "This is something you have to do on your own without my help, because this is your next initiation into the mystery."

I was reproached and reminded from the other side that this work was serious, challenging, and confronting at times, and if I wanted to be a part of it I had to surrender to owning my responsibilities. Qala was my beloved teacher but she could not do everything for me. Her role was to educate me—my role was to become a good student and eventually a chela to the Ancient Masters ... and travelling to Egypt was the golden key to opening this new door.

Dearest reader, why Egypt you may wonder? Because Egypt is the land of the last of the ancient advanced civilizations still existing on the geographical map of earth, the only remaining land on which we can still walk upon as Meruvia, Lemuria, and Atlantis are no more.

Almost a year later, Qala announced she would be leading a sacred journey to Egypt. I was no longer working full-time at *Harper's Bazaar*, having instead successfully combined freelance consultancy, TV appearances, and some editorial projects. I was earning a lot more money and was very much in demand, yet I fully responded to the Egyptian call because I knew, above all else, it came from beyond the veils.

The Pyramids and Temples of Egypt awaited me and yet unknown to my mind, a second powerful Awakening was looming; the Awakening of my heart.

ꓮWꓮKENING–
EGYPT

The signs of ancient karma marked my arrival in Cairo.

In the very beginning, I was led astray by some belligerent aspects of my consciousness that fueled an ongoing flow of Dark Illusions, stirring ancient memories that had been dormant. Consequently, I was propelled into experiencing a complete loss of faith, putting into further doubt all of my Spiritual Learnings.

For a start, my suitcase got lost leaving me in an uncomfortable state of being. Stripped of all my belongings, I was immediately hit with a temporary identity crisis as my beloved clothes represented the most superficial layer of the formidable mask of protection that I still had. The vanishing of my possessions threw me into a vulnerable position, taking away all possibility of hiding behind appearances.

This sudden event created a very unsettling launch to the already mysterious journey ahead, leaving me to wonder what madness had compelled me to even go to Egypt. The lack of faith was such that I almost left the country there and then while the various aspects of my consciousness pushed and shoved me in all directions.

Another destabilizing factor was that Qala's group was rather large, maybe around fifty of us. I hardly knew anyone and my patterns of disconnection and separation from others were immediately activated. My defenses were up and my first reactions were of a negative nature. *How am I going to survive almost three weeks in the company of these people, especially when they give me dirty looks each time I light up a cigarette or have a glass of wine?* Confronted with my addictions, I felt judged and became in my mind the black sheep of the group.

It was a strange sensation that made me feel like I belonged nowhere. Despite no longer being so entrenched with either the Fashion World or my old ways, I was still ruled by plenty of bad habits that made me feel less than the others, almost as if I was not pure enough to truly be a part of this sacred journey. In response to my thoughts and feelings, I sprang into judgment mode towards them, projecting upon my new companions a fake sense of superiority in order to overcompensate for my own deep insecurity and illusion of not being wanted.

In truth dearest reader, it was the closure of my heart that had chosen this great divide as it is only the glue of love that binds everything together. Without love there is only the experience of separation.

Though feeling lonely, judged, and still not fully aware that many of my aspects were creating havoc with my personality, in the end I decided to stay and fully engage all of my energies in the program Qala would teach us. In order to be initiated further into the mysteries, so much needed to be purged by the Light allowing me to then eventually advance to the next level. The bigger the initiation, the more profound the preparation process. My preparation work had already started well ahead of the journey, weeks before in Sydney. Many of us had acquired karma from previous

Egyptian lives, therefore we were asked to listen to some specific meditations prerecorded by Qala in order to start early on the deep clearing process. Although nothing could have prepared me for my first encounter with the Pyramid Portal as I was about to be ripped apart....

The first evening, staring out at the Great Pyramid of Giza from my hotel window, I was hit with a sense of great remembrance that I couldn't explain logically because it was not my mind remembering, but rather my soul.

The next day our profound teaching program began. The first part of the journey was to be in Cairo, at the Pyramid Portal; the highlight, a private meditation in the King's Chamber inside the largest Pyramid. But in order to get ready to be in the sacred chamber, we had to delve inside ourselves and receive three aspects of our previous Egyptian lives that could potentially be blocking the Spiritual Evolution of our current lives.

Qala taught us how to open our channels, importing the information in the manner of automatic writing. Being blessed with the gift of clairaudience, I could hear the *Enlightened Masters* dictating to me all the necessary information while my hand moved at the speed of light, recording through writing everything they were clearly transmitting to me.

After individuating the aspects and their different stories, we then sat together, meeting those parts of ourselves, connecting heart to heart, feeling our dynamics, pains, and losses.

In the midst of facing my aspects, something truly magical occurred through the reconnection to these parts of my soul consciousness that had lived in ancient times. Learning their poignant stories, I clearly saw parts of myself, the ones holding the deepest patterns reflected in them, and began to experience a profound sense of love and compassion towards my aspects—and for the first time ever, I also felt love and compassion towards myself. This helped me even more to understand the causes of my sufferings: why it was so hard for me to let go of certain things, why I could not express love, why I felt so lonely.

With revelation after revelation, a thick veil of stagnant energy began to release and dissolve from my core. Three days later I witnessed the *Ascension* of each one of these three aspects into the most radiant pink Light by the Pyramids. I was so moved that I could not stop crying while the gates of my heart opened, flooding every cell of my being with love. Something so old had been lifted from my soul, infusing me with a great sense of liberation literally humming inside my chakra system, raising my frequencies and instantly shifting my outlook on life.

It was a miracle of love produced by my own being, an internal experience that began to show me instantly that truly all we need is inside and not outside us.

This raised me into a state of joy and I became friendly and open with everyone in the group, apologizing profusely for my previously distant behavior. I recognized that I had judged them all because in the beginning I didn't feel accepted, choosing instead to align my beliefs with illusions created by my mind. The understanding of such truths made me realize how much the thread of rejection had been sown inside the dynamics of all of my relationships, especially those of an intimate nature.

In the middle of this intense transformation, my lost suitcase reappeared. It was rather strange to retrieve all my clothes just as I had gotten used to needing very little and understanding how wonderful it was to travel light. And yet, still unknown to me, this was only a taste of things to come

On our last full day in Cairo, I crossed the threshold of the Great Pyramid for our special meditation in the King's Chamber. There were so many different sensations that bombarded me as soon as I started to make my way inside. Surrounded by mysterious and perfectly smooth stones, my flood of ancient remembrances was equally matched by my flood of tears as those memories entered my consciousness in overwhelming full force.

Once we were all inside, Qala started her channelling and I instantly saw all the heads and sometimes whole bodies of the other members of the group start to disappear inside a very thick energy. It was like we were entering together into a different dimension, losing the sense of the present reality while simultaneously experiencing a parallel reality. It was a powerful collective experience and that night at dinner many, including myself, shared stories of what we had seen and felt at that extraordinary sacred site.

The next day, our journey proceeded south to the Temples of Luxor and Karnak and then to the Valley of the Kings. Egypt became my own Valley of Tears, as at every sacred landmark my heart opened a bit more causing me to cry, releasing through tears all that my soul had carried for so long.

These were not tears of sadness or anger. They were tears of relief, tears of realization, tears of liberation, and above all, tears of love. Because my heart was opening, the energy of Love was igniting the Light, taking the consciousness within me to a new level of expansion. I was gifted with a deeper level of understanding and acceptance of my own being through the flame of Love, Light, and Power burning brightly inside my heart. I came to realize that Light is pure consciousness, that Love is what unifies all parts of us into Oneness; the universal glue that both binds us and dissolves all feelings of separation. That Power is simply the full expression of our own energy, the full expression of what we may be able to create when fully attuned to our flame.

Dearest reader, this same flame is also in each one of your hearts, ready to be switched on whenever you are ready to educate yourself in a new way.

And in the wake of my heart opening so much began to activate in my consciousness, triggering the beginning of a massive shift.

Since we had arrived on the shores of the Nile, I could not take my eyes off the azure waters of the River of Light. My soul memories grew strong, especially when the birds flew above those sacred waters at twilight forming all sorts of geometric configurations across the golden evening sky. That particular scene evoked something so powerful within me that my heart instantly swelled with love and more tears flowed freely, washing away the Darkness and gifting me each time with a stronger sense of Lightness.

When we reached Aswan and the Temple of Isis, visions of dancing priestesses performing sacred ceremonies filled my eyes and I began to remember my childhood dreams. My soul knew well all of these places. I realized that as a child my dreams had not been random—I had simply been in touch with my soul's remembrances from another time.

The last stop of our trip was Mount Sinai. At sunset, Qala gave us another amazing teaching while we all sat in a circle inside the walls of an ancient fortress at the very top of the mountain. Later on, surrounded by a biblical landscape, our silent return journey on foot under the moonlight was pure magic. It was the perfect closing for this unforgettable sacred journey.

To walk again upon the Egyptian land opened inside of me the most important of all doors, the door to my own heart—nothing would ever be the same because the initiation of the heart is truly the turning point for each one of us. I thought to myself it's something that cannot be explained by the mind, but the heart simply knows.

When I landed back in Sydney, it was like three years and not three weeks had passed, and yet again I came back as a very different being. At first I felt utterly lost and exposed. The opening of my heart was also a physical experience. I was physically in pain and emotionally hypersensitive, as I had been ripped wide-open and many of my old barriers were in the process of being dismantled. Indeed, during the trip Qala and the *Enlightened Masters* had begun to reveal new information that scared me, as it all pointed towards a great change in my lifestyle. When I left for Egypt I was very successful, still doing special editorial projects, TV appearances, and working with an impressive number of fashion clients who paid me incredibly well. But when I came back from Egypt, everything started to change in ways I could never have imagined.

At first, I became somewhat of a hermit, closing myself off in my apartment for days on end, refusing to go to any social events or even to see my dearest friends. I only emerged occasionally to work but then went straight back to my hermitage. There was a precise reason beyond my sudden shift, as during a meditation almost immediately after my return I received an unexpected visit from *Master* El Moyra.

He had come to let me know that it was time to truly embrace my Spiritual Path. The Enlightened Masters had patiently waited four years for me to comprehend that all of my transformation was given to me for a specific Higher Purpose and not for my own indulgence.

El Moyra, who holds The Mastery of The First Ray, The Ray of the Will—The Ray of the Divine Purpose—told me that I could either fully accept my responsibilities right then, or not, in which case my momentum would be lost until my next life.

Flabbergasted by both his ultimatum and the idea of losing the incredible chance I had been given, in that seminal moment I knew the only response I could give him was YES. And so dearest reader, this is how I started my proper training with the *Masters*. Qala was my teacher in a human body and the *Masters* were my teachers in Bodies of Light.

In the beginning it was very difficult for my personality to surrender to this new state of being. After such a long period of independence, I was faced with an imposed discipline in order to align my human will with the Divine Will; a true shock to my system in all sorts of ways. El Moyra came to visit me everyday apart from when I was still busy with my fashion career. The Master trained me for hours till he was satisfied with my progress.

The first point of focus in his trainings was on my Light Body. My heart flame was weak, my pillar was small, and my chakra system was not developed enough according to El Moyra.

The heart flame holds all of our Love, Light, and Power of Creation. It is our own personal source of everything we truly need. The Pillar of Light is our connection to the earth and the Heaven, a luminous tube through which all universal energies and Higher Parts of our being can unify with our physical self. And the chakras are doors that can be compared to energy vortexes that allow us to access the infinite nature of our beings, our super-consciousness.

Day after day, I gradually got used to my new teacher who was as loving as he was severe. El Moyra was also counting my cigarettes, my glasses of wine, and my daily intake of coffee—all interfered with brain neurons and clouded my ability to be a clear channel. After many negotiations, my cigarettes were down to five a day, glasses of wine down to three a week, and coffee down to one cup a week.

Sometimes I cheated but always got caught. How can you truly cheat a Master? El Moyra simply informed me that every time I did as I pleased, I was performing an unkind act towards myself as none of my addictions were helping me to stay as crystal clear as I needed to be.

After about four months of training, all of my fashion work, previously abundant, began to slow down. I knew this was part of the *Masters' Plan* designed from above, but that knowledge did not prevent me from feeling less frightened or less livid as I realized I was no longer in control of my own life. In addition, I found myself in a very precarious financial situation where my expenses were much larger than my entries. The money I earned barely covered my basic expenses, reducing me to a state of perpetual fear of becoming destitute.

On top of this all my cleansing was so drastic that I found myself in the midst of what is spiritually described as The Dark Night Of The Soul—the dissolution of the ego—where Initiates of Light get stripped of everything that will not serve them for the next stage of their Spiritual Life. My deep identity crises was on the rise as I was no longer the person I used to be but I was not yet the complete new version either. All of my mental constructions were melting away, and my huge ego was gradually shrinking as Love and Light took over, ultimately loosing his place as the commander.

My whole way of being capsized. I was on shaky ground holding on to fears, struggling with everything transmuting so fast and feeling helpless to slow things down. I knew I had to let go and fully trust the mysterious process but this was incredibly challenging for my personality. As a control freak I clung to parts of my old self, old life, and old belief system.

Some days I felt the weight of the world upon my shoulders. Looking down from the thirty-fifth floor window of my apartment, I often thought that if I could find the courage to jump I would because life had became almost unbearable. The process was so intense, I did not know how or what to say to my friends anymore, feeling unable to explain what I was truly going through. And once again they were beside themselves in a state of frustration and worry as I had become even more reclusive often not answering phone calls for days.

But El Moyra just kept training me, encouraging me, and explaining to me that the way I was feeling was just temporary:"Beloved, you are like the chrysalis entering the metamorphosis stage and yet you are not the butterfly. But we promise that you shall become that butterfly and your new Lightness of Being will astonish you forever more."

One day, feeling especially low, I phoned Qala's office in Byron Bay. She had been in America to teach and to write her first book. I truly needed her advice and prayed that she had made it back and could answer the phone—I felt so lonely in the eye of this spiritual storm, a cosmic delirium that was pushing me towards a very uncertain future. But it was Amaya who answered as Qala was still away. That was an absolute godsend. As soon as I heard her voice I was so relieved to talk to someone I fully trusted. I poured my heart out, bombarding her with an infinite number of questions about my state of being. Very quickly, Amaya made sense of my river of words and put everything in perspective. The wonderfully wise Amaya is not just Qala's closest friend, but a teacher in her own right. She possesses an encyclopedic knowledge of spirituality. She described to me her own *Dark Night of the Soul* that happened to her many years earlier. She had also been confronted with suicidal thoughts, and explained some of us with the strongest minds need to receive this initiation in a stronger form.

She further told me that during The Dark Night of the Soul we are also meeting our deepest core wounds and this is why it is so confrontive, the pain so acute, and the wish to terminate our own lives can at times be present. She advised that the only way to get through it was to trust and not oppose change—to do otherwise would only make the process even harder. She also told me with confidence that the bigger the process, the bigger the gifts I would receive as rewards.

Amaya held me so very gently for almost two hours and when the conversation was over I felt uplifted. I understood again that all was indeed meant to be, and that my biggest lesson to learn was about TRUST—I was not alone anymore but in co-creation with Spirit, and I needed to count my blessings that the *Enlightened Masters* were my loving teachers instead of keep fearing the changes.

It was during this time that I had another insightful dream in which I was transported to a grand old house. The house seemed to be abandoned as all was dusty and in a state of decay. Suddenly I saw a light coming from one of its many rooms and started to walk in that direction. The door was semi-open and I heard several voices calling my name, asking me to come in. A group of very distinguished older-looking people were sitting around a table drinking tea. It could have been a scene from one of those movies portraying the British upper-class of the early nineteenth century. They kindly invited me to sit with them and have a cup of tea in the most precious blue and white porcelain cups.

Then one of the gentlemen asked about my relationship with the *Enlightened Masters* and how my training with them was proceeding. The group was extremely knowledgeable about the *Masters* and after awhile they mentioned several times the name of a very good friend of theirs, a writer named Helena Blavatsky, telling me that our paths had great similarities. I had never heard that name before so they made me promise that I would learn more about her.

That morning when I woke up I had a slightly distorted version of the name in my mind, as I could not remember the exact pronunciation. But just downstairs from my building was the biggest esoteric bookshop in Sydney called Adair. So off I went to inquire if they knew about this lady.

The shop assistant gave me a funny look and after correcting my pronunciation, started laughing. "Yes, of course I know Helena Blavatsky! Madame Blavatsky is a very prolific writer and the founder of the Theosophical Society. You're standing on the grounds of the Australian office of the Theosophical Society and Adair, the name of our shop, is the Indian city where Madame Blavatsky once lived!"

I was left rather speechless.

The very helpful shop assistant suggested I buy Madame Blavatsky's memoir since I seemed to be so interested in her. And what a fascinating story it was! Dear Madame Blavatsky was a messenger for the *Enlightened Masters*, a clear channel who wrote many books with their support ... still I was not so sure of how my path would cross with hers, but that was indeed the greater mystery.

One month later Qala returned to Australia from the USA bringing with her something extremely valuable—her first book. As soon as I started to read it a major internal shift occurred, opening my mind to the full realization that my new life would become similar to the one that my teacher was leading. I felt shocked but also intrigued by this new insight. My mind flashed back to four years earlier when an Angel had predicted that my life would completely transform in order to accomplish a special mission on earth. It was not like I hadn't being warned!!!

While this revelation was grounding within me, I joined Qala in the hills of Byron for a *"Divine Presence Retreat." In the middle of the Australian bush, I was about to receive my next initiation.*

My teacher had promised to give me a private session while there. All excited to receive more of her precious pearls of wisdom, instead I ended up at the center of a grueling training session for the Higher Purpose of taking others on seership journeys. Three hours later, exhausted but mesmerized by the whole process, Qala told me, "Honey, you are ready to give sessions to others." She said it in her usual way of making the most extraordinary appear so simple. "Now you must practice, practice, and practice."

During that seminal retreat I also finally pierced through the veils of the human illusion concerning birthright, the belief that leads many people to feel superior if born into certain families: the aristocratic, rich, powerful, and famous. This false credo was completely dismantled within my own consciousness after having been ingrained for so long.

In its place I understood we are all equally divine, equally loved by God and the Family of Light. In truth, it is only karma that determines which kind of life we shall live upon the earth for the purpose of our learning. We may be born kings in one life and unknowns in the

next—kings can feel miserable inside, while the indigenous living simply in the forest may feel much happiness every day surrounded by the beauty of nature.

I felt liberated by the Light of this truth and the Love in my heart continued to grow. My newfound awareness expanded to a new level though I knew also that the levels are infinite and I was not even scratching the surface.

I returned to Sydney and without wasting any time announced to my friends that I was going to start giving spiritual sessions. To my great surprise they all began queuing up and some even insisted on paying me. At last, my beloved friends were given a practical understanding of my own Spiritual Shifts and that made them so much more relaxed, realizing that not only was I rather sane, but I could also support their own transformations by healing them from the heaviness of their karma and internal patterns. So I started to live this curious double life—half Spiritual Healer and half *fashionista.*

In the following months I was guided to enroll in two more programs that Qala offered. The first one was called the *New Human* and involved just listening to recordings. This particular program propelled me into a much Higher State of Consciousness and profoundly helped me to comprehend and accept my own process with less fear.

There is something vital that I need to explain about Qala's teachings and all other Mentors of the Divine University—they contain High Frequencies of Light. It is not so much in the teachers' spoken words but in the frequency pauses between the words that hold and imprint the lessons within the students' consciousness.

The result is the teachings powerfully ground inside your cells, your DNA, your chakras, your organs, and your brain, manifesting each time a potent upgrade of consciousness and simultaneously dissolving and releasing all that is not needed in your being.

Fifth-dimensional teaching is exclusively based on frequencies of Love, Light and Light Technology. This is why transformation can be rapid.

The help is there for all of you. All that it needed is to give permission to the Family of Light and to your own soul to receive this magical learning called THE NEW EDUCATION OF THE DIVINE UNIVERSITY.

The second program was called *Sundarah*. Almost every year, Qala gifted humanity with these special blessings from the Family of Light.

It was 2011, a very important year of preparation for all of the Light Workers on the planet. *Sundarah* was to be held in Byron Bay, so off I went to stay at Coorabella for a whole week of intensive training. The marriage, the Oneness of the spiritual reality with the physical reality, was the subject of this program. It was so incredibly appropriate for that exact time in my life.

By then, I had become very comfortable in the ever-growing group of Qala's students, with a few of them becoming very close friends. My Egyptian journey had in fact also gifted me with soul reconnections with three beautiful women—Mary, Giulia, and Mother Mary, the last one renamed by me because she would later become a clear channel of this female *Ascended Master.*

Every night, after a very intense daily program, another special individual named Lelama gave me regular lifts back to Coorabella. Lelama, also a teacher at the *Divine University*, has an incredible voice. Presence sings through her in the most exquisite way. So every morning she opened us up and prepared us through sounding, before Qala started her daily teachings.

I, on the other hand, had been told since childhood that I was woefully out of tune. Though I loved singing, I didn't dare as I felt shut down by the constant judgment saying it would be best that I not make another sound. My throat chakra was still very much a work in process, as apart from singing, I also had blockages regarding speaking and accepting my own truth. Lelama explained

that sound is a powerful tool and expression of creation. Also that we all have the infinite potential to develop a beautiful voice—I stared at her in disbelief, not quite accepting that I could have a harmonious singing voice.

Though recently, it occurred to me that indeed something had unlocked suddenly allowing me to speak Light Language, especially when I gave my sessions. Light Language is specific channelled sound that carries High Frequencies of Light that assist in releasing blockages from the Light Body. Lelama was adamant that I could shift my voice to also sing. She said that she and Qala were due to co-teach an upcoming *Self-Mastery School of Creation* and maybe I was meant to join them. An important seed was planted inside me during those nightly car journeys with Lelama.

And this dearest reader is how creation works—there is the seeding first and the growth later.

During those uncertain times I talked with my mother and the rest of my family often. Throughout my years in Australia I had developed a new appreciation for them and my birthplace Florence. Having moved so far away from Europe, the dynamics of my family relationships transmuted. We truly missed each other. I thought of them frequently and they equally grew accepting of my Spiritual Awakening, mostly because they felt a shift in my heart. Even my father, a man known for being distant, often told me to come back to Florence; to always remember the family home was also my home.

This warmed my heart as the idea of having a solid roof over my head somewhere in the world gave me strength and a renewed sense of security. My money was disappearing fast but I was so exhausted by my fear of poverty that I reached a critical point and all of a sudden I let go—I let go of all of my fears and asked God and the *Family of Light* for help as I finally begun to surrender....

A month later, I received a very significant visit. Qala on her way to Brazil, stopped in Sydney to launch the new *Creation School*. When she had asked if she could stay with me during her short visit, I instantly knew the *Masters* had guided her to my door. Those few days in her Presence were incredible.

She came in the company of so many Angels who activated a much Higher Level of Light Frequencies in my home.. At night, the white-painted door leading to Qala's bedroom became purple in color—all sorts of other strange phenomena occurred too. But the most wonderful gifts she brought were her own amazing frequencies and friendship. She explained so much more and I understood so much more—slowly other pieces of the jigsaw puzzle slotted in.

One day during her visit, I was deep in meditation when I met another wonderful friend for the first time, the *Enlightened Master Paul the Venetian*. During a profound soul journey, I was transported to his ashram and realized only then that he was the same apparition I had seen many years ago in a childhood dream—the one in which I had climbed a very tall wall covered by rambling roses. My hands had bled but I also had felt no pain and kept climbing till I arrived at a secret golden door carved in the stone that lead me to a palace where many works of arts hung from the walls. Paul the Venetian was the figure I had seen smiling at me from the sky and the mysterious palace was his ashram, his residence in a Higher Dimension of Light, a Higher Plane of Consciousness.

In that instant I came to understand that I needed not worry, that I was being looked after and that my life road map had been designed a long time ago when I was not yet born; that I was indeed the co-designer with Spirit of my own destiny. That day, the realization that we are THE CREATORS OF OUR OWN REALITY hit me even more powerfully. I knew that the great shift was soon to arrive....

Just before leaving for Brazil, Qala gifted me with the reading of my last three lives on earth—a fundamental lesson that supported individuating where karma needed to heal the most in my present life. In addition, her next destination was a very special portal called Abadania, the home of John of God; a *Master Healer* that can incorporate certain Entities of Light to spiritually and physically cure thousands of beings who visit him from all over the world.

All of a sudden, I received a powerful insight. I also had to travel to that portal and be in the Presence of John of God and those particoular Entities of Light. I needed to keep dissolving my karma, and to stay in that portal was the fastest way to do it.

With little money left, I prayed to God to help me and somehow I knew in my heart that everything was already arranged.

AWAKENING—
BRAZIL

A few years earlier I had met two of Qala's students, the lovely couple Frank and Nicole. They had recently returned from the portal of Abadania, home to John of God. They carried with them a mysterious tool called the *Crystal Bed*. According to the two, the *Crystal Bed* holds miraculous properties which once activated, call in the Presences of the same Entities of Light that work alongside the *Master Healer* to perform Spiritual Surgeries on patients. Never one to shy away from trying a new esoteric experience, I immediately signed up, convincing my friend Donatella to come along with me on this Spiritual Adventure.

What followed was so phenomenal that we both became enthralled with the *Crystal Bed*. The benefits were immediately visible. Every time I received a session I would see Entities gathering around me, operating, sometimes on my Body of Light, sometimes on my physical body. Spiritual Anesthetic was dispensed first so that I would be comfortable—often I would taste its bitterness in

my mouth, immediately sensing that I was about to receive very deep surgery. Sometimes, after certain Spiritual Surgeries, I could hardly stand up, needing a few days to fully recover. The *Crystal Bed* was also extremely complementary to Qala's work because it helped me quickly clear the density, the deposits of cellular memories still remaining inside of my being, so that afterwards I could better receive the frequencies of her teachings.

But despite my love of *Crystal Beds*, for a long time I was utterly resistant to joining Frank and Nicole when they took groups to Brazil so others could also fully experience the magic of this portal. A part of me knew and feared that going to Brazil would be the catalyst to even greater change, and my soul was not yet ready to dig more deeply. Then in 2010, while I was in Egypt, Donatella traveled to Abadania and returned home a changed woman. Something had touched her profoundly and I was rather impressed by her experience.

One year later, when Qala had visited me on her way to the Abadania portal, I knew then that my time had arrived and this new journey was meant to be. I also knew that Nicole would soon after be leading her own small group soon to the portal. Miraculously, out of the blue, I received an offer to work with one of my fashion clients. The payment I received was exactly the amount I needed to cover the journey's expenses.

From a rational view of my finances, my decision was absolute madness. But my heart was open and overrode my mind. With hardly any money left, I applied almost all of it towards my Brazial trip. A few weeks later I was on the plane....

I arrived in Abadiania in the middle of the night after the longest journey across South America. Exhausted and yet very alert, I could feel so clearly the most amazing energetic current through the whole field of the small Brazilian village. The *posada* where I stayed was a spartan but clean place. A small bedroom with a single bed and minimal furniture was my home for the next couple of weeks. I truly felt like a pilgrim searching for the truth of the heart, the focal point of our inner being. That first night, as soon as I laid my head on the pillow to sleep, Entities gathered around me in great numbers, preparing me for the next morning when Nicole was to bring me in front of the *Master Healer*.

From first light, *La Casa de Don Ignacio*, the center of spiritual action in Abadiania, was already a beehive of activity. Once I got there, I could not quite believe how many people from all over the world patiently waited to pass in front of John of God and the Entities of Light.

Just witnessing the faith of others instantly moved me, helping me renew my own faith that at the time was still rather wobbly.

After hours of prayers and singing, Nicole and I finally joined the long queue. We walked across the Current Room, the special meditation chamber where spiritual currents build up. Many individuals sat in silent meditation helping *Jiao* do his sacred daily work. As I got closer to him, my heart pounded faster and faster, my legs became like jelly. I felt completely and utterly humbled by this man who had dedicated his life to an incredible mission to help humanity—a cascade of spontaneous tears poured from my eyes, such was the emotion I felt.

Finally I stood in front of him, my heart open to receive his Divine Message. That day *Jiao* was channelling an Entity called Doctor Augustus. The doctor looked straight at me through John of God's eyes and said in a firm tone just one word: "Operation." I was then directed into a smaller room with many others to receive collective Spiritual Surgery. While the Doctors of Light operated on us, I recited the mantra of three wishes that I had previously asked the Entities to grant me. One of those wishes was to fully embrace my Spiritual Path with no more fears …

I came out of that room in a state of trance. With Nicole's help, I barely made it back to my bed at the *posada* where I collapsed for the next twenty-four hours.

One morning I was meditating in the Current Room when El Moyra came to me. The *Master* was very present in that sacred place—his portrait hung from the wall closest to my seat. He had a proposal that needed my full approval as the *Family of Light* can't interfere with humanity's free will and must always ask if Spirit is allowed to help us.

"Are you prepared to give up smoking?" the *Master* asked me matter-of-factly. If I was, it could be arranged in such a way that I would never want to touch another cigarette in my entire lifetime on earth.

The Entities could cut off my addiction, snip it off like an unwanted thread in the hem of a dress.

According to El Moyra, having a nicotine-free existence was essential in order to be a clear channel; and if I was serious about embracing my Spiritual Path fully, then cigarettes needed to go.

For a second I almost said no, such was my attachment to the poisonous stick. Then thinking that it would be rather impossible to quit, I replied yes, almost challenging the *Master and the Entities* to prove their powers. They did.

I immediately lost my will to smoke. But such was my luck of trust, that on my return journey back to Australia I bought a new carton of cigarettes feeling convinced that I would go back to my bad habit. And as predicted, on my first night home I decided to have a smoke. Dearest reader, I could not even manage to open a new pack as a powerful energy repelled me from doing so.

In that instant, I realized there is so much assistance for us from the Worlds of Light. The key is simply to ask. Ask and you shall receive— this is not just a pretty sentence but a universal Spiritual Truth that belongs to us all if we just learn to trust Spirit.

From that moment, smoking was banished from my system. After such a ferocious addiction, I never touched a cigarette again, even to this day.

On another night in a dream, I soul-travelled to a Temple of Light in an alternative dimension. The temple was built in the middle of an opalescent lake—a crystal boat driven by the *Enlightened Master* Isis took me there. Isis, resplendent in her golden Light dress and wings, explained: "As your heart opens more a little bit at a time, your karma will also dissolve." Inside the temple, seven *Crystal Beds* were lined up and on them lay my seven Knights: Merlin, Gawain, Arthur, Lancelot, Percival, Tristan, and Galahad, all peacefully sleeping while Entities of Light worked on each of them.

When I woke up from my dream, I felt a new sensation of peace knowing that a big healing process had been activated between myself and all of these beautiful men I had cared for so much in different ways and at different times of my life.

That day, I wondered if karma would ever allow me to find the special one with whom I could share my life. Maybe this would be the beginning of a process of dissolution of all that kept me from being happy in love, this ancient karma with men. Just maybe, one day I would also experience the full blessing of an intimate relationship with the beauty of an open heart, without the shadow of the ego.

On my last day in Abadiania I was meditating in the Current Room with many others, when suddenly I saw through my third eye the immense Body of Light of San Ignacio, the Patron Saint of *La Casa*, hovering above me. Then he simply blessed me for all of my future Spiritual Work on earth, telling me not to fear the mysteries in front of me. I cried upon recognizing the sign. The big shift in my life was about to happen. That afternoon I went to say goodbye to *Jiao*. He held my hand for a while. Then, channeling one of the many Entities, he whispered with infinite love and kindness that he would help me and not to worry ever again.

My two weeks in the portal were the most profound spiritual acid trip ever. What I saw and what I received were priceless in terms of healing the profound karma still anchored within me. Being spiritually operated on, meditating in the Current Room, and bathing underneath a magical waterfall in the middle of the Brazilian countryside were all part of the cure, a true cure for the diseases of the soul from which physical illnesses may often stemmed. I had come to understand that the spiritual and the physical co-exist within each other, and when we learn to live in Oneness with both of these realities, we can truly experience fulfillment in every aspect of our life with deep peace in our hearts and minds.

In November of 2011, two weeks after my return from Brazil, I was sitting on the white leather *chaise lounge* in my home wondering about my future. Suddenly, several Pillars of Light appeared from nowhere and formed a circle around me—a group of *Enlightened Masters* literally materialized in my living room. Speaking in group consciousness they asked for my full attention as the message they wanted to share was the beginning of the Divine Plan for my new life on earth. I fully recognized that the time had come.

First, I was to give everything away. I could only keep what could fit in two suitcases. Everything else including other personal belongings, my apartment, and all of my furniture had to go. They said I would not have a home for the next few years and that material things would only get in my way. I needed to be unencumbered and mobile because I would be returning to Europe where my mission would start. Though I would remain in Australia for another year or so as Qala was to gift me the *Self-Mastery School of Creation*. The *Masters* wanted me to enroll in the school and become a Keeper. My *Keepership of the Rays of Creation* would be essential for the success of the Divine Plan.

During the duration of my schooling I was to live with my friend Alethea in Sydney, and with my friend Giovanni in Coorabella, for alternate weeks until it was time to go. I was to keep one suitcase with me in Australia and ship the other to Lella's place in London. Reading my mind, the *Masters* told me not to worry about my financial situation. "You will experience the full meaning of being a co-creator with Spirit. When you are following the Divine Plan, all is provided for. So much grace will come to you, supporting you to be able to do everything that you are asked to do by the *Masters*. So whatever you need just call upon us."

Then, as fast as they had appeared, the *Masters* vanished. This was the sign I had been waiting for—if I acted exactly as they told me, the great shift would manifest. What I was most aware of in that moment was my lack of fear, which had been replaced by a new confidence and absolute trust in the Spirit.

In the weeks that followed everything started to unfold. The grace, as promised, flooded in. As if by magic, it touched every single part of the Divine Plan. As soon as my darling friend Marina heard of the visit from the *Masters*, she decided to buy every piece of furniture and decor in my home; in one go she helped resolve my immediate lack of funds. Next, having just renewed the lease on my apartment, I wondered how that would work out—the lovely people at the Estate Agency understood my situation. No penalties were assessed and a new tenant was found at the speed of light. We agreed I would move out just after New Year's Day.

In the meantime, Alethea and her husband Eli, and Giovanni and his girlfriend Miranda, each of whom had been the most caring of friends, said yes to having me as a guest in their homes for the requested time. A few days later, I also received a telephone call from Rapheah, Qala's assistant, gifting me enrollment in the *the Self-Mastery School of Creation* as predicted by the *Masters*.

I was down to one more aspect to let go of and the one I felt the most attached to—my entire wardrobe that had created my Fashion Editor persona. It was my impersonation for so long, my fake identity that needed to be shed once and for all.

For days I worked through an arduous process of packing clothes, handbags, and shoes into my two suitcases. Then unpacked it all. I looked in desperation at my wardrobe that would be left behind. *What am I going to do?* This was so difficult for me as after twenty years in the fashion business it felt like I was giving away a part of myself. Ultimately, I had to bow my head and trust the meaningful and necessary clearing in order to birth my new life; I was guided to a perfect solution. I called upon my young friends Marina and Vanissa. Both had been my assistants at *Harper's Bazaar* and I could trust them to help me make the right sartorial decisions.

So, with my Fashion Angels, we devised a plan: I would give a portion of my clothes to charity, another portion would be sold, and the remaining portion would include what I truly loved and would be useful to me in my new life. And this was to be the key of how to choose well. In my new life I would not attend hundreds of glamorous events, not go to fashion shows, and not party all night long. I did not need my armor anymore—I did not need to have the latest fashion to impress others or to make me feel better. Buying a new pair of shoes would no longer be the highlight of my week. Filling my life with such things had only given a temporary rush of excitement before I needed the next hit in a vicious cycle of wants and desires that never did and never would offer my soul what it truly needed.

Instead, I would be a *Chela* of the *Enlightened Masters*, an Initiate of Light, employing my time in service to others and forgetting about myself. This was to be a time of humility, serving the Divine Plan for the benefit of humanity and Gaia.

There is nothing wrong with the appreciation of beautiful things or with wanting to be well-dressed. But if you are addicted to this condition as much as I was, then dearest reader you must understand that a dramatic shift has to occur to embrace your new Self.

My original personality held many addictions. I locked myself in a world of illusions that blinded me to many truths. Therefore, I needed to shed this layer, as without the full unraveling, the full deconstruction of my previous identity, I could not fully enter my new reality in co-creation

with Spirit. Sometimes we have to give away in order to receive back. I had no choice but to bow my head and trust this arduous process.

And yet, dearest reader, I would be lying if I said it was easy to embark on this Divine Plan. When the realization sank in that I was about to be homeless, stripped of almost everything I had once possessed, my reaction was strong and I cried for days on end. I experienced a kind of death, often mourning what was to be no more and what was to be left behind. But it was also in those moments that my beautiful friends and family showed me the most incredible support. They believed in the new me and in my new life devoted to helping others. In their eyes, a small miracle had occurred—I, one of the most selfish and self-centered of all, had made a real turn. Actually, some did not really believe in Spirit; but none could deny that something powerful had happened to me and so they gave me the strength to accept my new way of being, and supported me to be enlightened about the fundamental truth of living a Spiritual Life.

Spiritual Life is to fully embody every single word, thought, and action where the mind and heart align to serve a Higher Purpose.

Serving a Higher Purpose means expressing our full energy in alignment with our heart dream, without the restriction of fears, illusions, and boundaries of the mind when separated from the heart.

This is the true freedom that many aspire towards, when we are no longer slaves to our internal patterns, wants, and desires but rather guided by our Higher Self, or super-consciousness. This, dearest reader, was the biggest lesson I was about to learn and that I am still learning today.

Just before Christmas I received all of the new material for the *Self-Mastery School of Creation*. I could not wait to get started in a little over a week right after the new year rang in. This time, I promised myself to be a model student and to deeply apply myself to every single subject in the program.

In those final days of 2011 the *Masters* were around me at all times, consoling me when sadness overwhelmed me, and dispensing their wisdom when my mind tricked me into thinking my Divine Plan was nonsense.

Then another prophetic dream came ... I dreamed of Percival encircled by Angels, suspended in a blue and golden Heaven. One of the Angels was his mother who had passed away a long time ago. In the middle of that magical angelic circle she rebirthed Percival in full view.

I was so moved by the dream, that after a long silence, I called him straightaway.

What ensued was very much in alignment with the *School of Creation.*

I supported Percival on his next big project, channeling many things that were helpful to him. And for the duration of the new year we had a rich and fruitful exchange which gave me the opportunity to look deeper inside his beautiful soul.

The School of Creation would educate me to create in a new way and simultaneously teach me how to support others with their creations.

This, dearest reader, is the essence of the truth about Spiritual Power. It is not something to be kept for ourselves. Instead, it is something to be shared, as there is nothing that can fulfill us more than seeing others flourish and grow in the full knowledge of their own Love, Light and Power.

At the dawn of 2012 I moved in with Alethea and Eli. Their home was gorgeous, large, and very comfortable. I was put in a blue-colored room that became my sacred space where I could study undisturbed day and night. The Family of Light had arranged for me to live in that beautiful environment surrounded by loved ones. Everything was provided for me, even a cleaning lady, the wonderfully eccentric Berenalda, who lovingly made my bed and washed and ironed my clothes.

Also, as promised by the *Masters*, practical problems were taken away from me so I could devote all of my time to my Spiritual Studies. After the initial shock, I adapted fairly quickly to my new existence, even to the point of completely forgetting about my previous material possessions. In fact, no longer owning anything gave me a sense of freedom that I hadn't experienced since I was a child. I could not recall anything that I had once possessed. None of my previous belongings compared in importance to my acquisition of Spiritual Knowledge. Inside of me a new stillness of mind was manifesting. My worries regarding the future dissolved little by little as I learned to live much more in the present moment, fully witnessing what it truly meant to be able to co-create with Spirit and experience the amazing grace that came with it.

Soon after I travelled to Coorabella and stayed with Giovanni and his girlfriend Miranda. They provided me with a beautifully furnished pale-green colored room as a sacred space. To spend time in the luscious hills of Byron, in the heart of nature, was indeed a very nourishing and inspiring experience for my soul. I became an invisible guest, spending whole days buried in deep studies that shifted me powerfully. The *New Education* was a golden, infinite pool of teachings and understandings that opened me to my innermost truths and the potential of my being.

Also, to my utter delight and as predicted by Lelama, my voice was finally finding itself. I sang in the forest with so much joy in my heart to all the nature around me. I had no words to adequately thank the human Angels that made this possible. The names of Alethea, Eli, Giovanni, and Miranda are permanently imprinted in the core of my heart.

A couple of months into my new life and after returning from my second journey to the Portal of Abadiania, out of the blue came an offer for a TV role on a fashion program; it was the Australian version of the popular American reality TV show named Project Runway. I had known the producer for a while and had always really liked her. The work was not exactly complementary with my new Spiritual Evolution, particularly since I had gone through the difficult task of letting go of my possessions, including my most prized one: my wardrobe. But still I was so grateful to have been given this financial gift and considered it to be a godsend. In a short amount of time I earned enough money to sustain myself through my period of preparation, and also to cover the expenses of an upcoming retreat in Bali where I would fully activate my *Keepership of the Rays of Creation.*

May arrived and I was to share my birthday with the festival named Wesak— a celebration of the Buddha's birthday by all the Light Workers on the planet. Qala was to give a special Wesak meditation in Byron Bay, and as a birthday present, Giovanni offered me to stay at the River House, his other stunning property situated just down the road from Coorabella. I invited a few friends for my birthday weekend but in the end Mary and Alice were the only ones free to come up from Sydney.

In that particular year, the most spectacular supermoon announced Wesak. It was so big and shiny that on the first night of my girlfriends' arrival, we all decided to go for an after-dinner walk in the moonlight. It was while we were walking uphill along the road, under the platinum shadow of the Wesak moon, surrounded on both sides by the wild Australian countryside, that the three of us literally jumped dimensions.

Suddenly the road became flat—no longer an uphill climb as in our Earthly Reality. The nature around us also reached new dramatic proportions with the trees so much taller and the leaves so much larger. The energetic frequencies vibrated to a higher bandwidth. Then, from behind the trees figures of Aboriginal giant elders swiftly emerged, surrounding us with their powerful Presences. Soon after these Ancient Guardians started channeling an important message. I was to return to Europe that summer to start seeding my new reality there. I did not need to worry as everything had already been arranged by the Worlds of Light. "You must find the courage to jump," the Guardians revealed, "and you will land on soft grass."

Indeed, some fears had come up for me regarding my return to Europe—fears of being judged, of being misunderstood, and possibly of being cast out due to my new state of being. After all, I would be returning stripped of the glamour, success, and position that everybody had long associated me with. I felt naked and vulnerable.

However, the *Masters* fully guided me through that next part of the Divine Plan. First I was to travel to Florence. Then to Ibiza where many of the people I knew from London vacationed during the summer season. It was important to reconnect with as many as possible being my new Self in order to pave the way for others. Last, I was to fly to London and from there back to Australia to finish both the TV program and school.

All of my friends and family on the other side of the world were so excited that I was coming back. At that moment in time nobody cared what version of me would return. Arthur was thrilled that I could spend August with him in Ibiza. He announced it to anyone who would listen. So I took a deep breath and braced myself for the next part of my journey.

I had long-forgotten the beauty of European summers after living in Australia for ten years. Even though I traveled back and forth to Europe on a regular basis, it was never during summertime. The light in Florence was particularly breathtaking, but despite the warm welcome home, being back with my family was rather challenging. So much of our karma and genetic patterns still needed dissolving. And I knew already from the *Masters* that clearing my family karma would be one of my first spiritual projects once I was back in Europe full-time. Though one particularly positive thing did happen: my mother and sister asked if they could receive sessions from me, and as both are very open spiritually, they immediately recognized and felt the benefits within themselves.

This small step gave me great hope that more people would open up to receiving my sessions and accept the new version of me, that was in reality the original version of me—the one without the mask.

Once I reached Ibiza I was thrilled to discover that so many of my old friends and acquaintances were into Spirit at different levels, and to my even greater surprise, several of them wished to receive sessions from me.

Arthur's home is the most romantic place on top of the Old Town. Built around a Moorish-style courtyard covered in bougainvillea, with a multitude of brightly colored flowers scattered across luscious vegetation, this heavenly retreat has an old chapel downstairs that was hardly ever used. The *Masters* guided me to meditate in this chapel and when people started to flow to me, it became the perfect setting for my sacred work.

Arthur quickly recognized that something truly transformative had happened to me. I had developed a beautiful singing voice by then—the *Creation School* had fine-tuned my vocal cords every single day with a series of sacred practices. A rather practical man, he was taken aback by my new singing abilities. For him this represented a tangible sign of change, and because of this he decided to fully support the "new" me. His enthusiasm touched me deeply. I was so happy to have listened to Spirit's suggestion to commence seeding my new European reality. Slowly my beautiful mind also learned to let go more deeply and follow the inner wisdom of the heart and guidance of the Family of Light.

This whole journey was peppered with the most astonishing coincidences and encounters with people that I had known a long time ago.

In spiritual terms this is called Synchronicity. It is when time suddenly syncs with our path in the most perfect way, allowing many positive situations to unfold as if by magic.

I visited Percival during the last leg of my trip in London. He was tired and not entirely well so I gave him an impromptu session to perk him up. I would have loved to have stayed longer but time was not on our side. When I left I felt a longing for the closeness of our souls, and carried sadness that a karmic barrier remained between us that we could not dissolve.

But even if my heart was open, that was just one step in my Awakening to unconditional love—a faraway destination that I could only reach without my fears.

Time flew. As soon as the TV show was over I felt guided to travel back to Brazil again. I knew it was the only way to keep burning karma as fast as I could. By the time I returned to Sydney, the end of the year was fast approaching and with that also the end of the *Creation School*.

At the final ceremony, I was filled with infinite gratitude because even if what I'd received was far too vast to be comprehended by my mind at that time, the new knowledge and awareness of the truth was at least fully imprinted in my heart, DNA, and in Divine Time ready to be integrated into my daily life.

But my schooling was not completed. Soon after, a retreat in Bali awaited me—it was the last part of my present Divine Plan before jumping again into the unknown.

When time came, I travelled back to the magical Island of the Spirits to be reunited with other students from all over the world. Our common aim was to become Keepers of our greatest Spiritual Gift, to understand what our Keepership truly meant, and to learn to use it in service to humanity and Gaia.

I had often wondered about my sacred name and Keepership. All of my spiritual friends called me Ishkah, a name that indicates the vibrations and frequencies of my Divine Presence. But what was the meaning of my *Keepership of The Rays of Creations?* I could not wait to listen to Qala's recordings given to each one of us at the very beginning of the retreat that would explain it all.

When I finally did get to hear her recordings, so much more made sense to me.

The Rays of Creation are the Divine Lights infused in everything that gets created. These are safely kept in a separate dimension, and as the Keeper I would become the transmitter of these rays, helping both myself and others to create all that is needed in our reality according to our Higher Purpose. But firstly I had to embody the teachings myself in order to become the conscious example for others. Teaching humanity how to create in new ways was to be my gift to the world.

However, the recordings also filled me with fears: fear of mis-creations and abuse of power. In many past lives I had abused my power and disempowered others. I was fully conscious of this truth since my Egyptian journey during which much karma had been cleared. But thankfully, the *Masters* told me that in this life-time I would only help many to empower themselves. The lesson to be learned was one of understanding that the more our Spiritual Powers grow, the more we have to grow in humility and compassion to balance this power.

To birth my Keepership was indeed a complicated and harrowing process. I spent the first week clearing some daunting past lives—back at the cinema of my third eye, I watched the movies rapidly pass through while I cried and forgave all that had occurred.

Then I was told that my special project was to design nine templates of creations, sacred geometry art, through channeling the frequencies of my Divine Presence into ink and imprinting them on paper. It is called scripting, the sacred calligraphy of our Presence. When Qala began teaching how to script the frequencies, I just could not do it as I would not trust my own ability and let go of my mind. Every night I was transported to the *Divine University* dimension on Sirius, one of the Dimensions of Consciousness, where I would sit for hours with the *Enlightened Masters* El Moyra and Paul the Venetian, just scripting away, practicing for the next day. Yet, the following morning I was still blocked in the Earthly Reality. Plus, we were approaching the last few days and Qala was adamant that the first of the sacred art works had to be completed at the retreat—I was getting more and more stressed out and more and more into my mind.

One day, with the deadline looming, I was laying on a special bed of support when El Moyra came to me. He told me to just get up and do it! I was literally pulled back to my working table and started to design the template. Slowly but surely, all of my Presence's frequencies began to pour onto the paper with the scripting at last flowing freely. A few hours later my first template was completed to Qala's full approval and to my greatest relief. Later on that same day she honored me in front of all the other students, telling them how I had embraced the Spiritual Path fully by giving everything away, surrendering to my Divine Presence. My teacher's words gave me such strength that all the tribulations of the past few weeks disappeared in an instant.

Just before we left Bali, Qala took me aside and revealed how happy the *Masters* were with my work and not to fear as when we say yes to the Divine Plan it is a continuous path of grace. We hugged for a long time while I wondered *when will I see you again? Will I be strong enough without you?* Everything appeared so enormous in front of me: *am I really ready to go out into the world by myself?*

As soon I returned to Sydney, I received a visit from El Moyra. I was to go back to Florence and finish my entire Keepership Project. Afterwards the next stage of the Divine Plan would be revealed.

I was to depart from Sydney in a few weeks and leave ten years of my life behind. I quickly went to Coorabella to say goodbye to Giovanni and Miranda, and when I saw the property disappearing behind the last curve of the windy country road, my heart sank. I loved Australia, a country that tempered and shaped me in so many ways. A land that educated me to love the earth—Mother Gaia, dismantled my pretenses, and supported me to live in more open heart.

Then I realized there was somebody else I truly ought to see before my departure: Lancelot. My attachment to him was long gone, but somehow it felt like unfinished business and I could not leave without saying goodbye to the man who had inspired me to come to Australia in the first place. So after days of arrangements, off I went to his new property not too far away from Sydney.

Lancelot struggled to understand the new me, especially my disinterest in carnal affairs. It was also strange for me to experience such detachment from someone who, not long ago, held the power to capsize my life with the snap of his fingers. That night at his farm, alone in bed, a part of me truly mourned those passionate emotions that I used to feel for him. But I was also well aware that those were cellular memories having nothing to do with the actual truth of my relationship with him.

Through my training I had learned to discern the truth as opposed to my thoughts and feelings. Beloved reader, even if thoughts and feelings seem very real in the moment, they are not necessarily the truth.

The truth is instead buried deep within our heart and consciousness. Later on I understood that if you do love someone as much as I loved Lancelot, the love is always there. It just shape-shifts into a different form and the most beautiful friendship can flourish from the ashes of the old way of loving. Love is love and cannot be dissected or put in a little box with an expiring date etiquette..

I recognized though that Lancelot and I had some more work to do in order to be able to reach a new way of loving each other, so I prayed to God to give me that possibility in Divine Time and in Divine Order with our beings—those who have the patience to wait may one day reap the rewards.

During those last few days in Sydney I spent a lot of time with my Spiritual Sisters, dreading the reality that in Europe I would be unable to share all of my spiritual-centered talk so freely as none of my friends would be Awakened at that level. But I reminded myself: *upstairs they always have a plan, so I just need to learn to trust more.*

Just before my departure, I called Percival. I had dreamt of him in Bali. To my greatest surprise he promised to visit me in Florence. *Something to look forward to* I thought to myself with a mixture of excitement and fear....

Then the final day arrived ... that morning, all of my closest friends came to say goodbye. Peter, my beloved driver who had driven me around during my fashion heyday, took me to the airport. I was so moved by their love and a new insight....

In the end, what is a place without friends? And what is a life without love? Only the memories of those we love are what makes a place and ultimately our lives so very special. This is why, dearest reader, to love and to be loved is truly the only thing that our soul comes to learn and relearn upon this earth. All the rest are just details that may seem so important at the time, but in the end leave no traces, like dust scattered by the winds of time.

SURRENDER–
RETURN TO EUROPE

March 21, 2013. The *Masters* suggested this as the date of my return. They told me that it would be auspicious to arrive on the first day of spring so that my new life in Europe could blossom like nature in springtime. After ten years in Australia I was back in Florence where my Earthly Life had begun. *As a forty-nine-year-old woman with hardly any money, no home of my own, and no idea of how everything was going to unfold,* Florence would be where my new Earthly Life would commence.

In the very beginning, reuniting with my family was very special even if there were many karmic undercurrents with transformations needed in order to create harmony and an unconditional loving familial bond. At the time, my sister Francesca was navigating the treacherous waters of a very difficult marriage that brought upon her a constant dark energetic cloud, and the need to drink far more alcohol than was wise. Addiction runs deep in my family tree but as I started to clear mine, I hoped that through energetic cleansing the other members of my family would eventually also be free of theirs. Unfortunately, my mother was also attached to her glass of wine. But fortunately she was able to stay more present as she had powerful Spiritual Gifts of her own.

My father, as usual, lived in his own world, oblivious to everything that did not interest him. He also often fought with my sister.

Something old and decayed lay at the core of the channels of communication between all of my family members. Distortion of the truth shaped by the projection upon each other of negative thought forms was laced with judgments and unforgivingness. I could see clearly the dynamics of all of our aspects and often prayed to God and the *Family of Light* to guide me and support the dissolution of the genetic karma in my family tree. In fact, each time I went to Brazil I would take their pictures to be blessed by the Entities of Light. I was well aware in my heart that somehow the process had already started and that I needed to be patient and to trust. To rebuild a clear and loving relationship with my family would take time, but at least I was more conscious of what was truly needed to shift these old energies.

There were however two young family members who gave me a lot of joy. My niece Angelica and my nephew Gabriel, both imprinted with the codes of the new children of the earth. Gabriel was still too young, but Angelica, together with my mother and sister, often asked to receive my sessions and in Divine Time a great improvement started to manifest. My father, an atheist, was not so keen but sometimes I did ask permission to do some energetic work on him and he would agree even if he had a complete lack of understanding about it all. I knew I had personal karma with my father from my third to last life on earth and was determined to clear it before his passing—my karma with men also stemmed from my paternal relationship. In fact, I realized that generally I did not understand men, often felt deeply distrusting of them, and consequently judged them with no compassion.

I thought deeply about this. How could I ever engage successfully in a romantic relationship with all of this unsolved energy in my own being? My father was the perfect mirror from which I reflected all of my insecurities and anxieties while my ego pushed away everything that could potentially hurt me, in particular previous lovers, because I had felt fundamentally rejected by him since I was a child.

I was given my grandmother's old bedroom, a beautiful room with a garden view, where I immediately created a new sacred space, built an altar to anchor a Pillar of Light, and started to design the rest of the templates of my Keepership project. I could feel the frequencies pouring through my being, activating all of the new centers in both my physical and Light Body.

In the midst of all of these activities, I was guided to call Percival as I remembered his promise to visit me. It was Easter and I knew he was recovering from a grueling schedule in his country house in Italy. A plan was swiftly arranged and a few days later my old friend arrived in my city of birth. He took up residence in an old patrician grand house that was remodeled into a luxurious hotel. Surrounded by the most enchanting ancient gardens this was to be the backdrop for our unconsummated love. You see, dearest reader, Percival had come to me with a certain degree of heart openness and almost certainty that the promise of romance would be fulfilled.

At the beginning of his visit, he spoke his truth but I could not speak mine, resulting immediately in an imbalance and disharmony between us. In spite of my Spiritual Education I was still dealing with the deepest form of my personal karma, causing me to feel unwanted and terrified of showing vulnerability. As a result I went into judgment mode and ultimately pushed him away. It was not premeditated in anyway, but I couldn't refrain from using my power to control the situation through fear, instead of letting myself go with the mysterious infinite potential of such a situation. I was so blinded by the illusion of protecting myself from any form of suffering that I didn't even recognize I might had hurt him badly. A rejected Percival left Florence immediately. Being still unconscious about the deeper meaning of my action, I was left behind in a state of great disappointment.

Fresh from becoming The Keeper of the Rays of Creation, I was shown a great lesson about creating, with Percival as my teacher. We are the Creators of our own Reality in every given moment, therefore it is vital that we all learn how to create consciously and with love to avoid unnecessary states of sadness, anger, and disappointment so that misunderstandings can be avoided with those we love.

Fear, at times, can manifest some damaging consequences and there is no worse fear than that of not being able to express the truth of one's own heart.

After his visit to Florence, Percival more or less ignored me. But one day another Spiritual Journey would illuminate my heart and consciousness to discover more of the truth of this matter of the heart.

During my second month back in Florence, the next part of the Divine Plan was finally revealed to me. El Moyra told me to go to London, as this was the primary city of my mission. Everything would develop from there as it had already done once upon a time with my fashion career. There I was to start giving regular sessions in support of others' Spiritual Awakening. This would also help me sustain myself financially and spiritually.

His request was not a big surprise as I already had an instinct that London would be an important key to the Divine Plan. Yet how to achieve the desired results was still a mystery. London is one of the most expensive cities in the world and my financial situation was disastrous. So how I was going to afford renting a place was a big concern. During my last months in Australia, knowing that I couldn't stay at my friend Lella's place because of the size of her small apartment, I had already started to inquire with my other friends if an alternative accommodation could be found, but nothing had materialized.

This mission was rather daunting at times, as I was really living by purely trusting the *Masters* and the Divine Plan, trying often to avoid questions from my family and friends regarding my future. I never knew how to answer them anyway—I always thought that the truth would be too much for them to understand and accept. I laughed to myself imagining telling my father: *sorry Dad, I am waiting for El Moyra to come up with a practical solution to my financial problems and the rest of my life....*

In truth, my mother was the only one who really believed that everything made sense, and she sometimes helped me to trust even more. Soon my Angel friend Freya also immediately embraced my new way of life without question, and with infinite faith even started to support me financially when it was badly needed.

But a few days after El Moyra's latest visitation, as if by magic, I was offered the perfect space in London. The previous summer in Ibiza I had met the beautiful Amanda and Sebastian, a married couple who instantly became my friends and clients. Sebastian's father was an old friend of Arthur's and mine from way back. At the time my new friends lived mainly in the country, but they also owned a townhome in London in the middle of Notting Hill Gate. That fated day Amanda rang me as she needed a long-distance healing session. Afterwards I simply asked her if she knew of a place where I could stay and receive my clients at the same time. The response she gave me was the answer to my prayers as she invited me to stay at their home. She told me that she and Sebastian were not in London that much and they would both be very happy to help me out, as they also firmly believed in my Spiritual Gifts.

So with hardly any money, I went back to London with so much hope in my heart like I had as a young girl so long ago when I left Florence in search of my destiny and wondrous adventures.

London that June was a vision of the spontaneous generosity of nature. The weather was marvelous and Notting Hill Gate an explosion of rambling roses growing lusciously in the well-manicured gardens that surrounded the elegant buildings of the famous neighborhood. My temporary new home was so much more than I could have wished for. Amanda offered me a spacious and gorgeously designed bedroom on the first floor. It had many great features including a fireplace that I loved and upon which I built a powerful new altar.

I was so grateful to her and Sebastian. I learned to trust a bit more every day that the Divine Plan was not a figment of my imagination, and that Spirit was truly co-creating this new reality with me; therefore I should just let go of my worries and enjoy the process. Yet, I faced another big mystery. *Where will my clients be sourced from?* But even this question was soon answered as so many wonderful beings just appeared out of thin air. Some of my friends became my first supporters like the beautiful Leila. The fiery Charlotte brought to my healing space every other member of her large family. As news spread a bigger wave of clients started to manifest.

I used no advertising and no sales techniques of any kind to either gather more clients or to keep the ones already with me. The *Masters* simply asked me to draw a new template of sacred geometry with a special mantra designed to attract all the souls of those who specifically needed my help—then everything was truly left to the Presence of others to guide them in my direction.

I am a doctor of the soul, helping the souls of others heal from internal mechanisms, supporting them to shift their consciousness and to understand that each one of us is indeed a powerful being. That all we need is already inside of us.

So there was no chasing, only receiving within my heart those who were truly meant to come to me. That time back in London became the blueprint of how my life would unfold in the following few years. Shuttling between London and Florence and a few more places around the globe, this moving around the spiritual portals became a very significant part of the Divine Plan.

Towards the end of one of my London visits, El Moyra advised me to return to Ibiza and deeply meditate in the ancient chapel where another important piece of the jigsaw puzzle would be given to me. I knew better than to say no to my beloved *Master* and dutifully let Arthur know that I was coming back to the enchanted island, a powerful portal magnetizing to its shores many individuals, unconsciously or consciously, drawn by its powerful energy.

Another portal leading to another door would bring me a big surprise....

SURRENDER–
IBIZA

Ibiza, the most famous of the Balearic Islands, has been a second home to me since I was nineteen years old. At the beginning of the eighties I fell in love with Ibiza at first sight. Then, the island was still a refuge to bohemians and hippies who inhabited its ancient villages and walked barefoot on its reddish land where pine, olive, and fig trees had grown undisturbed for centuries amidst the untouched beauty of the silvery-green Mediterranean landscape.

Today much has changed, but Arthur's magical castle on top of the Old Town still stands, untouched by time. It has been the constant backdrop for several decades of my life, filled with innumerable events, too many to even remember. Crumbling old walls protect this exquisite oasis from the indiscreet and curious eyes of many tourists on the other side of an imposing iron and wood door. It's an enchanting place, an island within an island, which embraces me upon each entry with the perfume of its flowers, the harmony of its designs, the warmth and comfort of its interiors.

All welcomed me back home from nights of endless fun, the memories of my youth imprinted on every stone in every room of that wonderful house, but had since grown to offer me a very different experience of equal if not greater importance.

After many years I discovered that the unused chapel is a small and powerful portal which I had reactivated energetically with all my meditations and sessions. Here many sacred ceremonies occurred in ancient time. I found this out one day when, to my greatest astonishment, the *Old Guardians* of the portal thanked me for my sacred work by paying me an unexpected visit. And it was here, inside this portal where El Moyra promised me I would obtain a vital piece of new information.

One early morning while the rest of the household was still in dreamland, I made my way to the chapel for my daily meditation. As soon as I started to go deep into my core and heart flame, a *Council of Enlightened Masters* made their Presence felt very clearly. I knew this meant the moment had arrived to receive the next part of the Divine Plan. The *Council of Masters* announced that I was to write a book. The book would be the first of many but that was just a little bit of extra information that I did not need straightaway.

In this first book, I was to write about my life and Spiritual Awakening, not as a pretty picture, but as the absolute truth of my being; so that people could be inspired by my story and realize that they too can liberate themselves and fulfill their infinite potential and Power of Creation to manifest the realities of their heart's dreams here on earth.

They told me that the book would be channelled and contain special Light Frequencies so that the reader could shift and have plenty of their own realizations while reading it. That was the Higher Purpose of my book which would belong to a new breed of manuscripts for humanity, carrying High Frequencies in each word.

In completing their message, the *Masters* said that the book had to be written in English, and finally, that I had one year to

prepare myself, opening up more of my channel so I could fulfill this sacred task. They advised me to go to India with Qala on
her next sacred journey and to also return to Brazil as part of my
preparation.

*Well dearest reader, now you know the truth of how this book came
about and that was not at all my original idea!!!*

In the meantime, back in the chapel I fought with the *Masters*,
the whole of my being unable to accept what I had just heard.
Write a book in English? Were the *Masters* out of their minds?
Who would want to read it anyway? And what could I possibly
say? Huge chunks of my memory bank were gone, wiped out since
my Awakening. Oh God!!! Nothing made sense to me anymore so
I ran upstairs in absolute distress wondering how I was going to
deliver this part of the Divine Plan.

Arthur was up drinking his cup of tea while contemplating
how to improve the already stunning garden in the courtyard. He
was a vision of calm in total contrast to my rather agitated state of
mind. Since day one I could always count on Arthur for anything,
and without wasting one more second, I immediately poured my
heart out to him!

To my infinite surprise he just stared at me and told me in a
firm but loving way that before I could not sing but now I could,
before I could not draw to save my life and now I could design
amazing templates with the precision of a Leonardo da Vinci. So
why did I think that the book would be a problem? After all, it
seemed to him that by some mysterious force I was managing to
do rather well at everything I could not do previously. *Are the Masters talking through Arthur? I wondered with suspicion....*

But he was right. There was no reason why I could not channel
the book. There were plenty of reasons for my mind to freak out,
however when trained to go beyond the mind, as I was, surely I

could do it. I had already forgotten that I was not creating alone, but rather working in co-creation with Spirit because it was simply this co-creation that was the explanation behind my newly acquired voice and skills at designing sacred geometry.

The *Enlightened Masters* also announced that I needed one year of preparation, so I confessed to Arthur the second part of the story—I needed to travel to particular portals in order to be able to channel the book. I told him about India and Brazil and my frustration of how I was going to get there with hardly any money in my bank account.. With his kind heart, Arthur promised that he would pay for my Indian journey.

In a split-second the Divine Plan had turned my life around once again. I was to become a writer and soon I was also to be reunited with my beloved teacher travelling across India on the sacred journey of a lifetime. So, dearest reader, I had to keep moving forward both my trust and courage, delving deeper and deeper into the mysteries without fear. All the help and support were already there— my duty to keep walking upon my life's map according to the very specific requests of the *Family of Light*.

Once I had left Ibiza I felt immensely grateful and well prepared for the next stage of my journey: I had one year to birth the writer in me and suddenly I felt joy in my heart remembering that I had always loved writing and reading the many wonderful books that had shaped my life. Then the memories started flooding back as I saw myself in my early twenties, dreaming for a fleeting moment of writing a book but unable to do it because I had no faith in myself.

So, in truth I had always carried the dream of being a writer in the deepest recesses of my heart, and now it was time to fulfill this forgotten aspiration.

I am sure, beloved reader, that buried deep in your own heart too are many forgotten dreams and aspirations just waiting for a ray of faith to

illuminate and bring out of the shadows something that is truly dear to you. But that you have put aside thinking you couldn't do it, thinking that it was impossible to live your heart's dream.

I am here to say however that you are simply bound by an old belief system like I was, and that when you open yourself to Spirit and to your magnificent heart anything is possible. When we co-create with Spirit, magic and grace shall touch our lives in the most improbable ways.

SURRENDER–
INDIA

One of my greatest fears about my return to Europe was that I would not be accepted by others, nor be able to share my Spiritual Truth without being misunderstood or judged. One of my own lessons though was learning to accept that not everyone believed in my transformation. My lesson was to not judge, and to be able to stand in my Light and heart no matter what, even if other people were indeed pointing their fingers at me.

Sometimes I succeeded. Other times I failed and got incredibly defensive instead of recognizing that my detractors were in fact my teachers, teaching me to be more compassionate and forgiving. This was all in Divine Order for both myself and the other parties involved. After all, the greatest challenge is to keep our hearts open even during the harshest disputes; and I would be tested several times on this very subject, because to embody the teachings is a never- ending process.

In truth, to aspire to be perfect is also an illusion while we are still in a physical body. The Spiritual Path it is not a path of perfection. It is simply a path of learning, a path of surrendering to love, and I still needed to surrender so much more.

In Florence, the reconstruction of my family bond had also extended to my auntie and cousin. With the death of my uncle, a process of reunion between the two sides of our family had commenced, and much needed to be forgiven.

Bringing my family together remained one of my primary aims, as peace in our families is a vital step towards peace in the world. If peace can't be achieved amongst family members, what hope do we have to achieve peace on a larger scale?

Yes dearest reader, to be peacemakers is an essential role for each one of us, a process that starts with seeking peace within ourselves. We must first find peace in our own hearts so that we can transmit it to others. To be awake is to truly understand the importance of peace and that everything is sourced from within to then be given out for the benefit of everyone. To help others is to help ourselves and to give to others is the greatest gift that we can give ourselves.

Every day I was learning a little bit more, letting go of a little bit more of my fears, doubts, and old identity. I often compared myself to the humble onion as this was my daily sacred work—pealing away my many layers of protection, cellular memories, and old beliefs to eventually reach the pure essence of being. My own revelations were aided by the *Masters* training me in the art of detachment. To have given away my material possessions was only the starting point as I had also adopted a plan to sparsely buy only what was strictly necessary.

After awhile, this rigorous discipline made me realize how much I had accumulated when it is very possible to live happily with so much

less. It was not easy to contemplate this truth in our consumerist society, where to possess a lot is seen as a sign of wealth and success. I began to apply this knowledge to helping my clients. Clearly giving away everything is not practical for most, but taking steps towards a sense of restraint from satisfying so many wants and desires is. The result is a heart filled with Love and Light rather than one filled with illusions.

While I learned to discern between true needs and wants, something rather wonderful manifested unexpectedly. Certain individuals suddenly gifted me with all sorts of things like designer clothes, luxurious beauty creams, a new iPad, money, and more. These were all people receiving spiritual support from me who responded to a heartfelt call to support me in their own way by providing again all that I had given away. It was quite extraordinary to receive such spontaneous generosity coming from all these beautiful hearts. Grace was touching my life in ways that I could never have imagined and for this I was immensely grateful.

I received another precious present too—the friendship of two special women; Laura who was married to my cousin Simone, and Fiammetta, a childhood friend who came back into my life via a series of fated events. Both were on their own Spiritual Paths, dispelling my fears of not being able to find any sisters in Europe with whom to share my credo.

Of the two, Fiammetta was especially attracted to Qala's work, and had decided to travel with me to India in order to experience her teachings. So in early October Fiammetta and I left for India, the Country of the Light, where new powerful initiations were awaiting us.

I had travelled to India twice before when I was still unconscious. But even then I was moved by something inexplicable, something in every molecule of the air and earth of the country; an immense Light kept alive and in perpetual growth by the absolute faith and spiritual daily practices of millions of devotees.

The journey started in Delhi. Qala's channelling of the *Masters* offered us quite a program. On the Yogi's Path, we received the activation of how to live on Light if this was our future wish. Like alchemists, we were also taught how to make special waters infused with High Frequencies of different qualities of Light in order to initiate our system to achieve this goal in Divine Time. But that was just one aspect of our learning as the Yogi's Path, above all, is meant to cut through all wants and desires, liberating the mind and body from the realm of illusions. My so-called onion was about to receive a drastic exfoliation—to carry on my Spiritual Path and write this book I needed to achieve a crystal clear consciousness not tainted by such illusions.

From Delhi, our group was to travel to three specific portals that held the special Light needed to both activate and seal the program in our systems as required by the *Masters*.

Geographically it was to be a colorful journey, visually stunning and highly entertaining as there is no place like India to witness the absurd but to also touch human nature with such a vast spectrum of emotions.

But this time, spiritually, my journey was arduous, confronting me every day with those trickiest aspects still subtly attached to beliefs from my old life.

It was in Dharamsala, home to the Dalai Lama, underneath the high white peaks of the Himalayas, where I discovered that despite all the grace I had received, parts of me still grieved for my previous existence. I missed the financial freedom, my influential position, and even drinking, smoking, and partying. I missed all of the material things I had given away. Everything that was buried in some remote part of my consciousness pushed its way back to the surface and exploded with negativity, regrets, and attachments. I became angry and frustrated. *I'll never see the end of this. When one layer dissolves, immediately there's another one and another one....*

I was coming to terms with the real nature of the Spiritual Path in which our initiations are never-ending, no matter how high we may go into the Light. It is a path of eternal learning. Once we embrace this truth with humility there is equally no ending to the gifts that we may all receive upon this sacred journey.

Struggling all the way through India, I was so grateful to be in the company of Qala. My teacher reminded me that if the *Masters* asked me to write a book, it was because I had the ability to do so. Her encouraging words helped me a great deal as in truth I was filled with doubts.

Amaya was also travelling with our group and was such a helpful Presence, especially with Fiammetta, who was opening up like a blossoming flower in springtime. It was nourishing for my soul to witness my friend be touched by the magic of Qala's work. To see her flourishing gave me hope. I had to be more patient and understanding towards my own deep and painful cleansing process.

One evening, after we reached Varanasi, I was finally graced with the shift in consciousness that I had been waiting for. It was dusk and our group was on a boat sailing down the Ganges, absorbing the magical atmosphere—along the shoreline the last sunrays painted the temples and its sacred waters with the most delicate shades of pink and golden hues. Time seemed to stand still, suspended between past and present as at the river's edge wise ones performed ancient ceremonies; covered in the shadows of decaying buildings which reflected their faded beauty into the gleaming water.

Inspired by the sacredness of that moment, I started to perform my own ceremony. Taking off one by one some precious bracelets that had adorned my wrists for a long time, I offered them into the golden water of the Ganges. I came into the full realization that I was letting go of so much more than jewelry.

I was letting go of memories and the many illusions of what those memories had created in my mind: romantic visions of the past that had nothing to do with the truth of how I used to really feel, suffocated by the constriction of my fake identity. In that moment I saw clearly that I had not been free but simply a prisoner to all my addictions and illusions.

Dearest reader, there is no quick fix on the Spiritual Path and to believe that to transform ourselves is a speedy process is also an illusion. But if there is a will, there is a way, a graceful way that once tried and tested will leave you with wanting to experience much more of the Love and Light in offer....

That evening, sailing on the Ganges, at last I put my past to rest and surrendered more deeply to the Divine Plan.

A few days later we arrived at the legendary Bodh Gaya, the last leg of our journey. Waking up every morning before dawn, we begun each day sitting in deep meditation underneath the Bodhi Tree where the Buddha had received enlightenment thousands of years earlier. To be under that tree in the company of hundreds of monks was a very significant experience. One morning a monk came towards me, telling me in broken English that he could see my Light. I was so humbled by his comment that I promised myself *Light and Love are to be my only focus as what I am learning is so much more precious than all of my illusions.*

In the last few days in India under that sacred tree I suddenly received an immense gift. I was graced with fully experiencing ONENESS. This was such a revelation that I could never go back to where I once was. In an instant, a vast expansion of my consciousness showed me that there is no right or wrong, good or bad, as all is ONE and all is DIVINE with its own holy purpose. That the real nature of our beings is divine even if we have been told the opposite. Not even one of us is marked by an original sin. Yes, we have karma, but it can be dissolved

to reveal the truth that we are indeed very powerful, with our own direct contact to Source, to God, therefore to our own divinity.

This mind-blowing experience of ONENESS supported my acceptance, without too much judgment of myself and of all others. Yet, there were still moments when I did slip back into old patterns. But they were brief as something so strong had been seeded within the fabric of my consciousness, a new way of looking at everything.

Step-by-step with the help of Qala, I slowly progressed and received more from that Infinite Source of *Love, Light, and Abundance* that is in the Universe, available to be shared by absolutely everyone.

I arrived back in London with much to process, integrate, and ground. But it wasn't the time for this as I immediately jumped on a train to Glastonbury to join my dear Australian friend Mother Mary in yet another portal—the magical Avalon....

SURRENDER–
GLASTONBURY

$\mathcal{M}$ary had just returned from a European tour, or more accurately, a European pilgrimage. She had just spent a few weeks in France following *Mary Magdalene's Trail*. Along the way she had visited innumerable portals, retrieving gifts and parts of herself.

Those of us who feel guided to travel to these portals do so because the Higher Spiritual Planes offer our beings something significant that is not found elsewhere. So if we visit such portals with awareness, magic happens and many new revelations may touch our hearts and connect us more deeply to the many gifts of our Ascended Consciousness. This means that if we go as normal tourists, we can't expect to be connected to our lost gifts through the retrieval of those parts of ourselves still locked in those Higher Dimensions of Light. Thus, I was inspired to journey from portal to portal in search of the many pieces of the puzzle from my soul having travelled back and forth from earth to the Dimensions of Light, and vice versa during several lifetimes.

Mary and her husband Michael were waiting for me at the charming country station close to the picturesque town of Glastonbury, the focal point of my new Spiritual Adventure. My heart was filled with gratitude towards both of them, as it was their kind invitation that allowed me to explore a place that had often come into my dreams.

Avalon, once the sacred island of ancient ways, the Druids' way, the legendary England of Arthur and Merlin, still exists although on an alternative Dimension of Consciousness. Through connecting with our Spiritual Power, we can consciously soul-travel interdimensionally, but it is only through studying the mysteries that the needed deeper knowledge can be acquired to enter Cities of Light like Avalon.

To access the portal of Avalon also signifies a deeper connection to our own heart chakra and to the Holy Grail; the mythical golden chalice of the Christ that symbolizes the flame of Christ Consciousness, a special quality of Light that carries all of the attributes belonging to the Christ such as love, faith, charity, compassion, forgiveness, humility, and divinity to name but a few.

And this was exactly the reason why I had been guided to join Mary at this specific portal. I was badly in need of receiving the keys and codes of Love and Light that would support opening my heart more profoundly. I was also guided to ground, grow, and expand the Christ Light within in order to birth more qualities of pure Christ Consciousness.

These beautiful qualities ultimately guide us to evolve into *New Humans*—the Christ Light being one of the key activators necessary for such transformation so that we may learn to act, think, and speak through the way of the heart.

In my numerous portal journeys there have always been spectacular visual elements that enabled me to see the Worlds of Light through the lenses of my brow chakra. But most importantly, there have also always been the retrieval processes of keys, codes, and aspects of my Higher Consciousness that ultimately helped me shift much more quickly so that in return I could also help others. My trips to the portals represented an intense period of energetic transmutation to then transmit to others all that I was given.

That first night in Glastonbury I dreamed of the Golden Cup of the Holy Grail, receiving a deep transmission of Christ Light in preparation for my next few days in the portal. I also became acutely aware that my soul had lived in Avalon in ancient times. Such memories were first triggered when I read a wonderful book entitled *The Mists of Avalon,* a novel that must have been channelled by its writer. The story brought a very different imprint to the already well-known Arthurian tale. The character Morgan le Fay was not portrayed as an evil sorceress but as a high priestess trained in the ancient ways. An inspiring piece of literature, every word in the book spoke to me and several visions of Avalon followed through the years till the time arrived when I finally reached the physical place of Glastonbury. The days that followed were wonderfully intense and filled with profoundly deep realizations that completed the process firstly activated in India.

One early evening while we were walking up to Glastonbury Tor, the veils lifted and I was presented with a scene from long ago. In a parallel dimension, a procession of priestesses were also making their way up to the Tor holding torches of sparkling Light, their long white gowns floating in the wind. Around them, winged fairies danced, and while pirouetting towards the top of the hill, the evanescent otherworldly creatures created clouds of golden and silver fairy dust all along the crest. Overwhelmed by a vision of such beauty, I started to cry softly, my soul recollecting that particular lifetime when I had served Gaia, our Mother, according to the old ways of the magical island of Avalon. This was also my original connection to why the English land was so close to my heart.

In that moment I reclaimed another aspect of my Ascended Consciousness left behind in that specific dimension thousands of years before. Piece by piece, I am reconstructing myself in the way of my original soul blueprint, where many aspects of my being hold expanded consciousness and an abundance of Spiritual Knowledge. This is my true identity, a collection of all different parts of my consciousness held across the Universe from the earthly to the starry portals that with time are reuniting within me, reshaping the Oneness of my being.

The way of Love and Light is simply the way that takes us back into our heart, as ONE with all parts of ourselves. To enlighten each one of these aspects of our consciousness is the Ascension Process, which may take many lifetimes to be achieved. The person I had been grieving for while I was in India had never been the absolute truth of my soul because there was so much more to me as there is so much more to you dearest reader, so much more then you can possibly imagine. Once we rediscover this hidden reality of ourselves, it is possible to manifest a life totally aligned with our heart dream; our Higher Purpose, the one that will fulfill us the most.

I returned to London feeling much lighter and preparing myself to follow the next step of the Divine Plan taking me back to Brazil.

I was asked by the *Masters* to spend six weeks in Abadiania. Of course there was always a Higher Reason for celestial requests, though parts of me were not looking forward to being there for so long, nor to being confronted with the laborious process of purging myself of more karma and all else that was needed to keep advancing on my path. But I accepted the challenge and returned to the land of John of God and the Entities of Light. And thank God I did.

Until Abadiania, this book was just a remote concept. I knew that somehow I needed to manifest it, but the process was still wrapped in thick veils of mystery that often left me questioning

myself: *how am I even capable of fulfilling such a task?* Constantly doubting myself, the idea of this book put me in a strange mood, often leaving me forgetful of the fact that it was meant to be a co-creation with Spirit and I was therefore not doing it on my own.

On the very night of my first Spiritual Surgery, El Moyra and a *Council of Masters* lifted the veils that had prevented me from seeing my future creation. They clearly explained that the book needed to be divided into a prologue and three parts. Then they proceeded to give me the titles of the prologue and three main sections. Everything was clearly detailed, including the number of chapters for each one of the main sections plus the titles for each of the chapters. Afterwards, in a firm tone, I was advised to write the prologue first, followed by the rest of the book in chronological order.

The *Masters* then told me that in the upcoming nights I would dream about my story starting with the prologue: "Yes, you will consciously dream it beloved; dreams are where all future creations are first seeded."

So I dreamt of which moment in my life the prologue needed to express, and each night a new chapter unfolded during my conscious soul-travelling. Afterwards, everything was seeded and sealed within my consciousness in order to be used at a later date. A few weeks later, the *Masters* revealed that this book was to be the first of a trilogy, and the first of many more books.

I was also asked to do one more thing. Qala and Amaya were about to open a new school: the *School of Loving Presence,* and the *Masters* highly recommended I enroll. I accepted their words, thinking *it's going to be rather wonderful to start writing my book while the school will hold me in group consciousness, fast-tracking my whole being to the next level. As usual, all was perfectly arranged upstairs.*

When my time in Brazil was over, I went back to Europe with lots of answers and a heart overflowing with gratitude. The Divine Plan was indeed unfolding with grace and clarity. Having the

Masters reveal to me the structure of this book was a turning point in my level of trust towards them, and through the *Universal Law of Reflection* towards myself.

SURRENDER–
GENEVA

My new life began to take shape in front of my incredulous eyes and became as busy as my previous life. But gone were the glamorous events, shopping sprees, and turbulent affairs of the heart. In their places were my schoolwork, emotional investments in close relationships, and focus on helping others. Slowly but steadily, I fully accepted my new reality where the barometer of my happiness was measured by the improvement of my clients and the well-being of my family and friends.

When spring arrived, I was guided to visit Geneva where a school buddy, the beautiful Dorothea, was hosting one of Qala's workshops. I travelled there with another dear friend and fellow student Sarah, a very gifted being, who like me had a successful career before her own Spiritual Awakening. It was very special to reunite with my Spiritual Sisters on the shores of Lake Geneva— another powerful portal.

At the very beginning of our visit, Qala mysteriously asked us for dinner. She had some important news to share and was exited to have the opportunity to do it face-to-face. I was curious but didn't give too much importance to her invitation.

In the meantime the workshop confronted me with something very deep, my relationship with God, therefore my relationship with all there is.

It dawned on me that I was fundamentally angry with God, only connecting with him very occasionally when I was in great need; but even then mainly calling upon the *Enlightened Masters* because I loved and trusted them more than I trusted God. I was stunned to find out the truth about my relationship with Source. But within my heart I had already known since childhood that my rapport with God was challenging, especially because I held God personally responsible for every loss that I had endured in the course of my present life.

And yet, it is only when we are truly ready to delve deeply within that we may discover the absolute truth of what holds us back, provokes internal defense mechanisms that may cause us much grief and anger. Courage is needed to confront the Darkness in our being but afterwards the rewards are immense because they bring us liberations.

The *School of Loving Presence* had slowly started to activate this very process within me but it was that latest workshop which brought the deepening of the question about the true nature of my relationship with God.

I was confronting the fact that at some stage my soul had suffered from a severe disconnection from Source, causing me the pain that I presently felt. This disconnection led to my core soul wound of loss of innocence, creating the loneliness in my soul. Because when I lost my innocence regarding love, I experienced separation from Source, and when I felt separated from my own Source, I experienced loneliness.

I also understood that the core wounds from what originally happens to our souls is what is then reflected in our present life in a myriad of ways until we are finally healed and returned to a state of Oneness. Our present life is simply a reflection of our relationship with God, constantly holding up a giant mirror reflecting all of our internal makeup and everything outside of us with the result being a range of consequences.

The beauty was that my healing process—mending all of my diseases and conditions accumulated through all time, space, and dimension—was a positive consequence of my supporting the souls of others. Progress had certainly being made but still so much more was yet to transform ... Will I now be able to see and feel the Light of God in everything? Can I lose my blindness by recognizing the divinity in myself and in all others? Will I take full responsibility for my own karma and not blame God?

A few days later at a pretty restaurant in a small fairy-tale-like village by Lake Geneva, unexpected news were about to be revealed to three unsuspecting women. Qala sat across the table from Dorothea, Sarah, and me. She started the conversation with news of a 2016 launch of a free membership website called the *Sirius Library: The Web Portal of The Divine University*. In time, it would hold all of the teaching programs that she brought to earth in the last fifteen years for the benefit of humanity. The three of us immediately began congratulating Qala for creating a space where so many could be introduced to the *New Education*.

But she cut short our celebratory response saying there was more. "I will not be the only one carrying the project forward. The *Masters* have chosen a group of individuals to join me in introducing this work to the world, and to preserve and grow the legacy of what has become a very important body of spiritual education here on earth." She paused, seemingly to let this sink in, and then: "The three of you are to be part of this group if this is what your souls wish."

The delicious chocolate dessert in front of us had suddenly lost it's allure and sat untouched, as silence descended upon our table. Qala continued, "In order for each of you to achieve the *Divine University Connection* you will have to go through an intense eighteen- month training with me and the *Enlightened Masters*. I do not yet know all of the details, but a pre-training will happen in the summer. That will give you a much clearer view of what is going to be required for October when the proper training will commence."

This was certainly a most unexpected proposal and the three of us were stunned, lost for words. I was so taken aback that a part of me did not know how to deal with such a commitment. At first I felt almost casual about the whole affair, simply thinking *oh well, I'll wait a few months until summer arrives and see what I truly want to do. I mean, is it ever going to end?*

So I went back to London and attended to my clients and carried on studying the school program. When summer came I returned to Florence to begin writing this mysterious book.

Besides, that was the year of my fiftieth birthday, a significant passage that would mark the initiation of a very important time in my life, the time of discovering what truly lived beyond the physical me.

July in Florence was hot and humid. Everyday I sat in front of the computer writing the book that you are now reading. The *Masters* had asked me to start with the prologue as it was already clear in my mind and just needed to be transcribed—so that was easier to channel, while the rest of the book was completely unknown, meaning I knew the timeline but had no preconceived ideas on how to fill it in.

In the very beginning I was petrified of failing, fearing that nothing would flow through me, that it was just a big illusion, and that I could not truly write. My mind played up, interfering with the sacred work—once again I forgot the book was a co-creation with Spirit, and that I was not writing it with just my own resources, not with just my mind alone. When I finally let go and my mind became still, the magic started and the book finally began to take shape. The process was multilayered—every time I went back and reread the material I was shown something was not necessary or something needed to be developed more.

What I learned right away from this process was that every word, sentence, and paragraph had to have a purpose—it was not enough to just be pretty, it had to be essential to the story. A spiritual book is created to give special messages that may assist the reader in the Highest Way and the consciousness of the writer needs to hold and reflect great clarity and integrity.

My tale needed to be about the truth, not the embellished truth but the core truth of my being and what had really happened to me internally and externally. I had to strip myself in a most profound way and expose myself deeply. Yet, doing so also triggered my fears and insecurities as I had been so used to wearing a mask. And now, the Enlightened Masters had asked me not just to unmask myself privately, but to do it much more publicly so that many others might also see themselves through my experiences. Hopefully then they would be inspired to seek liberation from their own constructions and constrictions.

When the book was still in its infancy stage, the moment came to focus upon Qala's intriguing invitation to join the Mentorship Training Program. Soon, time arrived to listen to the pre-training webinars, and what I heard was so astounding it triggered all sorts of rebellious reactions within me.

We were given only the outlines but I already knew that the journey would be mysterious and many doubts assaulted me because the level of surrender required was far beyond what I was used to.

I trusted Qala and the *Masters*. But I questioned myself: *could I really devote myself to such a huge commitment when I don't even know*

half of the other Mentors involved, let alone be in group consciousness with them?

On the other hand, I knew that *The Divine University* truly represented a pure example of a Fifth-Dimensional Form of Education for absolutely everyone on earth who was ready for the *Path of Ascension*. And undoubtedly, to become a Mentor would propel me into a much Higher State of Consciousness very quickly.

I was utterly confused and decided to sit on it.

Then El Moyra paid me a surprise visit. In spite of Qala's clear statement that my soul had to fully agree to this mission, my beloved *Master* told me point-blank that I did not have a choice and that I had to simply trust him as this training would support me in reaching a new level which I would never be able to achieve on my own. He said I needed to just accept this truth with great humility, and it did not matter if my mind was aligned—he added that later on I would thank him deeply. When El Moyra left I became angry—angry that he was taking away the choice I had been promised. *This was hardly fair* I thought in total exasperation.

After El Moyra's visit I felt I had enough. Quite frankly I just wanted to run away. So I did, sort of. I left the torrid heat of Florence and joined my parents holidaying at the seaside.

Upon my arrival at the pretty seaside village, my mother immediately noticed something was troubling me. She knew how to extract my deepest thoughts, those that sometimes I did not even know I had. Since Giovanna had started receiving my sessions, not only had she stopped drinking but she had opened up even more to her own gifts. I was well aware that she was somebody I could completely trust because of her expanded view of seeing beyond the veils. So I explained to her my opportunity to become a Mentor, about all my doubts attached to it, and about El Moyra's latest visit.

In an instant my mother was even more adamant than El Moyra—"You have to do it. You trust everything else he tells you, why don't you trust him now?" I had to admit there was logic to what she said.

Still, I was not completely convinced until El Moyra came back soon after to support me in clearing some old Atlantian Records; a time in which I had sat in councils with others and felt betrayed. Those memories of betrayal helped explain my reticence to not trust being in group consciousness with all the other Mentors. After dissolving those ancient memories, I felt lighter. The rest of the summer went quickly until finally I concluded it was my soul's wish to become a Mentor of *The Divine University*.

Soon after I was again walking up the dusty Egyptian road leading to the Pyramids amidst the sand dunes and ancient stones, the silent keepers of endless mysteries and forgotten secrets.

Returning to Egypt was very special because a few of us who had already committed to the Mentorship Program reunited in the land of the Sphinx. It was truly wonderful to bond with members of our future Mentor Family. I was now certain this was utterly meant to be, that this mysterious turn on my roadmap was utterly necessary for my *Path of Ascension*. I also felt infinitely grateful to both El Moyra and to my mother for encouraging me to join the training.

Sometime fear can play dangerous games, taking us away from our true path. To live life conditioned by fear is to not allow ourselves to live our life to the Highest Potential of what we may be able to create and manifest without such fears.

In the first part of this Egyptian pilgrimage, I connected with twelve unresolved aspects from past lives and was able to bring them into the Light, one after another. This gifted me immediately with a new lightness of being. But it was another extraordinary event that touched me the most, showing me for the first time some of the ancestors in my starry soul lineage, revealing who these beautiful Beings of Light were, what amazing gifts they possessed, and where my soul was originally birthed,

This encounter came to me in 3-D as if I was inside a hologram. I had met the *Masters* a few times in that way, but somehow the meeting with my soul lineage was even more dramatic as they entered my hotel room in the middle of the night, galloping in on winged horses. Because of the thin veils between realities, they were able to travel inter-dimensionally. These Bearers of Light dismounted their horses—I could feel their weight sinking into the mattress as they sat around me on the bed. I was so taken aback that I could hardly breath.

At last one of them who appeared to have almost man-like features spoke with kindness and love: "We are going to extract some old stuff from a specific point in the back of your neck called the Zeal Point chakra. Do not be afraid as this is for your Highest Good."

As soon as he touched me with his long thin fingers of Light, I was aware that he was performing Spiritual Surgery, extricating a long tape of ancient beliefs and cellular memories while the others were working on different parts of my being. When they finished, they left in a great swirl of Light, promising they would come back to visit soon.

I wondered how that all could have been possible. But I reminded myself *I've been experiencing the most sensational of occurrences since I was a child, showing me time after time that life on earth is only one reality. This life is a world within so many other worlds and many other souls are Awakening to there being so much more beyond the material and physical—and many of them will have their own stories to tell just as I have been asked to tell mine. Of this I am certain.*

I stayed in Cairo for a few extra days to spend more time with Qala. She saw in my crown chakra three books—a trilogy— that I would write. In truth, each had already been written in the World of Light, including this first one you are reading now. Through channeling, I was simply going to manifest them in the Earthly Plane. I knew what Qala said was directly from Spirit. I knew this is how creation works.

Everything is first created in the Realms of Light and that is why it is so important to dream consciously, as when we dream consciously we start to seed in the Light. Consequently, the dreams are woven into manifestation if they are aligned with the destiny that we have chosen for ourselves. Whenever we truly feel something deeply in our heart and soul, it is most probably because we have chosen it before and this is a sign that we must follow it. It is also a time when fear usually comes in, interfering with our heart dream, telling us that it is impossible to create the reality that we really wish for.

It is this discerning of the fear, the heart versus the mind, that will support us to learn how to create from a state based on no such fears. This is exactly what the New Education has been teaching me—to liberate myself from all illusions created by such fears. To be truly free doesn't mean having enough money to buy anything we might want. To be truly free means to not be affected by fear, and even if this sometimes still happens, through Spiritual Knowledge we are ultimately able to discern the truth from the illusion.

It was this freedom that I was starting to experience on a daily basis—peace of mind, happiness, and lightness in my heart as my soul slowly progressed on the Path of Ascension.

When I returned to London, mixed news greeted me. The bad news was that my beautiful friend Lella had just been diagnosed with cancer of the colon. Apparently it was curable, but to see my Angel so consumed by pain was a harrowing sight for me. She was so determined to not let the cancer get the best of her that I was utterly inspired by her Light—no matter her state of being, she gave me so much joy. The good news was that my friend Freya had just moved back to London. Another cancer survivor, she supported Lella as much as she could, as well as being a column of strength for everyone around her. My old friends were still my Angels and often my teachers.

Crispin, for example, was a constant reminder of how everyone has his or her own Spiritual Evolution—each different but nevertheless equally divine. Crispin and his beloved partner Alexander were blessed with a deep connection to Gaia, the Earth Mother. Their garden in the countryside was attended to with the greatest of love and care—each plant, each flower, each tree, had a place in their hearts.

When I visited them we would go out to the garden together and pay our respects to nature by smelling the aroma of roses and wandering through the green maze they had created with so much passion. And nature spoke back to them, flourishing in all her beauty to touch their hearts. Of all my old friends they were the most skeptical about my transformation and spirituality and instead relied more on science. Even so, in my eyes their love towards Gaia made them very spiritual indeed. Also, their devotion to each other taught me that a relationship in which a couple lives and creates together in harmony does exist and that is possible to dream about this kind of partnership.

Dearest reader, the purpose of an intimate relationship is evolution, to evolve together. My friends gave me hope that one day I would also experience the blessings of being in a sacred partnership with someone. They simply experienced God through nature and their love for each other. This was profound to witness and one of many examples showing us the infinite ways of expressing the divine.

The wheel of time was turning at great speed and another year was upon me, marking my return to Brazil.

I managed to do a little bit more work on this book too, though really I was far from completing my sacred task. So I returned to

Abadiania with the intention of concentrating fully on writing. But the *Masters* explained to me that the real reason I was there was to heal my Spiritual Pain, the loneliness of my soul, and therefore, my separation from God. Since Geneva, I had already faced the fact that my relationship with God was in need of transformation, and that I needed to have the humility to see the divinity in everything.

Yes, there were certain qualities I had fully embodied, like the power of my Spiritual Will. But there were others that I had only partially embodied, like vulnerability, compassion, and patience—I struggled with these in my day-to-day life, especially in certain situations where those qualities were most needed. I thought of Percival, Lancelot, and all my other Knights who at times reflected all of my insecurities and unresolved issues. I thought of my family, especially my sister, who I had treated so uncompassionately since the day she was born, only because she had been born. It was time to make amends to those I loved and I knew that in Divine Time I would be gifted with the opportunity to do this with each one of them.

I was also given by the *Masters* a work structure for the six weeks of my stay in Abadiania and so the process of healing my Spiritual Pain and writing started again. One day while on the *Crystal Bed* I received an impromptu visit from the Spirit of the great Brazilian medium and writer Francisco Xavier. To my greatest surprise and delight he was encouraging me to write, to give my message to the world through books. He told me he would come and sit on my bed regularly while I was in the portal to check on me, but he especially emphasized that I should have no fear of being judged.

He revealed to me he had been judged harshly during his lifetime, and that unfortunately judgment is a part of human nature but it cannot stop those who do sacred work on earth. "Everyone is bound to have different views, different truths, and above all a different expansion of their consciousness and levels of openheartedness. If you can remember that," he told me, "while they are judging you, you shall not judge them but will instead just send them love."

I was so touched by his words. In truth, I held a deep fear of being judged, and also I remembered well that I constantly judged others. It was difficult for me not to judge, to only see the divinity in others, to see God in them. Can I really reach that state of being? Can I really send love to those who point fingers at me? Suddenly I came to a full realization: I had first judged God because of the Spiritual Pain created by my separation from him, from my own Source, and that is the reason why I ultimately judged everyone and everything else.

To learn to be more humble was the door I needed to enter in order to achieve a deeper state of cosmic love. I didn't need to wait longer to find that entrance as one day, while meditating in the Current Room, a portal opened above my head and Saint Francis descended from the Heaven bringing me a very specific message. As one of the Over Lighting Entities of *La Casa*, the Saint asked me to go to Assisi specifically in the company of my friend Fiammetta where we would both receive some precious new insights.

I left Brazil with a sense of accomplishment. I had progressed with my writing and clarity and wisdom were received aplenty.

The sweet hills of Assisi awaited to gift a new piece of the puzzle for the healing of my soul.

SURRENDER–
ASSISI

My return to Florence was marked by the dissolution of some of my deepest family karma. In a floods of tears, I made amends with my sister asking her to forgive me for all of my wrongdoings. I admitted to Francesca that I had been a terrible sister, blinded by my ego and constantly judging her harshly. I confessed I had resented her from the moment she was born because I wanted to be the only daughter, and I saw her as stepping on my already established position in our family. I explained that I had constantly accused her of being jealous of me, truly missing the point that by the Law of Reflection I was actually the one who was jealous of her. That blessed day the whole truth poured out of my heart.

Through her own tears, my sister summoned the level of humility that I was still striving to achieve. She opened her arms and forgave me. "Don't worry," she said. "I love you and understand you." The simplicity of her words touched my heart in such a profound way and in that instant, I understood that simply by making amends I had allowed a great energetic shift to occur in our relationship.

To forgive ourselves and to ask for forgiveness from those we have denied love to, in the end, is an essential key to our freedom and lightness of being.

Without forgiveness there is only life with regrets in which a combination of resentments and carelessness lead to the same result of a closed heart that will block our ability to fully give and receive love.

From that moment on, my rapport with Francesca greatly improved as a bond between us that never existed before was forged. I felt grateful to have a sister and at last, I looked upon her through Spiritual Eyes, seeing her fragility and strength, and fully accepting her back into my heart.

The dissolution of the karma with Francesca was the first in a long line of people with whom veils were lifted and I saw their truth, not what I imagined their truth to be. My uncompassionate opinion of others was hardly the truth about them, it was more the truth about me—I had made quick judgments from my own projections upon others instead of looking at them from my heart. And it is only by looking at another from our heart, that we can witness the preciousness of this person and understand more of their nature in a deeper way.

Many parts of my old consciousness were finally in the process of great transformation. All that I learned at the *School of Loving Presence* was gracefully integrating and I felt the results deeply in my heart.

The Mentorship program I was immersed in also revealed much more truth about my own nature and the future of my Spiritual Life. One day I was listening to teachings when El Moyra appeared in 3-D. He was so close, all I could see were his giant fingers handing me a Pen of Light. But as soon as he touched me I passed out—the energy he generated by his Presence had overwhelmed me. When I regained consciousness, he was gone visually, but I still heard his telepathic message: "You are now holding in your Body of Light the pen of the scribe." What I had received was indeed the initiation of the Spiritual Writer, or Spiritual Novelist as the *Masters* liked to call me. Afterwards, I began to sense that both teaching and writing were to be the next key elements on my Spiritual Path.

There is always a Divine Time with everything and while I was letting go of the old and surrendering more to the Spiritual Truth, I suddenly remembered that I had to travel to Assisi.

Fiammetta and I were enjoying a walk together, witnessing the beauty of all that spring offered if we just cared to observe it. Walking through the ancient country lanes of the streets of Florence, at every corner we stopped to smell the sweet scent from cascades of violet wisteria; floral waterfalls rippling off of the ancient walls of villas and churches. And it was during this walk, surrounded by the rebirth of nature, that I informed Fiammetta of Saint Francis's message.

My friend had also experienced the power of the Abadiania Portal and immediately agreed to the sacred journey. A couple of weeks later, Fiammetta and I were on our way to Assisi.

On the initial night of our journey, during a profound conversation with my beloved friend, I received the first of several insights while I was pondering all that I was still struggling with—meaning humility and divinity. In a flash, Percival came to mind and I was hit by the truth of a practical lesson about divinity as time after time I had failed to see the divinity in him. Instead, I constantly judged him for his womanizing, for his cynical view of life, for his sense of self-importance, and whatever else I decided to judge him on in an uncompassionate way. *Did I ever truly see the truth of his soul?* I don't think so, dearest reader, as I was too busy concentrating only on the negative side of his being,

The way of the heart was now showing me that it is easy to blame others when we avoid looking deeply at our own projections and reflections, preferring instead blindness to the truth of our unresolved energy. With awareness also comes the full responsibility to own our actions. Percival was again the teacher of a lesson that was still personally hard to learn.

The following day, Fiammetta and I drove to Assisi, both getting lost in the beauty of the ancient Umbrian land, kissed by the sun and loved by many Saints. Assisi, perched on a hilltop, displays medieval perfection having been untouched for hundreds of years and still stands in its pure essence of Spiritual Citadel.

Surrounded by an enchanting countryside covered in spring flowers, we arrived at a small church built by Saint Francis in the very beginning of his conversion from rich and spoiled young man to loving monk. To pray and meditate in that holy space was powerful. Once inside the chapel, I could not stop crying—the Presence of Saint Francis felt by me as never before. I asked the Saint to make me see as he saw during his magnificent but short life. Like him, I also had given away my possessions to be able to step on the Spiritual Path. Not for one moment did I compare myself to Saint Francis but somehow I felt aligned to him as in different times we lived through similar experiences. But unlike him—he had surrendered himself to humility and divinity in such a spontaneous and irrevocable way—I felt still as a beginner, so far away from achieving anything of the kind that he had.

And yet a magical process unfolded in that tiny church, adding another piece of the puzzle on what firstly was brought into my consciousness in Geneva. The healing of my separation from God, my own Source, was now well on the way ... I also realized, in full awareness, that I had never forgiven God for taking my beloved grandmother away from me when I most needed her—she was the person I loved more than any other, and in fact, her passing marked the seminal moment when I closed my heart to God and consequently to everyone else.

The next day, another powerful insight hit me all of a sudden and led me to mend something else still unsolved in my consciousness:

I deeply healed my hatred of the Catholic Church because I recognized that I have been judgmental of all religions. Saint Francis explained me that every church, synagogue, mosque, or temple on earth equally receives Light directly from the Enlightened Realms, so to be respectful of other spiritual beliefs was fundamental to my own growth.

The ways to God are infinite and the frequencies of faith and love are equally present in all places of prayer and veneration of the divine as when we honor God, we honor ourselves. It doesn't really matter which is the chosen channel. The truth was that I had karma with the Catholic Church created from past lives that bound some of my gifts, and only forgiveness and acceptance could dissolve it.

In Assisi, both Fiammetta and I felt truly touched by Saint Francis who for centuries had poured from his luminous essence the Infinite Source of Love and Light to touch all those who sought Spiritual Truth.

I was a pilgrim of the heart and my quest was far from over.

In the months that followed I returned to Bali to learn about my next level of Keepership and in August all Mentors were due to travel to Montana for our first retreat. A new chapter of my mysterious existence was about to unfold.

Back on the Island of the Spirits, my understanding of the meaning of Spiritual Power or Power of Creation revealed to me many more insights.

During the Keepership Retreat, I came to understand even more deeply that Spiritual Power always needs to be shared and used with utmost sacredness, especially in holding awareness that the Love of an open heart is the alchemical ingredient that always keeps the Light in balance.

Since I was young, I had some sense of this power but was not aware enough to fully comprehend the responsibilities that accompany it. I had been able to create new realities for myself without even realizing it at that young age. I was already a Reality Shapeshifter through the powers of imagination and visualization. But it never resulted in a full manifestation touching every aspect of my life in equal measure. Until we learn to co-create consciously with Spirit, life will always be with some kind of incomplete manifestation.

Since coming back to Europe I had learned to create in a new way and gradually grace appeared to touch those parts of my life where karma had ruled before. I was releasing one by one the knots of my souls, making peace with myself, my family, and many people around me. And so much financial grace had been dispensed by the Family of Light, gifting me a life where everything was provided for and showing me repeatedly how powerful we truly are.

But the more we advance on this path, the more we need to be truly responsible for every thought, word, and action. This was especially true as I also undertook the immense responsibilities of being a Mentor at the Divine University.

After Bali, I returned to London to prepare myself for the next big journey: The Mentor Training Retreat. This great new initiation was around the corner, waiting in the middle of the American Great Plains.

SURRENDER–
MONTANA

On the flight to Montana, I was blessed to encounter a powerful collective experience that touched me deeply.

There was a long wait at the first airport I was passing through before connecting to the next flight. So while I was entertaining myself walking around the shopping area of the airport, unexpectedly the veils lifted to reveal a hidden reality. But this time were no World of Light or Being of Light shown to me. Instead I began to see without filters inside the people around me.

Many of them were marked by the signs of an unfulfilled heart, not loving themselves or their realities. Simultaneously, I was also struck by the realization that these lovely humans were in the dark about the real nature of their souls beyond the boundary of the mind. They ignored the truth of their Light and Power of Creation because they simply were not aware of it.

Immediately I was reminded of myself before my own Spiritual Awakening and how unfulfilled I used to be when ruled by karma and plenty of other internal mechanisms. Though, by then I knew a cure truly existed and that great changes can occur if each of us takes responsibility for our own shift of consciousness as this is simply the key. To transform the old consciousness does liberate us from all old paradigms. It shows us how to become conscious creators, able to operate in a new format without the conditioning of fears and all kinds of negative thoughts forms. All that we need is the will and faith to do it as the Family of Light always supports us with the rest to create the magic.

In that moment, I finally realized that my book had a real Higher Purpose. To help others to also walk upon their Golden Path of Self-Realization. If I did it, I thought, anyone could do it!!!

With a renewed sense of purpose to share the Spiritual Knowledge I had gained, I arrived in Montana. Our host and fellow Mentor was a unique being called Katherine. She owned a vast property bordering one of America's most spectacular national parks.

I was assigned a bedroom that displayed remarkable paintings of American Indians. Their very distinguished faces stared at me with enigmatic expressions, but as soon as I went to bed and closed my eyes they came alive, resulting in my first Spiritual Contact with the natives of North America. What followed was pure magic.

I soul-travelled with them somewhere up in the mountains where they showed me how to dance with fire. During this wild dancing they explained that I was preparing myself for a different kind of journey in which my animal spirit would be revealed. Next, I shape-shifted into a silvery wolf, running across the dark landscape with a pack of wolves. It was an amazing sensation to be inside a wolf's body, feeling its strength and agility, running so fast and free in the thickness of the forest and past a glistening lake under the shadow of a pale fluorescent moon. Then suddenly the pack came to a halt in front of a large teepee. We entered the tent, shape-shifting one after another back into human form. An elder wearing the most beautiful feathered headdress asked us to sit in a circle and began to teach us his indigenous wisdom. After awhile I became unconscious, passing from a state of pure awareness into a dream state.

When I woke up at dawn and saw from my bedroom window the beauty of nature that sprawled in front of me, my heart sang. The sun was rising above a lake encircled by majestic mountains and vast lands stretching for miles in all directions with forests and open plains naturally creating a picture of wild beauty. I realized it was the landscape of my dream.

This land is very sacred indeed, and Katherine's labor of love could be seen across the property. Many years ago, as her first Keepership project, she was asked by the *Masters* to build a starry gateway on her land to be supported by many other smaller specific portals. She had brought tons of crystals to the land in order to create this multiple Stonehenge-type setting, grounding the vast project in the fabric of the Earthly Ley Lines. The result is sensational and over time she has welcomed many international gatherings of great importance, especially those with indigenous people sharing their wisdom. Now the High Frequencies of this magical land were assisting us to shift more gracefully, because we were required to birth a new and mysterious part of our consciousness that would also support each of us in recalibrating our Body of Light in order to achieve our Mentor status.

Day after day, initiation after initiation, we were all pushed out of our comfort zones in order to be able to birth this new, larger part of our consciousness. On this sacred land I was given the understanding that each one of the Mentors had such extraordinary gifts, and that all together we formed a powerful Spiritual Army to go out into the world and help as many as possible. The Family of Light had the perfect plan, giving us back the full power of our individual gifts but also equally sharing them in group consciousness with all other Mentors so that our Spiritual Power could be balanced and managed to serve the multiple needs of humanity. This first retreat truly gave us a vision of the great potential of our future mission together, while a deep bonding process of love and trust was woven between our hearts and minds.

I returned to London as a new being having received my most powerful shift yet. Then only a few days later another present from the Universe arrived. I was to meet the Dalai Lama, as arranged in the Heavens via a couple of beautiful Earthly Angels named Zach and Jan.

We were privileged to receive a *Private Blessing* from him—his transmission of such pure Light Energy immediately sent me into the Spiritual Stratospheres. In fact, when the time came to sit in the large auditorium filled with thousands of people, I could not hear a word of what His Holiness was saying because the aftereffects of his individual blessing were so powerful, they had taken me straight to a Higher Dimension of Consciousness.

I could see myself sitting in the audience while in my Body of Light I was floating somewhere above in the ethereal planes. That was the first time I was aware of being completely detached from my physical body, and I have to admit it was hard to come back down because the experience was just sensational.

In that instant I realized that we must never fear death. To start with, our soul is immortal—our permanent life is up there in the Higher Dimension of Light. We are only visitors on Planet Earth, living here temporarily learning whatever it is we have come back to learn.

That same night in the comfort of my bed, I soul-travelled back into the Inner Planes of Light where I received a surprise visit from the Dalai Lama and more beautiful teachings I am still so grateful for.

All of a sudden, I got news that Lancelot had arrived in town. This caused a cosmic commotion inside my heart. I wondered *am*

I ready to stand in front of him in the complete truth of my being?

After almost three years of silence, I was in a cab on my way to meet him for dinner. It was a rainy October evening and the traffic was appalling, giving me plenty of time to experience the flood of surging memories. I remembered that young girl who had fallen hard for a man who was never destined to be hers.

And I remembered the passion and equally the pain that made feel so raw and alive. But quickly I was shown my own blindness and stubbornness in deceiving myself and not seeing the truth of Lancelot's soul. As I came back into the present moment, I pondered:

To understand the soul of others is vital, as we can't change them into who we would like them to be. That was my fundamental mistake with all of my Knights, not fully accepting the truth of their souls. Instead of being able to love them unconditionally, I had always wanted to adjust them according to my own desires. I promised myself to never again lose this awareness.

When I arrived at the luxurious hotel where he was staying I immediately spotted my old friend seated in the lobby, completely absorbed in a telephone conversation. Unobserved, I just looked at him for a while—this man, for twenty-five years of my life, had represented the most unfulfilled of my desires. Yet, in that instant I saw him in a completely new way with my open heart, understanding that I truly had a chance to heal my karma with him once for all.

We talked for five uninterrupted hours during which I made amends for all the times I had judged him without understanding his soul. Now we could truly be friends. I even wished for him to finally settle down with the right partner—that showed me all forms of jealousy were finally transformed. At last, I completely let go of wanting him and through this action I obtained my freedom.

Liberation came to my heart in a powerful way. With the dissolution of karma, I felt that my heart was now free and ready to receive whomever was eventually meant to come into my life as my romantic companion.

I also realized that men were no longer an enigma to me. I could see them as they truly were with all of their fragilities and their dreams. For the largest part of my life I had envisioned them as eternal adversaries, trying to outdo me—woman versus man, the feminine versus the masculine, without realizing that we all carry both sides but in most of us it is unbalanced. Thus, we have a choice to do the work to achieve balance, Oneness between our masculine and feminine.

For example, my most prominent side has always been the masculine that never showed any signs of vulnerability, leaving me in a perennial unfulfilled state with all of my partners. All that I wished for was to be taken care of, but all that I manifested was exactly the opposite. If I had let my feminine also express itself, the result would have been more graceful without a doubt.

Happy to have received these fundamental new understandings, I poured more focus into both this book and the Mentorship Training Program. The first section of the book was almost finished but certain parts felt very incomplete. In truth, my consciousness was evolving rapidly. I had previously written some pages when my consciousness was at a lower level of awareness. Also, my training had intensified and El Moyra's Presence graced me day and night. I used to say jokingly to the other Mentors that the *Master* had moved in with me. El Moyra always had plenty to teach me and his guidance was truly appreciated. My trust in the *Masters* was now absolute.

One day, El Moyra advised me to stay longer in Egypt where I was due to return again to graduate as a Mentor of the *Divine University*. The reason was to keep writing my book as it was still an unfinished task. Of course I said YES!

It was during that time when I also started to witness the Awakening of some of my friends and clients. Especially Freya after she came back from a journey in South America ripped open. I was happy to be with her in that moment as Spiritual Awakening can be overwhelming.

Dearest reader, my heart truly goes out to everyone who is Awakening right now and particularly to those who do not have somebody guiding them through the massive shifts. I remember meeting a few of these souls while I was at John of God, all trying to make sense of what was happening to them and being in fear of their new state of being; becoming very unsettled as a bombardment can occur in which it is hard to discern what is true and what is not. In my case, I was lucky to have been familiar with Spirit since childhood, and above all, I had been blessed with the infinite grace to have found Qala as my guide and teacher.

That same year the Sirius Library was launched on the web, providing some more of the guidance needed for all Awakening and already Awakened Beings, and also for those not yet open but searching. Dearest reader, my advice is to became a free member of the Sirius Library and enroll in a program called The Master Meditations in which Qala will take you through all of the basic principles of how to turn your attention inwards, learning the functioning of your Light Body, in order to kick-start your own transformation.

The magic of Spirit was all around. Lella was slowly getting better having survived another terrible year of radiation and chemotherapy. My prayers had been heard once more. I was more grateful to God. More fully aware of the divine in all beings and all things. More accepting of Earth and Heaven being so bound together, that all is ONE without separation. More knowledgeable of the lesson that giving and receiving Love and Light is our true purpose

Through an Easter dream I also came to see a more caring side of Percival. One that he always kept well-hidden to protect himself because underneath that crustaceous shell was indeed a very tender heart, frightened of being hurt. His cynicism was simply a consequence of the fear of opening his heart. I could now see clearly that he had been hurt a fair bit and the more one is hurt the thicker the protection becomes. He was by then the only one of my Knights with whom I had not received closure of some kind and so I committed to making amends, to speaking in open heart.

A few days later we finally talked on the phone. I said, "I am sorry to have judged you." But my dear friend sounded so exhausted by his relentless work schedule, I could not go as deeply as I wanted to. Nevertheless, I could feel a surprised tone in his voice because the cynical man still held some innocence which helped me realize that my past actions reflected a time when the truth was a very vague concept in contrast to my present actions reflecting so much clarity.

I prayed that one day, in Divine Time, I would be offered the chance to truly receive closure and a new beginning with Perceval.

Finally, the moment of my departure back to Egypt arrived. I was leaving from Florence and the morning of my departure, every member of my family, including my father perceived that this journey would be different from all of the others and that whatever I was going to do in the land of the Pyramids would be of great significance for my future.

When I boarded the plane, a remembrance came strongly into my mind, the memory of boarding another plane ten years previously. As I knew then, I knew again in that moment a new mystery was about to unfold. This trip though I was more trusting. The passage of time, the evolution of my soul, was showing me that to live a selfless existence in the Love and Light of all there is, is the most rewarding life I could experience on earth.

SURRENDER–
THE
EGYPTIAN MYSTERY

I arrived in Cairo feeling unusually emotional, recognizing that my journey would culminate in my graduation as a Mentor of *The Divine University* in a ceremony at the Great Pyramid of Giza. The anticipation was simultaneously exciting and challenging.

The majestic Mena House Hotel, an oasis of peace in the bustling district of Giza, was the Mentors' residence for the duration of our retreat. Set amongst the exotic landscape of a vast and impeccable garden, the old palace was chosen because of its prime position at the center of the Keystone Portal.

Almost every room has a spectacular view of the Pyramids and there was nothing I loved more than sitting for hours in a comfortable chair on my bedroom terrace contemplating the sacred geometry of these astounding structures. I thought often of my first time in Egypt, remembering the powerful effect that journey had on me, changing the entire course of my life. Here I was again at another pivotal point on my Spiritual Path, free-falling into the unknown of the Egyptian Mystery while still questioning many of my own unresolved personal issues.

Dearest reader, at times we might fear our own power therefore our own ability to create, as ancient memories may be still connected to the ways we misused our Power of Creation in past lives. This is what I was simply experiencing in that moment, the fear of confronting the unveiling of the deeper truth of who I was, the real essence of my soul, and my Highest Form of Consciousness, my Divine Presence. Suddenly the explorer was in fear of her own discoveries, because my mind was producing the fear that I could be overwhelmed by my own Power of Creation.

But despite my temporary distress, much rose to the surface for the purpose of clearing the way to become a Mentor. Therefore, all of my worst apprehensions unraveled at great speed—such as the illusion of losing my humanity. That particular fear had been with me for a long time. I had progressed quickly in my evolution, causing me to feel increasingly distant from my original personality as often I could hardly recognize myself.

This strong sense of detachment confused me at times, while in fact I was simply learning to live and love without wants and desires. This dichotomy pulled me in two different directions that created fear around my yet to be discovered power and true self. Indeed, the biggest mystery was held within me. The lesson, one of utter surrender, was aligning my will much more deeply with Divine Will. I was also still adjusting to my new reality, integrating parts that had not yet reached the Light. Above all, I was coming to terms with the concept of unconditional love that at times seemed like an insurmountable wave. Ultimately I still had some attachments to the old self, and consequently to the old way of being.

While I was immersed in this washing machine, clearing my various aspects and fears in the strong light of the portal, one by one the other Mentors arrived from all corners of the earth. What joy it was to see all of my brothers and sisters gathering together for this unique event, each one of them bringing to our collective their beautiful hearts and souls. In their company, I slowly calmed down and acknowledged that I was not alone in dealing with integration and surrender—it is an ongoing process that touches everyone on a Spiritual Path.

Under the leadership of our beloved Qala, along with the ninety-six *Enlightened Masters* over-lighting *The Divine University*, we worked tirelessly everyday for many hours guided by a very deep and advanced program. A few days later we left Cairo for Luxor where we boarded traditional Egyptian boats and travelled on the Nile all the way down to Aswan and then back up. As the training grew in intensity, stretching us in many new and unexpected ways, sailing upon the sacred waters of the River of Light soothed our souls.

While on the boat, every morning before dawn I regularly meditated out on the main deck. Surrounded by a mantle of blackness that made everything invisible, I could not see what was hiding within the night sky. But later on, the early sun began to reveal, bit by bit, sceneries of breathtaking beauty, uninterrupted landscapes where nature reigned supreme, only at times dotted with a few huts and even fewer local people dressed in their traditional clothing looking after cows and goats.

Time stood still, as past, present, and future blended as one and everything else seemed so far away, until suddenly a magnificent temple appeared on the riverbank. This enchanted vision from another era reminded my soul of the many past lives touched by the power of these temples that offer immortal wisdom to those who can read the magical codes hidden in their walls and chambers, the secret language of a world that is no longer physical, only ethereal. I and all of the other Mentors were reclaiming this ancient connection in order to support our modern society to also reconnect to the wise ways of a forgotten spirituality.

The New Education of the Divine University is one of the timeless education systems that disappeared from earth with the advent of organized religions thousands of years ago. These ancient teachings were never lost but simply preserved by either specific portals or by members of secret societies

One day, all of this knowledge was destined to return to humanity when the time was right, and that time, dearest reader, had come.

The Golden Age is simply the name to describe Spiritual Awakening. It is an individual internal experience that will also reflect in Divine Time the wider Awakening of humanity. The secret teachings of Love and Light are available now immediately to all those drawn towards studying them. They are to be openly shared with anyone who wishes to truly open his or her heart and enrich themselves on the Path of Self-Realization.

The role of the Enlightened Masters, the enormous consciousnesses holding the Divine Plan for humanity, is to guide us with loving care towards the Golden Age and therefore towards a world without war, without poverty and greed, where everyone acts in open heart, and karma, aspects, fears, and patterns do not burden us anymore. Future generations will have the possibility to enjoy such a new world if we all start to take responsibility for our own shift of consciousness. The Masters' deepest wish is simply to see the shining hearts of everyone on earth switched onto the greater Light, Love, and Power that reside within each of us....

It was the 5ᵗʰ May 2016, the day before my Birthday. Once we disembarked in Luxor, everyone went to their hotel rooms for a well deserved rest. But once I reached mine, while I was staring from the fifth floor terrace at the blue sacred waters of the Nile, I was suddenly hit by a deep internal process.

Guided by my Presence I began to make amends with all of the people I had hurt or treated unfairly in my entire life. Hundreds of faces were presented at the forefront of my mind, while through floods of tears I repeatedly apologized to each one of them from the deepest core of my heart. The list was incredibly long but some inexplicable force pushed me to carry on. When this was done, an even bigger process started because I finally had the humility to make full amends with God. Hours later, when the full process was completed, and after fifty-two years of struggles, at last I made my peace with God and myself; forgiving myself for every ill act and deed I had committed in this lifetime and in all past lives.

I felt so profoundly peaceful. Something had clicked, truly shifted ancient forms of separation in my consciousness. At last I felt ONE with God, with Source. I was reborn in the true essence of my being, ready to do sacred work with no more fear of being judged by others because of my Spiritual Path. I knew my truth and was ready to exercise it with full conviction, including by completing this book. Before I had been secretly worried about what others might think of it, a fear that slowed down my process of writing. But in the end we can never please everybody. We can only hope that someone will be in resonance with the truth of our heart.

Later on that day, the *Masters* came to tell me it was time to remove from my wrist a very heavy silver identity bracelet that I had bought at Tiffany's in 2010 just after my first trip to Egypt. On the bracelet my sacred name **Ishkah** was inscribed to always remind me of my Spiritual Identity. The *Masters* said that I was becoming **Ishkah** and the bracelet was to be offered in ceremony to the Nile because it was not needed anymore.

The absurd thing was that because the bracelet had never left my wrist for six years, the clasp was jammed and wouldn't open. After endless attempts I asked for help from some of my sisters who swiftly escorted me to a jeweler across the road from the hotel—eventually the kind man succeeded in unfastening the clasp. When this was done, not just my wrist, but also the whole of my being felt instantly freed. It was similar to what I had experienced a couple of years before in India when sailing on the Ganges, but even more potent.

At twilight we ran down to the river, and after some deeply felt prayers, with no more regrets or attachment towards my old self, I launched the bracelet straight into the waters of the Nile and experienced immense happiness and gratitude. My true identity, the one concealed underneath my temporary human identity, had at last been utterly embraced. Now I was truly ready to celebrate both my Birthday and my Rebirth!!!

After almost two years of intense training and a few days past my fifty-second Birthday, we finally became Mentors of the *Divine University* in a ceremony at the Great Pyramid of Giza. The graduation was powerfully surreal in its potency—the sense of achievement and wonder in our hearts was deeply imprinted in each one of us. We were like family now, reunited across all times to support humanity and Gaia with the *New Education*.

While the other Mentors returned to their countries, I stayed for the specific purpose of writing this book. I had one more month in the Pyramid Portal as Amaya's guest.

Her apartment was situated in the middle of Giza. I love her home—an angelic white space that energetically holds the frequencies of the Divine Mother, a consciousness of pure love. And with Amaya's caring and nurturing ways this was the perfect support system for my sacred writing process.

Everyday, held by a special Light Chamber, I worked for twelve hours straight, only interrupting for short lunch breaks in order to sustain my body. I chose to sit in a comfy white wicker armchair opposite a large window opening to one of the most enchanting views our planet has to offer. Standing proudly in front of me were four of the Pyramids of Giza and the enigmatic face of the Sphinx, the powerful Ancient Guardians of my project. Each day under the watchful eyes of the Sphinx, I witnessed the creation of the flow of words become new paragraphs, new chapters. My life unraveled in ways I could not have imagined—I was a vessel through which Divine Presence and the *Enlightened Masters* passed. My memory vortex opened up to the exact moment in time needed to describe a precise passage of my life story, and accordingly, each one of the Spiritual Messages. Till one evening I realized to my greatest astonishment that I would complete the book before my return to Europe.

The ancient land of Egypt, the sacred Keystone Portal of the Pyramids of Giza, had given me a new way of being that gifted me with the ability to finish my book in one month, despite having spent almost two years in writing only the first part.

Through all of the different phases of my Spiritual Awakening, it was when I walked again upon the Egyptian land that it all started to truly take structure, as the magical Portal of the Pyramids empowered me to manifest my first creation for humanity, this very book.

It has been a long journey to get to this moment and one that I truly cherish as the hardest moments were simply those of greatest learning. Completion was only possible with a new understanding of co-creation with my Higher Consciousness and the Family of Light.

And from the very beginning of writing this book, each word has been dedicated to you, dearest reader, from my heart to yours.

Once upon a time there was a young girl who did not know how to love and yet love was all that she ever wanted. But the girl felt no love for herself and could not express her love to others.

She was sad and lonely as the mystery of love was utterly consuming her. Love was in truth her greatest fear and her greatest ambition, a distant soul memory of something so magnificent but unattainable, lost in a forgotten corner of her heart that she could not access no matter how hard she tried.

But she could not admit to this. In fact, she could not admit to any kind of weakness or failure—this was a grave and hopeless situation that constantly hurt her, shattering her dreams of achieving happiness.

Then one day a small miracle happened, love swiftly revealed itself and burst the girl's heart open, showing her a truth she never thought could exist.

Suddenly her being was experiencing a new reality where all was seen and observed from a very different perspective in which the heart was the shining star in her life.

Sadness and loneliness were no more, having been replaced by a deep peace and a great desire to let everyone know that her life was no fairy tale, but a true story because those who search will always find.

I believe we all share the same dream of love, no matter who we are or what we do. But to know real love takes a commitment of the heart. My story is simply an account of the search for such love that took me on so many adventures and so many twists and turns until I discovered that to truly know the meaning of love I had to look deep inside of myself and no longer look outside.

How can you truly love others if you can't love yourself? And how can you truly create your heart's dream if your heart is not open to it?

Dearest reader, I leave you with these two fundamental questions. Love is the key to everything. Only through love can everything be healed and transformed so that you may live the life you once dreamed of when you were a child still untouched by the deepest conditionings.

I hope that one day soon we will meet so that we may continue to share all the wondrous and Spiritual Riches of the Worlds of Light and the infinite wisdom of the *New Education*. My dearest friends, the *Enlightened Masters* will accompany me on my journey step-by-step as my support system so that I can help others with ease and grace.

The Angel prediction came true and my full mission is about to start, the mystery is still unfolding.

May the end of this book be the beginning of a new and rich phase in your life where the preciousness of your heart shall be your guide to the map of your own existence, leading you upon the Golden Path to realize all of your dreams.

With immense love,
Ishkah and the *Enlightened Masters*

THE DIVINE UNIVERSITY

Dearest Reader, If you feel guided to discover more about
The New Education System of The Divine University, please
explore our website and enjoy learning and receiving
the sacred work of Qala and the wonderful Mentors.

thesiriuslibrary.com

GLOSSARY

Enlightened Masters

Huge consciousness of pure Light that holds the Divine Plan for humanity and all beings. Each one of these consciousnesses has mastered different qualities. For example, El Moyra is the Cohan of the First Ray—the Ray of Divine Will—helping humanity to align its will with Divine Will. Each *Master* merges consciousness with us depending on what we need to learn the most about at that moment in time. Some of these great *Masters* came to earth reincarnated in human bodies to support us in opening our hearts to the Love and Light as the Christ, Mother Mary, and Buddha, to name just a few.

Family of Light

A conglomeration of the consciousness of the pure Light of many different natures. For example, there is Angelic Consciousness, *Enlightened Masters Consciousness*, Galactic, Celestial and Universal Consciousness, Ancestral Consciousness, Middle Earth Consciousness including fairies and all nature spirits, Gaia Consciousness, and so on.

Light

Light is simply consciousness. Not just human consciousness but the consciousness of everything there is.

Love

Love is the glue and the greatest healing force that unifies and heals all parts of our consciousness and gives us Oneness with all that there is. Contrary to standard beliefs, love can be produced internally by us and it is not just something that is given to us by others.

Dimensions of Light

Different realities of consciousness/awareness. They represent a Higher Dimension of Consciousness to the human consciousness usually guided by the mind. All human beings can access their Higher Consciousness through the study of spirituality and through meditation.

Body of Light

We are all equipped with a physical and a Light Body even if many lack this awareness. For example, the chakras are an essential part of such Bodies of Light as the doors to our Universal Consciousness. The foundation of Spiritual Studies is always centered on the knowledge and the functioning of such Bodies of Light that connect us to our Higher Consciousness.

Higher Self

Every human being has a Higher Self, their own super-consciousness that can be reached by opening the channelling canal we each have. The Higher Self is that part of our Body of Light that brings us back to truth and eternal wisdom from the Higher Dimension of Light. Even if we are all channels in one way or another, to open our Divine Channel requires Spiritual Discipline of some kind.

Divine Presence

Our Universal Consciousness, our own *Master Consciousness*.

Divine Order

An order of states of being or actions and events that has a Higher Reason to be a certain way and in a certain order, even if it does not make immediate sense to our mind because of our wants and desirers.

Divine Time

Always the perfect timing for things to happen or not to happen according to the Highest Potential of our being, even if our mind doesn't agree or understand because of wants and desires.

Divine Plan

In our present incarnation we have two choices. To live according to our life plan or to live according to our Divine Plan, meaning our Spiritual Path. One path is not higher than the other but simply a choice made by the soul for that particular incarnation.

Akashic Records

The records in our soul that reveal to us our past lives.

Frequencies

Frequencies of pure Light that pulse inside every part of our being like cells, DNA, brain, organs, and so on, imprinting teachings of Light/consciousness and dissolving patterns, blockages, cellular memories, negativity, and so on.

Chela

A dedicated student of spirituality usually studying with the *Enlightened Masters*.

Soul-Travelling

The ability of the soul to leave the body and travel to other Dimensions of Consciousness, that may be of the Light or of the Darkness. Usually the soul-travel experience is a very conscious one for those who have an open Spiritual Channel. Dreams are simply unconscious soul-travelling.

Aspects of Consciousness

Those parts of ourselves that are still locked or frozen in unresolved past lives that influence us negatively. They are simply very ancient and powerful thought forms, cellular memories that produce our patterns, blockages, fears, and anxieties and may limit our minds through all of these internal belief systems and dynamics.

Universal Laws

These are the sacred laws that truly govern the Universe and all in it, including humanity. Learning *Universal Laws* is essential to understanding the Spiritual Truth of how everything really works within us and in our lives. To live according to *Universal Law* is among the deepest learning along the Spiritual Path.